Sociobiology & Mental Disorder

A New View

Sociobiology & Mental Disorder

A New View

Brant Wenegrat, M.D.

Addison-Wesley Publishing Company
Medical Division · Menlo Park, California
Reading, Massachusetts · London · Amsterdam
Don Mills, Ontario · Sydney

Sponsoring Editor: Nicholas Keefe
Production Editor: Ron Newcomer
Cover Designer: Sharon Smith
Book Designer: Sue Harrington
Copy Editor: Libby Pischel

Library of Congress Cataloging in Publication Data

Wenegrat, Brant.
Sociobiology and mental disorder.

Bibliography: p.
Includes index.
1. Mental illness—Genetic aspects. 2. Mental illness—Social aspects. 3. Sociobiology. 4. Psychiatry, Comparative. 5. Behavior genetics. I. Title.
[DNLM: 1. Behavior, Animal. 2. Genetics, Behavioral. 3. Mental Disorders. 4. Social Behavior. WM 100 W4693s]
RC455.4.G4W46 1984 616.89 84-12377
ISBN 0–201–09686–2

ABCDEFGHIJ—AL—89876543

Addison-Wesley Publishing Company
Medical/Nursing Division
2725 Sand Hill Road
Menlo Park, California 94025

Contents

muzzle to earth at his feet
an animal rests
unaware of having been born

Jean Follain
(translated by W. S. Merwin)
Transparence of the World

Preface

This book applies modern ethologic and especially sociobiologic ideas to human mental disorders. It does this systematically, so that the particular hypotheses developed ultimately form a more or less coherent view of abnormal functioning. Many books have been written applying ethologic and sociobiologic ideas to normal human behavior. Mental disorders, though, are generally not mentioned, or at best are given just a few sentences. A small number of articles in medical journals have applied ethologic and sociobiologic ideas to particular abnormal behaviors. However, no generalized framework is developed within which specific applications can be systematically treated. Accordingly, there is a piecemeal quality to those articles, which never permit a view of the subject matter as a whole. Mental disorders are not only intrinsically fascinating, but they may also reveal otherwise hidden facts about normal mental functions. Therefore, it seems particularly important to develop a generalized framework within which powerful new ideas from ethology and sociobiology can be systematically applied to them. The framework developed here can be applied only to certain mental disorders, and an ethologic and sociobiologic model embracing the whole range of abnormal behaviors may not be practical. However, disorders encompassed by the framework developed here include the most common psychological problems, and within this framework, these disorders appear in a new light. Old concepts take on new meanings, causative factors and disorders interrelate in unexpected ways, and prognosis and treatment methods are freshly illuminated. Tentative and necessarily limited in its scope, a new viewpoint appears, together with a new way of talking about abnormal behavior.

This book is written so as to be accessible to both professional and nonprofessional readers, particularly if the latter have some enduring interest in problems of human behavior. Students, whether at graduate or undergraduate level, should also be able to follow this book. Technical terms are kept to a minimum, mental disorders are usually described, and much of the more technical material has been placed in appendices. Readers who want to learn more about the topics discussed in this book will be aided by an extensive bibliography.

Undoubtedly, no reader will agree with all the points in this book. Application of ethologic and sociobiologic ideas to normal human behavior has been controversial, and there is no reason to believe application of these ideas to abnormal behavior will be any less so. In fact, it may be more controversial. In a sense, abnormal behaviors seem even more specifically "human" than many normal behaviors, so that application of ideas developed in the study of animal behavior may seem overly simple to many readers. Other objections will be to specific points, particularly to the widespread reassessment of Freudian and behaviorist ideas implied by the approach taken here. The emphasis placed on mental life may estrange those who advocate a purely neurologic approach to psychiatric disorders. Even those who pursue a more ecologic approach—attachment theorists, for example—may be disturbed by my emphasis on group-related and sexual-competitive strategies. However, the wide range of behaviors discussed in later chapters illustrates the value of the ethologic and sociobiologic ideas I have attempted to apply. Whatever the general framework in which they are applied to mental disorders, these ideas should no longer be neglected. In later volumes, these ideas and the basic framework developed here will be carried still further into areas of abnormal mental functioning beyond the scope of this particular text.

• • •

Friends, relatives, and colleagues, as well as numerous authors cited in following chapters, contributed to the writing of this book. Authors are given some credit in the bibliography, while the friends, relatives, and colleagues are not. A few words here—though they carry my heartfelt feelings—are paltry indeed beside the aid and encouragement these many fine people have given me.

First, I was greatly aided by Anne O'Reilly Wenegrat. Her patience, encouragement, and sound advice made the writing of this book possible. Her kindness and consideration made it bearable.

Second, Adolf Pfefferbaum, Walton Roth, and Peter Finkelstein, who separately and together represent the best of psychiatry as I see it, have each in his way contributed enormously to this project. Without their encouragement, discussion, stimulation, and material support, I could not have persevered. I am also indebted to Bert Kopell, Irvin Yalom, George Gulevich, Floyd Estess, Jim Hawkins, and numerous others. As teachers, friends, and colleagues, their generosity and encouragement have played essential roles in my professional education and in developing much of what follows.

Third, Charles O'Reilly provided information and contacts when I needed them most. Stephen Kallison kept me from abandoning this project when I otherwise might have. My son Jacob taught me some important sociobiologic principles and entertained me in the process.

Finally, Nicholas Keefe, Sue Harrington, and others at Addison-Wesley provided encouragement and guidance. Their experience and expertise transformed this project from a private to a collective endeavor.

—Brant Wenegrat, M.D.

1

The Aim of This Book and Some Remarks on Its Ethical Implications

The Aim of This Book

The aim of this book is to examine human mental disorder from the viewpoint of evolutionary biology. This in itself is nothing new. Sigmund Freud, influenced by Charles Darwin, applied the evolutionary concepts of his day in his earlier theories, and others have since followed the same path. In each case, application of evolutionary concepts has led to new models with limited but real utility in explaining psychologic disturbance. In recent years, though, increasingly powerful conceptual tools—products of modern ethology and sociobiology—have greatly extended the range of behaviors potentially explicable in evolutionary terms. A new look at psychopathology is therefore justified, in hope that the new conceptual tools will shed further light on its phenomenology and causes.

Because the ideas and terminology of modern evolutionary theory are unfamiliar to most of those interested in mental disorder, and because current ideas on behavioral evolution have seldom been applied to topics of psychiatric concern, some background ideas will need to be introduced. The first of these, which will be called the *genetic viewpoint,* is an essential framework common to modern ethology and sociobiology alike. Comparison of the genetic viewpoint with more familiar conceptual frameworks, and with certain preconceptions about genetic explanations, will clarify what may be new in modern evolutionary thinking and will lead naturally to other crucial topics. Of the latter, the most important will be the *genetically transmitted response strategy,* which is the basic functional unit in most sociobiologic theories. In spite of their seeming newness, genetically transmitted response strategies can be systematically related to perceptual, cognitive, and emotional mechanisms long familiar to students of mental disorder. Next, specific genetically transmitted response strategies will be described, in relation to which normal and at least some abnormal behavior patterns can be shown to systematically differ. These response strategies have been widely discussed in the sociobiologic literature, but their description here will emphasize topics of special psychopathologic interest.

Finally, mental disorders themselves will be discussed with respect to the genetically transmitted response strategies outlined in previous chapters. Evolutionary biology, like other conceptual schemes applied to human behavior, cannot explain everything. Therefore, it should not surprise us to find that certain mental disorders are only clumsily described using sociobiologic notions. Because they involve dysfunction of many different response strategies, these particular syndromes are best described in other terms entirely, as indicated in later chapters. Other disorders, though, involve dysfunction of specific response strategies and therefore may be efficiently described from an evolutionary biologic viewpoint.

To aid the reader in following it, the argument here has been divided into three parts. In Part I (Chapters 2 through 5), basic ideas are introduced. These include the genetic viewpoint at the heart of modern ethology and sociobiology, response strategies and their use as analytic units, and criteria useful for determining their likely genetic transmission. A simple model illustrates how genetic factors, acting through mental processes, might produce adherence to response strategies. Numerous other issues are also touched upon. These include the place of culture, ultimate and proximate causation, inclusive fitness, and evolutionary stability. Biologic ideas are not exhaustively surveyed but introduced only insofar as they will later prove useful.

Part II (Chapters 6 through 11) describes specific genetically transmitted response strategies that are useful for explicating both normal behavior and psychopathology. Strategies surveyed include those governing attachment behaviors, hostile interactions, sexual competition, group formation, and altruism. Specific mechanisms contributing to each response strategy are briefly discussed, as are some of their psychopathologic implications.

Part III (Chapters 12 through 15) discusses mental disorders. Chapter 12 is devoted to mental disorders not efficiently described in the social strategic framework because their behavioral manifestations involve diffuse strategic dysfunctions. These include organic brain syndromes, psychosis, and infantile autism. Chapters 13 through 15 discuss disorders related to the dysfunction of specific genetically transmitted response strategies. These are syndromes efficiently described in an evolutionary biologic framework. Syndromes referable to attachment-related strategies include agoraphobia, pathologic mourning, unipolar depression, and borderline personality. Schizotypal and paranoid personality disorders are referable to group-related strategies. Oedipal and sexual disorders of varied kinds can best be described in terms of sexual-competitive strategies. In many of these same disorders, hostile and altruistic strategies also play critical roles.

Finally, Chapter 16 discusses the implications of a strategic, evolutionary viewpoint for public mental health.

To further help the reader follow what may be unfamiliar ideas, each of the following chapters is prefaced by a brief summary. More specialized topics, which will likely interest only the more serious reader, are covered in extensive appendices that are referred to in the text. Finally, the number of formulae has been kept to a minimum. Because sociobiology is a quantitative science, at least some formulae are required to fully illustrate certain concepts. Yet, even those phobic of mathematical formulae should be able to follow the arguments, or at least the conclusions, which have been rendered as precisely as possible in plain English.

Lastly, some of what follows is necessarily speculative. Hopefully, the speculations outlined here are more amenable to empiric testing than psychologic speculations have generally proven to be. Although the accounts given are true to empiric data as the author knows it, others may have better ideas of how particular disorders may be placed in the evolutionary framework. Nothing should be set in concrete. If the present study convinces at least some readers that evolutionary biology can now contribute substantially more to the efficient description of mental disorders than once seemed possible, its purpose will have been served.

Some Ethical Considerations

Since Wilson (1975) first brought them to public attention, evolutionary concepts of the kind we will later employ have been the object of considerable controversy. Some of this has been scientific, but much of it has been ethical, and even ideologic in its substance. Belief that these concepts may undermine political freedom and rationalize injustice has led many to denounce entirely their human application and to view those who use them as socially regressive. Here we will not only use them, but will also apply them to ethical injunctions themselves, in order to study conflicts important to mental functioning. Accordingly, brief remarks—to the effect that the ethical issues are more complex than may be apparent—are in order before beginning this study. However, the reader must form his or her own opinion, which, in any event, is an obligation no one can escape.

First, it is important to realize that although the current debate centers around sociobiology, the issues involved were actually set in motion by Darwin (1874) himself, when he used "heredity" to support Victorian social prejudice. Quickly, so-called "social Darwinists" adopted his theory for their own ends. Nonetheless, Darwinian ideas were also readily adopted by left-wing philosophers, who saw in them a potent weapon with which to assault religious conservatism. Both Engels and Marx were strongly influenced by Darwin, to whom *Das Kapital* was nearly dedicated (Breuer, 1982). Unfortunately, the social Darwinists seem to have won custody of evolutionary theory, at least as it applies to behavior. Seventy-five years after Darwin's remarks, Pastore (1949) found that conservative scientists largely believed in the power of genes and liberal scientists in the power of the environment to determine behavioral traits. With the development of modern ethology came simplistic overgeneralizations tending to further disparage the possibility of social change. Thus, popular books variably asserted that men are born killers, capitalists, or wife-beaters, depending on whether hunting, territoriality, or sexual relations were being discussed. In classical dominance theory, now less highly valued by ethologists themselves (Reynolds, 1981), right-wing intellectuals thought they had found a biologic rationale for economic repression. Sociobiology, in turn, has been expropriated by fascist intellectuals, particularly in England and France (Montagu, 1980), who imagine that it justifies their own racism.

However, even theorists with no ax to grind find in sociobiologic or ethologic concepts potential justification for racism, inequality, or violence. Thus, Washburn (1980), a highly respected anthropologist, argues that kin selection implies diminished ethical responsibility for those genetically dissimilar. Kin selection, which is discussed in later chapters, is a sociobiologic theory predicting that individuals will be more altruistic toward their genetic kin than toward those to whom they are genetically unrelated. King (1980) and Barnett (1980) both see the sociobiologic view of human relations as Hobbesian, meaning that social interactions are portrayed as a war of "one against all" in which few if any grounds exist for genuine cooperation. The reward of victory, they argue, is a greater degree of inclusive fitness (see Chapter 2). Nor have the political views of certain prominent sociobiologists contributed to the stature of that science among those concerned with social issues (see Rose, 1980). One ethologist recently argued that the "coming of age" of ethology signals the end of the Enlightenment (Reynolds, 1981, p. xi). In fact, the Enlightenment view of man has long since expired at the hands of Freudian theory, and the moral and political consequences of this event, whatever they may be, cannot be laid at the feet of modern behavioral biology. Claims of this sort, however, conjure images of a new dark age brought on by overzealous biologists. Small wonder then, that the possibility of a human psychology based on modern ethology and sociobiology has seemed to many a nihilistic and ultimately antisocial endeavor, one that would hinder rather than help the cause of humanizing society.

As usual, though, another side exists to each of these fears. Popularized ethologic conclusions have always been more sensational than accurate. On a more serious level, that kin selection implies diminished ethical responsibility for anyone is also highly problematic, as the reader can judge on the basis of later chapters. The social Darwinist notion that selection of the fittest justifies unbridled selfishness was long ago discredited, and Washburn's criticism of kin selection theory may actually be a rehash of that notion, updated in sociobiologic terms. Similarly, that humans in most environments will behave to maximize inclusive fitness says nothing about their desire for conflict. As demonstrated in later chapters, motivational structures associated in evolutionary history with enhanced inclusive fitness are as likely to favor interpersonal cooperation as conflict. Ironically, the kin selection theory attacked by Washburn vitiates the notion that sociobiologic concepts are Hobbesian. Competition for inclusive fitness, moreover, occurs between genes, not between individuals, a point made in the title of a well-known book, *The Selfish Gene.* To portray inclusive fitness as a resource for which individuals compete is to miss the point of sociobiologic theory entirely. A related error—that individuals somehow calculate inclusive fitness consequences of their various actions—has been made as well, even by those who would further apply sociobiologic notions (see McGuire and Essock-Vitale, 1981; McGuire, et al., 1981).

Finally, regardless of historical polarizations and attempts by modern fascists to expropriate these concepts, a sociobiologically and ethologically informed view of human nature may protect personal freedom far more effectively than the tabula rasa views traditionally favored by liberal thinkers. Tiger (1979), Wilson (1978), and Chomsky (1975), for instance, have each argued that psychologic theories that depict human nature as capable of unrestricted modification readily serve the ideologic interests of ruling classes. If human nature is wholly contingent upon societal exigencies, then society itself defines psychologic normalcy. Those who fail to conform are by definition abnormal, since no higher standards of normalcy exist than those provided by society. In this way, granting society the power to define human nature leads to invidious treatment of those finding fault with social mores or institutions. In the Soviet Union, by way of example, an official tabula rasa psychology and incarceration of dissidents in psychiatric hospitals go hand in glove with each other.

Even in psychology, tabula rasa theories have obliterated distinctions previously drawn between social convention and moral behavior (Turiel, 1978), and between social conditioning of constructive and destructive kinds (Wolff, 1978).

Sociobiology, by contrast, argues for human values and needs that may or may not be satisfied by any particular society. These are shared, moreover, by members of every race and social class. Radical social criticisms, insupportable from a tabula rasa viewpoint, are thereby made possible. Tinbergen (1976), for instance, suggests such a criticism when he describes mankind as "disadapted" to modern life. The results of such criticisms also differ, depending on their theoretical origin. Tabula rasa theorists envision utopias in which men and women are engineered to fit society (see Skinner, 1948); sociobiologists and ethologists must hope for utopian societies engineered to fit men and women. The reader may decide without difficulty which utopia is more likely to respect human rights.

As for the nihilism supposedly inherent in sociobiologic notions, knowing how genes create human nature in particular environments may actually help humanity foster the best in itself and make of itself that to which it aspires. The so-called "naturalistic fallacy"—which takes the naturally given for the morally good—is part of neither ethology nor sociobiology, in spite of those who claim to find it in them (see, for example, Fried, 1978). Knowledge of gene-environment interactions could help guide the creation of truly humanizing cultures, cultures in which men and women are not racist, sexist, violent, or exploitative, cultures that the world, tragically, has never really seen. To know the beast—if there be such within us—is not to embrace it, but to more effectively renounce it.

I
Basic Ideas

2

The Genetic Viewpoint I

Its Definition and Place in Behavioral Science

The "genetic viewpoint," an heuristic device at the heart of modern ethology and sociobiology alike, is described and illustrated. From this viewpoint, behavior is considered a genetic response to particular environments. The genetic viewpoint makes no claim concerning statistically measured environmental or genetic control and should not be mistaken for a simplistic form of genetic "determinism." The genetic viewpoint is more familiar to students of mental disorder than is at first apparent.

In Ethology and Sociobiology

Among those dealing with mental disorders, genetic influence and therapeutic nihilism are frequently equated. Insofar as genes control behavior, it seems, there must be less justification for environmental interventions of the sort now used to treat most mental disorders. Seemingly, extreme degrees of genetic influence might call into question individual, family, and group psychotherapy, supportive living arrangements, sheltered workshops, vocational counseling, and even human goodwill itself, at least as efficacious means for relieving psychologic distress. Clinicians might become mere diagnosticians, and treatment might give way to resigned acceptance of genetic fate. Those with problems—and their children as well—would necessarily be deprived of hope, at least until genetic engineering could take the place now occupied by predominantly environmental therapies.

What many fail to realize, though, is that neither ethologic nor sociobiologic concepts imply a competitive relation between innate and environmental behavioral determinants, a relation in which the greater efficacy of one implies the lesser efficacy of the other. A "competitive" framework of this sort is actually encountered more often in behavioral genetics than in modern evolutionary thinking (Alexander, 1979). Instead, ethologists and sociobiologists alike have sought to describe how genetic and environmental factors interact to promote behavioral development, the results of which might be altered by contributing determinants of either kind (see Schneirla, 1966; Tinbergen, 1968; Eisenberg, 1972). A pioneer in this effort has been Konrad Lorenz (1957), who coined the term *instinct-training interlocking* to describe the intercalation of learned behaviors into instinctive behavioral ensembles. A closely related concept, the *open* behavioral subsystem (Mayr, 1976), has been used to describe the same phenomena, while a somewhat different model, but nonetheless useful for conceptualizing gene-environment interactions, is provided by Waddington's *epigenetic landscape* (1956). It is discussed in Appendix A.

Among the learned behaviors inserted into instinctive ensembles are certain species-typical acts, which are nonetheless dependent on specific postnatal experiences for their development. In birds, for example, species-typical mating and territorial songs depend on exposure of the fledgling to normal adult vocalizations (Marler, 1979). Mallard fledglings must hear their own voices to recognize species-typical calls (Gottlieb, 1976). Among various carnivores, both the manner of killing live prey (Leyhausen, 1973) and what prey is appropriate (Eibl-Eibesfeldt, 1975) must be learned from universal experiences akin to those responsible for song acquisition in birds. Human language acquisition most likely depends on interaction of innate mental capacities with environmental events so ubiquitous as to define the environment of human adaptation (Papousek and Papousek, 1979). Other primate social behaviors also rely on coupling of innate dispositions with environmental events. In fact, the uncoupling of normally interlocking factors may result in social disability, the topic of later chapters.

Only the difficulty of following complex interactions prevents application of the instinct-training interlocking concept to the whole gamut of animal and human behaviors. Even the most complex of these depend on precisely the same interaction of innate and environmental factors responsible for development of bird songs, carnivorous habits, or language use. For example, automobile driving requires use of landmarks, traffic laws, and road signs, not to mention the automobile itself. None of the skills prerequisite to driving are likely represented in the genetic code, even of the average American. Yet, men and women drive because they are slow, bipedal animals, because they have the intellectual capacity to master operation of machinery, and because they depend largely upon visual pathways to monitor their environment. Moreover, auto trips themselves invariably serve goals more or less directly related to human organic structures. People drive to buy food, to make trysts, to escape cold weather, or to be with kin, among other reasons. Sometimes they drive for the sake of sensory stimulation, required by their complex nervous systems, or to rest their legs. Even business trips, like business itself, ultimately subserve biologically determined goals of one kind or another. Since bipedalism, cognitive capacities, dexterity, vision, and the desire for food, sex, warmth, kin, or sensory stimulation are all dependent upon genetically encoded information, genes are as necessary for driving automobiles as are the skilled uses of roads, maps, or traffic laws. Within the same Lorenzian framework applied to bird songs, driving an automobile can be described as an activity that results when animals with human anatomy, cognitive capacities, and motivational structures are reared in environments that teach use of roads, maps, traffic laws, and automobiles.

Within an interactionist framework of this sort it is as illogical to quantify the relative contribution of purely genetic and environmental factors to particular behaviors, whether that contribution is expressed in terms of statistical means or variability, as it is to assert that the operation of a radio is seventy percent determined by wire and thirty percent determined by transistors. Quantitative statements of this type may serve specific scientific purposes but should never be mistaken for true developmental facts. For example, that ten percent of the children of schizophrenics will themselves become schizophrenic is of obvious public health significance (Gottesman and Shields, 1982). That identical twins are more similar on personality scales than on intelligence tests provides useful information on gene-behavior mediation (Farber, 1981). The extraordinary gestural and mimetic coincidences occasionally reported between identical twins reared apart provide valuable insights into the peremptory force of genetic action expressed in certain environments (Farber, 1981). Yet, it must remain logically and scientifically true that to become schizophrenic, develop a personality, or make gestures, both environmental and genetic processes are required, and that no component of schizophrenia, personality, or gesture can be isolated, which, in any sense, is the result of purely one set of processes or the other. Collusion of environmental and innate factors is requisite to the occurrence of any characterizable behavior, whether considered as a whole or in any of its facets.

Not only are simple statistical approaches to gene-environment interactions not logically sound, but their empirical failure can be demonstrated as well. One such failure, with respect to traits of psychiatric interest, is illustrated by personality testing of various sets of fraternal and identical twins. The usual assumption made for statistical analysis of twin data is that variation occurring between members of twin pairs may be either genetic or environmental. Genetic identity is expected to eliminate intrapair variation resulting from genetic factors; being reared in the same home is expected to diminish intrapair variation resulting from environmental factors. Thus, identical twins reared together and fraternal twins reared apart should be most and least similar of all twin pairs, respectively. Identical twins reared apart and fraternal twins reared together should show intermediate levels of intrapair variation, their ranking with respect to each other being dependent on the relative strengths of genetic and environmental influences. Although these predictions are frequently correct, on some important measures identical twins reared apart are actually more similar than identical twins raised in the same home. Newman and coworkers (1937) and Shields (1962), for example, both found that rearing status of identical twin pairs had the opposite effect on personality differences than that predicted by the straightforward statistical model. Farber (1981) reviewed all extant reports of separated identical twin pairs and found the same pattern. Her analysis suggested that propinquity before the age of ten years was associated with differentiation of personality traits, which nonetheless could proceed even in adult life if twins were reunited.

In contrast to the simpler statistical models, an interactionist model predicts no behavioral effect of any single innate or environmental factor acting independently of factors belonging to the other category.

If neither innate nor environmental factors—acting in isolation—can be said to have any behavioral effect whatsoever, then efforts to disentangle the causative web responsible for even simple behaviors would seem considerably less promising. It has proven difficult enough to discover innate or environmental influences on particular behaviors without the additional burden of describing how those influences interact with all other influences of the same and opposite class. The problem of tracing etiologic roles from an interactionist framework of this sort would seem to defy practical resources. No scientist could have the time, nor any journal the pages, to fully describe the complex gene-environment interactions responsible for even the simplest human behaviors. Fortunately, however, causal interactions can be more easily followed if heuristic strategies are used to reduce the number of critical variables. Typically, strategies of this kind treat only one class of etiologic agents as truly active. Other agents are considered merely contextual with respect to the active class.

By way of illustration, since no biologic process can play an etiologic role except by interaction with environmental determinants, biologic factors could be relegated to a background role in behavioral analyses. This, in fact, is the practice of many social scientists who study the effect of environmental determinants occurring in a certain biologic context (see Bock, 1980). Even highly specific subcategories of environmental determinants, such as economic factors, are routinely made the objects of active study by considering all other factors contextual. Remaining factors enter the field of study only to provide the backdrop against which economic forces must act.

If social scientists place environmental factors at center stage, ethologists and, particularly, sociobiologists do the same with genetic ones. This is what will henceforth be called the *genetic viewpoint.* From the genetic viewpoint, all other biologic and environmental factors are merely contextual with respect to genetic activity. However, though it treats behavior as the genetic response to particular environments, the genetic viewpoint is not a claim about behavioral causation, nor about where the sources of behavioral variation, statistically conceived, may actually lie. It is an intellectual device, not an etiologic attribution, and the measure of its ultimate success must be an intellectual, not merely statistical, one. The genetic viewpoint has as its primary purpose achievement of descriptive simplicity.

Because the backdrop against which genetic activity occurs is comprised of environmental factors, the genetic viewpoint does not disparage the possibilities for environmentally induced behavioral change. Behavior that is considered the product of genes in a particular environment may logically be altered by environmental manipulations. The genetic viewpoint is therefore consistent with practice of environmental therapies.

In Psychology

Although the genetic viewpoint characterizes modern ethology and sociobiology, the two sciences that have most successfully exploited it for behavioral analyses, the same heuristic strategy actually has a long history in psychologic theory. Recent scholarship, to give one example, reveals the extent to which Freud was influenced by Darwin's essays on behavioral genetics. For this reason, Sulloway (1979) described Freud as an *ultimate causal,* rather than *proximate causal,* "biologist of the mind." These terms, which are commonly used today to distinguish between evolutionary-selective and mechanistic-physiologic explanatory schemes, signify a distinction that will run throughout this study. Others, too (Bock, 1980; Leak and Christopher, 1982), have noted the close affinity of Freudian and sociobiologic agendas. That Freud's theories miscarried by modern biological standards owes more to the dearth of material he had to work with than to any lack of biologic interest. Facts required for progress in ultimate causal behavioral biology—including the extraordinary homologies between primate and human behaviors—were unknown in Freud's era. Also lacking were conceptual tools requisite to exploitation of the genetic viewpoint. The notion of inclusive fitness, to mention one particularly telling example, had not yet supplanted that of reproductive fitness.

Inclusive fitness is at the heart of sociobiology (see Caplan, 1978), so its definition, and the way in which it differs from *reproductive fitness,* justify a brief digression. Reproductive fitness refers to the number of genetically related offspring left by each individual as the result of particular traits (behavioral traits in the present context). The value of various offspring in calculations of reproductive fitness are frequently depreciated to account for genetic relatedness. One child, for example, might be worth two grandchildren, each of whom is worth two great-grandchildren, and so forth. When this is done, reproductive fitness measures the number of copies of his or her own genetic material each individual leaves among direct descendants as the result of particular behavioral traits. Inclusive fitness differs from reproductive fitness in that it also counts genetic material left behind in other than direct descendants. Accounting for genetic material in other than direct descendants acknowledges the fact that particular behavioral traits may affect not only the individual's reproductive history, but the reproductive histories of those companions who share his or her genes. For this reason, inclusive fitness can be used to account for evolution of behavioral traits whose reproductive benefits are reaped by kin, rather than just by the individuals who actually manifest them. Altruistic traits in particular have been explicated in this fashion (Hamilton, 1964).

A central tenet of modern sociobiology is that individual behavior has been selected to maximize inclusive fitness—the number of copies of an individual's genetic material existing in future generations. Insofar as it is heritable, individual tolerance for behaviors detrimental to inclusive fitness will have been weeded out by natural selection, at least in environments resembling that in which the behaviors evolved. In this respect, inclusive fitness is perfectly analogous to reproductive fitness, which individual behavior was previously thought to maximize, but which is now known as an incomplete measure of genetic selection. Nor is conscious consideration necessary to maximization of inclusive fitness, which follows as the indirect and unselfconscious result of behavioral goals of a more specific kind (Chapter 5). That individuals act to maximize their own inclusive fitness will be mentioned repeatedly in later chapters, consistent with its importance in modern behavioral biology.

Because reproductive fitness alone was thought to determine genetic selection, Freud's emphasis on reproductive motivation was a logical consequence of his interest in Darwin. Because sexual motives, in turn, were thought to be the mental representatives of reproductive imperatives, it follows also that Freud eventually saw sex at the root of all mental life.

However, not only has reproductive success taken a back seat to inclusive fitness in modern theories of behavioral selection, but reproductive fitness itself is no longer thought to depend very much on frankly sexual motives. Instead, it likely relies on motives more distal to the reproductive act than those considered by Freud. An individual biologically predisposed to consider only genital acts would be quickly outcompeted by others willing to consider the reproductive problem more broadly. The latter, willing to consider resource allocation, competition, diplomacy, and cooperation, among other issues, would far more likely find partners with whom to share genital fantasies than would the narrrow-minded sensualist.

At first glance, sublimation—or the transformation of sexual drive into wider interests—might seem to save the Freudian paradigm. Yet, modern ethology and sociobiology indicate that concerns with resources, competition, and alliances are fully as innate as sexual preoccupations. The facts of behavioral life cannot be explicated by artificially considering one interest or the other more fundamentally given.

Other examples of Freud's genetic viewpoint, and remarks on other theorists, are found in Appendix B. Suffice it to say that what lies at the heart of modern ethology and sociobiology, which is called here the genetic viewpoint, is no stranger to psychologic theory, regardless of contemporary prejudice.

3

The Genetic Viewpoint II

Implications for the Nature of Behavioral Organization

To apply the genetic viewpoint, an analytic unit is required, for which the "response rule" serves admirably. Response rules are genetically or environmentally transmitted and are hierarchically superior or inferior. Hierarchically superior rules will be called strategies; inferior rules, tactics. Broadest application of the genetic viewpoint requires that the highest order response strategies be genetically transmitted. Genetic transmission of response rules is complicated by culture and ethical ideologies.

Response Rules

First and foremost, application of the genetic viewpoint requires specification of the analytic units to which it is relevant. This specification, however, is fraught with potential hazards. If units are chosen to represent discrete actions—paying for hamburgers, for example, or turning door locks—then their analysis as manifestations of genetic activity in particular environments will obviously become farcical. As our common sense informs us, paying for hamburgers or turning door locks cannot depend on genetic activity except in the most distal sense. If units are chosen to represent global tendencies—survival, for example, or interaction with other people—then their analysis as manifestations of genetic activity will become merely trivial. Survival or interaction may be closely dependent upon genetic activity, but no one would or should really care that this is so. But if intermediate units between discrete actions and global tendencies are required for psychologic application of the genetic viewpoint, then which of the many possibilities should be chosen?

Fortunately, the genetic viewpoint itself suggests an appropriate analytic unit. Insofar as genetic activity produces particular behaviors in specific environments, then the genes are essentially acting to provide transformational rules by which environmental configurations produce corresponding behavioral patterns. Natural selection, moreover, ensures that the genes assign a behavioral pattern comprising an adaptive response to each environmental configuration. Exceptions to this rule occur only when the environmental configuration is one with which the genes have no selective history. If genes specify adaptive *response rules,* a formulation of genetic activity known as the "norm of reaction" model (Kurland, 1979), then the obvious analytic unit for application of the genetic viewpoint is the response rule itself.

As analytic units, response rules are also exceedingly flexible. They may be of widely varying scope and temporal extension without losing their basic character as response rules and may be sequentially or hierarchically arranged to comprise the flow of ongoing behavior. For example, both "castle if the king is threatened" and "launch missiles on evidence of enemy attack" are response rules, in spite of their greatly varying consequences. Two everyday response rules that sequentially govern behavior are "brake if a traffic light is red" and "accelerate when the light turns green." Both of these response rules are also hierarchically inferior to other response rules, such as "drive if your destination is further than you can walk."

When response rules are hierarchically integrated, which is the norm rather than the exception, a useful distinction can be drawn between superior and inferior response rules with respect to delimited areas of behavior. Thus, with respect to war-related behaviors, "launch missiles on evidence of enemy attack" may be taken as the highest level response rule, while response rules governing specifics, such as final targeting, may be taken as lower level rules. Higher level response rules are commonly called *strategies*, or *response strategies*, while lower level rules are called *tactics*. In military usage, for example, strategy refers to the larger movements and operations of a campaign, while tactic refers to deployment of particular forces. The distinction between response strategy and tactic may be ambiguous, particularly since strategy with respect to one behavior may be tactic with respect to another, but it proves valuable if used with some caution.

A second useful distinction between response rules is in their transmission to the individual—via environmental or genetic channels. Although response rules require both environmental and genetic preconditions for their behavioral manifestation, the rules themselves may be characterized as *environmentally* or *genetically transmitted* without violating the interactionist dictum described in the previous chapter. Thus, "brake if a traffic light is red" requires for its realization that the light be seen, that the color be noted, that the foot be capable of reaching the brake pedal, and a host of other preconditions more or less dependent upon prior genetic activity. Yet, the rule itself is environmentally transmitted. Rules of this sort will only be transmitted by and to creatures genetically capable of using them, but in this case genes play only a permissive role. Response rules more specifically transmitted through genetic channels, and criteria by which they may be distinguished from environmentally transmitted response rules of the sort already mentioned, will be discussed in later chapters. For now, however, the reader must assume that behavior is governed by both types of response rules, and that consistent criteria can be used to separate them.

An heuristic condition for the broadest possible genetic analysis of behavior is that the highest order, or strategic, response rules be those that are genetically transmitted. Otherwise, the genetic viewpoint could explain behavior only on the tactical level, offering no insight into its strategic organization. If this condition is met, however, behavior can be broadly explicated from the genetic viewpoint regardless of the human propensity for acquiring novel response rules. Hereditary and acquired response rules, in other words, must be hierarchically ordered; the highest level rules being hereditary and the lower level rules being either hereditary or acquired. In terms more familiar to behavioral biologists: For broadest application of the genetic viewpoint, environmentally transmitted response rules must be limited to control of instrumental, facultative (or optional) behaviors, the obligative (or invariant) functions of which are represented by the innate strategies they subserve. Later results will justify or condemn this assumption, according to their success or failure.

If response rules are hierarchically arranged, then the highest level rules will ultimately generate extremely variable specific behaviors (Appendix C). If these rules are genetically transmitted, then genetic activity must be manifested via highly flexible processes. The well-known spinal reflex, for example, will provide no guide whatsoever to the mechanisms responsible for higher order genetically transmitted response rules. These mechanisms, however, are the topic of a later chapter.

Genetic Transmission and the Problem of Culture

Before looking further into criteria and mechanisms for genetically transmitted response rules, some clarification is required of genetic transmission itself. If genetic transmission of response rules were confined to pathways dependent upon immediate protein synthesis, no such clarification would be required. Seemingly paradoxically, however, genetic transmission of human response rules may occur via pathways dependent on previous, rather than current, genetic decoding. This is because human beings live in cultures that are environments systematically modified by the behaviors of previous generations. Insofar as earlier generations have shaped it, the human environment itself contains previously transcribed genetic information. Thus, response rules acquired by humans as the result of environmental influences may be those encoded in their own genes.

The difficulty may be better understood by considering culture an information channel parallel to conventional genetic transmission (see, for example, Reynolds, 1981). Conventionally decoded genetic programs into which extragenetically acquired information can be integrated to produce environmentally responsive behaviors are known as *open* programs (Mayr, 1976). These admit the possibility of extrasomatic channels of cross-generational information transfer. Nonhuman primates are known to be capable of limited cross-generational information transfer through extragenetic means (Itani and Nishimura, 1973), but evidence for the systematic exploitation of an extragenetic information channel first occurs in early hominids (Freeman, 1980). Among modern humans, information transmitted extragenetically through culture, together with information acquired through conventional genetic decoding, comprises the total information content passed from one generation to the next. Insofar as culture manifests previous decoding of the same information materially transmitted in the genes, the cross-generational messages on extragenetic and conventional genetic channels will duplicate each other. The extent of that duplication is of considerable relevance to the theory of innate response rules.

Unfortunately, the extent to which extragenetic and conventional genetic information channels duplicate each other has been the topic of bitter debate among social scientists. Numerous social theorists, for example, have found it necessary to demonstrate that cultural features cannot be wholly determined by genetic activity (Harris, 1979). From there it seems an easy leap to the closed cultural determinism dominating social science since Durkheim (1950). Actually, that genetic factors cannot rigidly determine human culture has been known to biologists since before the turn of the century (Huxley, 1894). No additional ground has been covered by latter day theorists, some of whom seem to have capitalized on misreading Wilson (1971). On the other side of the fence, though, evolutionary biologists have made equally spurious points. So-called "memes," or self-propagating cultural features said to be "parasitic" on human beings, have been deservedly criticized (Midgley, 1980). The meme concept extends an evolutionary model to cultural phenomena dependent on entirely different rules.

Fortunately, a theory has now emerged that accounts for cultural evolution in a new way. Rather than considering culture the product of competing determinants, the relative strengths of which are championed by one or another academic discipline, this new theory considers it the result of ordered interplay. Material, ecologic, and historical forces produce cultural possibilities, which are then *selectively retained* by individuals pursuing genetically determined personal motives appropriate to their environment (see Alexander, 1979; Durham, 1979). All new cultural features, according to this view, are eventually screened for concordance with evolved social motives. Thus, cultural evolution may be driven by processes that are

Lamarckian, nongenetic, and reversible (Medawar, 1976), but it is nonetheless constrained by Darwinian, genetic, and irreversibly established individual preferences.

The most thoroughly developed form of the theory of selective retention is offered by Lumsden and Wilson (1981, 1983). Their arguments are well worth sketching here, since they illustrate the basic principles involved in any theory of this type. Lumsden and Wilson first define what they call *epigenetic* (or developmental) *rules.* These are genetically determined and result from many different kinds of innate characteristics. Innate perceptual processes, stimulus and aesthetic preferences, gestures, fears, and cognitive tendencies may all determine epigenetic rules. These and other potentially innate characteristics also likely result in adherence to genetically transmitted response strategies (see Chapter 5 and Appendix E).

Epigenetic rules fix the probabilities that given *culturgens* will be selectively retained. Culturgens, which are basic cultural subunits, include physical artifacts, acquired behaviors, and *mentifacts.* The latter are ideas, myths, or religious and scientific beliefs. Therefore, epigenetic rules will exert pressure on cultural choices, shaping them along lines congenial with the panoply of innate perceptual mechanisms, preferences, evaluative processes, and cognitive functions from which they result. Although Lumsden and Wilson fail to discuss it in much detail, new culturgens are presumed to arise by generative processes intrinsic to culture so that a static condition—in which all remaining culturgens are equally compatible with epigenetic rules—will never occur. Furthermore, since cultural evolution alters the environment to which genetic adaptation must occur, epigenetic pressures on culturgen acquisition eventually result in evolution of new epigenetic rules, and the process becomes truly coevolutionary.

Lumsden and Wilson's model may seem like an unnecessarily complex way of saying that fashion is more likely to dictate two-legged than one-legged pants, and in some sense a reductio ad absurdum of this sort does capture the essence of their argument, but Lumsden and Wilson have also quantified their model. As a result, they are able to draw nontrivial inferences of real interest, if somewhat beyond the scope of this study. From the present point of view, the drawback of Lumsden and Wilson's model is not excessive complexity, but that it fails to fully develop the very aspect of selective retention that may prove of greatest psychiatric interest. This is that culturgens may be congenial to epigenetic rules for some individuals in a society precisely because they are incompatible with the same rules for others.

For example, among the culturgens selectively retained by epigenetic rules are those mentifacts comprising an ethical ideology (see Wolff, 1978; Markl, et al., 1978, for application of "selective retention" to moral injunctions). Rules, taboos, laws, and moral strictures fall into this category, together with ideals of conduct, tales of heroism, and religious precepts. Previous generations of biologic theorists have all too blithely equated altruism with ethical precepts, as if the latter always served the former purpose (see, for example, Wynne-Edwards, 1980). Yet, because failure to conform to ethical standards invites punitive aggression, only those individuals with the greatest power in any given society are actually able to formally or informally discard specific ethical precepts. These are the same individuals who may impose new precepts, or precepts only they wish to retain, on society as a whole. Therefore, selective retention of ethical rules is potentially a means by which the powerful in any given society mold the behavior of other individuals to promote their own innate preferences (see, for example, Alexander, 1979; Kurland, 1979; Breuer, 1982). The weak, by contrast, cannot impose ethics on the powerful. Furthermore, since no behavioral molding would be required if innate preferences were unanimous, ethical ideologies often apply to situations in which the weak, following their own epigenetic rules, might choose other behaviors than those preferred by the strong.

Among the ethical rules illustrating this principle are those imposed by parents on their offspring, when inclusive fitness interests (Chapter 2), and therefore innate preferences, of parent and offspring diverge. Innate preferences for certain social arrangements result in what may be called "prereflective" ethical dispositions, which are later elaborated in moral codes (see Nagel, 1978). Specific parental injunctions serving to mold children's behavior in ways favorable to parental inclusive fitness interests are described in later chapters. Not surprisingly, children who rebel against these injunctions eventually promote them as right and proper for their own offspring. This transformation, however, does not result from introjection of the parent into a developing superego, as Freud argued, but from the gradual shift of inclusive fitness interests—and therefore innate preferences—to coincide with those that had once influenced their own parents' moral choices.

In addition, if ethical ideologies manifest epigenetic conflicts between the weak and powerful, then ethical precepts serve to tame biologic impulses, but only those belonging to the weak. The notion that culture and nature stand in general opposition, which is central to Freudian theory and has since been echoed even by prominent biologists (see, for example, Lorenz, 1960), must be critically qualified. Even as they oppose epigenetic preferences of the powerless, stable cultural dictates inevitably conform to the preferences of those empowered to influence cultural choices. Cultural dictates that are an anathema to the very individuals who can enforce them are eventually weeded out. Therefore, apparent conflicts between ethical precepts and innate impulses are actually no different in principle than other frequently encountered conflicts between individuals motivated by differing preferences. They are merely apotheosized in the ethical strictures, punitive aggression, and rebellious countermoves that are most visible to the cultural observer. Various complications on this scheme are introduced to the extent that power of cultural choice in a given society is shared by individuals with divergent interests.

Not only is selective retention theory relevant to interpersonal, social, and, ultimately, intrapsychic conflicts at the heart of abnormal psychology, it also lends itself to description in terms of hierarchically ordered response rules. Response rules, as described, are analytic units uniquely suited to the genetic viewpoint. Broadest application of the genetic viewpoint requires that the most superordinate response rules be genetically transmitted. To recast selective retention theory in terms of response rules, notice should be given to homologous uses of very different cultural artifacts in particular societies. Americans, for instance, kill with firearms, tribal Africans with spears, and Amazon Indians with poisoned arrows. Yet very much the same sexual, competitive, and self-serving motives account for homicide around the world. Likewise, Americans practice actual or serial monogamy, Turkmen polygamy, and certain Ceylonese polyandry. Yet similar sexual, jealous, possessive, and parental feelings are served by marriage practices in every society. Readers interested in how particular marriage practices interact with economic and political exigencies to satisfy these motives are referred to Chagnon and Irons (1979). These and many other examples indicate that cultural artifacts, whether physical or ideational, fail to alter what have previously been discussed as high level genetically transmitted response strategies. Instead, they make possible new tactical response rules for realization of strategies in a given society. That cultural innovations are limited to the tactical suggests that selective retention depends on innate strategic needs in particular social environments. Cultural innovations that provide tactics useful to innate strategies are retained; all others are discarded. In this way, innate strategies shape cultural evolution to their own ends.

4

Genetically Transmitted Social Strategies

Criteria are needed to distinguish genetically and environmentally transmitted response rules. "Universality" and "evolutionary stability" serve this purpose well. Yet, evolutionary stability limits attention to social response rules. A hypothesis is suggested: Universal, evolutionarily stable social response strategies can be found that account for both normal behaviors and at least some of their psychopathologic variants.

Universality

An endless variety of response rules govern human behavior. By what criteria, then, can higher order genetically transmitted response strategies crucial to broad application of the genetic viewpoint be distinguished from environmentally transmitted or lower order tactics? First, the organizational primacy of any particular response rule must be judged on the particulars of its manifestations. Higher order rules will be manifested through many different behaviors consuming much of the individual's time and resources. By contrast, hierarchically subordinate response rules will manifest themselves only occasionally, or in response to time-limited exigencies, and will appear subsidiary to higher order goals. Their behavioral correlates will be less diverse than those associated with superordinate rules and will consume less of the individual's total resources. In the absence of valid and reliable quantitative measures, judgments of behavioral manifestations must remain impressionistic, which is nonetheless adequate for psychologic purposes. All the response rules considered in later chapters are such that their hierarchic primacy is obvious in light of their diverse behavioral manifestations.

In contrast to judgments of organizational importance, distinctions between genetically and environmentally transmitted response rules pose substantial problems. In large part, these result from redundancy between extrasomatic and genetic information channels, so that cultural transmission of a response rule fails to rule out its simultaneous genetic transmission. Since genetic transmission would occur even in a different culture, duplicated response rules are properly considered genetic regardless of their apparent cultural sources. The origin of redundancy in cross-generational information transfer is described in the previous chapter. If cultural transmission is little guide though, two other criteria are of more value. For reasons described later, response rules that are both *universal* and *evolutionarily stable* are likely to result from genetically transmitted predispositions, at least in the environment of adaptation. The strength of those predispositions, and their capacity to produce particular response rules in other environments than that of adaptation, should be judged individually.

Universality, as it applies to response rules, can never actually be proven. Mere ubiquitousness must therefore suffice. Higher order genetically transmitted response strategies should be ubiquitously manifested both within and across known cultural groups. Members of extinct cultures, insofar as their behavior is known, should also manifest these strategies, as may some nonhuman primates. Chimpanzees, the nonhuman primates genetically closest to homo sapiens, and baboons, who occupy an ecologic niche most similar to that of early hominids, are of particular interest in this regard. Apparent continuities of human and nonhuman primate behaviors, some of which were noticed by Darwin (1872) himself, demonstrate the great antiquity of certain response patterns. Some response rules, of course, may be absent among nonhuman primates for species-specific reasons, and others may be obscured for definable reasons in particular cultures or individuals, but all these reasons must invariably "prove the rule" if response strategies are truly ubiquitous.

Certain theorists argue that universality, much less mere ubiquitousness, is no proof of genetic predisposition (Gould, 1980; Simon, 1980). Review of their argument, which is quite correct, will point out the need for another criterion, evolutionary stability. Basically, they argue that invariant aspects of the natural world constrain human alternatives in a manner that produces universal behaviors. For example, at least since the Garden of Eden, all human environments have been such that food gathering requires some effort. Consequently, all human groups labor in some fashion to obtain food supplies. For universality to indicate biologic predisposition requires that behavioral characteristics continue to be in evidence even when the natural environment allows for alternatives. Behavior, that is, must confine itself to fewer degrees of variation than those permitted by the natural world. An interesting aspect of this argument, which leads to the subject of evolutionary stability, is that the social environment may also restrict alternatives available to individuals. Rather than environmental constraints being imposed by nonhuman factors, they are imposed in this case by the behavior of others.

Evolutionary Stability

Response patterns that are evolutionarily stable selectively penalize, in the evolutionary sense, individuals failing to manifest them (Maynard Smith, 1978; Davies, 1982; for a more complete discussion, see Maynard Smith, 1982). Generally, evolutionary stability characterizes certain response patterns only when they are frequent, or nearly ubiquitous, in the population under consideration. Evolutionary stability, therefore, corresponds to a special type of environmentally caused behavioral constraint. Untoward behaviors are permissible, but genes predisposing to them will be ruthlessly eliminated. The constraining factors, moreover, are not natural but consist in the ubiquitous response patterns that alone confer selective advantages.

As an example, a complementary set of male and female mating stratagems would be evolutionarily stable if neither males nor females could depart from them without suffering selective penalties, assuming the other sex continued en role. This would be the case, for instance, if females attempted to mate with competitively successful males, while males competed for control of useful resources as a way of attracting females. A female who failed to prefer successful males would be reproductively penalized insofar as her mate commanded fewer resources for her future use. She would also be reproductively penalized insofar as her mate's failure was transmissible to his sons. On the other hand, a male who failed to compete would be reproductively penalized by diminished mating opportunities. Even if he found a female willing to mate with him, he would remain penalized by his inability to command resources and by the potential genetic handicaps of his own children. Therefore, any genetic mutation acting to promote either new female mating preferences or male aversion to competition would be selected against, provided that the mating behaviors had already reached a threshold frequency for their evolutionary stability.

But evolutionary stability is not limited to sexually related behavior patterns. Response strategies far removed from mating and reproduction might nonetheless be evolutionarily stable if frequent in a given population. One such strategy, which has been widely discussed under the rubric *reciprocal altruism,* is the tendency of unrelated members of a social group to do favors for each other except when the potential recipient has failed to be altruistic in the past. This strategy is more comprehensively reviewed in a later chapter. The selective *cost* to the altruist of any particular favor is assumed here to be less than the selective *benefit* it confers on the recipient, an assumption that is true for many if not all generous behaviors. If they lived in a society dominated by reciprocal altruists, both those who refused favors to demonstrably altruistic recipients and those who dispensed favors without regard to the recipient's prior history would be selectively disadvantaged with respect to average persons. Those who refused favors would save the costs of altruistic acts but lose the potentially greater future benefits dependent on the recipient's goodwill. Those who ignored the recipient's history would incur altruistic costs for which future compensation was unlikely. Insofar as the costs and benefits of altruistic acts are disparate, the selective penalty for excessive generosity will be less than that for excessive niggardliness, yet in both cases individuals would do better to conform to the prevailing standards of altruism. Genetic mutations or drift predisposing to deviations from these standards will be weeded out.

Another nonreproductive response strategy likely to be evoutionarily stable is the tendency to peacefully associate with similarly acculturated individuals, while excluding or even attacking those acculturated differently. Like reciprocal altruism, this response strategy is more comprehensively discussed in a later chapter. Given an initial fragmentation into similarly acculturated groups, significant selective penalties would be exerted against individuals who allocated friendly and hostile behaviors according to different criteria. On the one hand, failure to maintain friendly relations with similarly acculturated individuals might leave the deviant estranged from any social group, members of which might readily attack him. On the other hand, failure to shun those acculturated differently might expose the deviant to attack by normally avoided, and potentially unfriendly, members of other groups. Failure to shun those acculturated differently might also distinguish the deviant from others in his own cultural group, thus carrying the risk of alienation. As in the case of reciprocal altruism, it is probable that risks of deviance are asymmetrical, with failure to peacefully associate with one's own group more stringently penalized than excessive pacifism toward outgroup members. Yet, genetic mutations or drift predisposing to deviations in either direction will again be weeded out.

Evolutionary stability in and of itself does not indicate likely genetic transmission. Just because a response strategy is structured to weed out genetic variations less conducive to its execution, it does not mean that it is genetically transmitted to begin with. To the contrary, a response rule may be environmentally transmitted and through evolutionary stability could prevent genetic change that might otherwise compromise it. In that event, evolutionary stability is a means by which environmentally transmitted response rules are protected from genetic mutation or drift, or by which culture imposes itself on reluctant nature. Scenarios of this kind are easily imagined, including some that turn previous examples on their heads. For instance, if members of an isolated community unanimously decided that males should mate only those polyandrous females who could compete with other women for the right to bear children, and that offspring from other matings would be murdered, then the resulting behavior patterns would be evolutionarily stable. Both males who mated unsuccessful women and women who failed to compete for the right to bear children would see their offspring killed. Therefore, evolutionary stability would seem to ensure that a decision taken for cultural reasons will remain safe from future genetic subversion.

Universality and Evolutionary Stability

If neither contemporary and temporal ubiquitousness nor evolutionary stability singly establish the likely mode of transmission of particular response rules, together they do indicate a role for genetic channels. A thought experiment will illustrate this principle. If the community described above could remain isolated for many generations, and if no upheavals disrupted the consensually approved mating system, then evolutionary stability would no doubt produce men and women more amenable to its rather odd regimen. Insofar as genes may affect sexual preferences, those inclining males toward uncompetitive women would have long since vanished. Insofar as genes may affect temperament, those inclining women toward pacificism would also have disappeared. Were ties reestablished after this long period with members of other groups, no doubt both the sexual propensities of the formerly isolated males and the aggressiveness of the formerly isolated females would prove remarkable to their new acquaintances. In other words, if response patterns are ubiquitous, so that selective pressures associated with their evolutionary stability are maintained for extremely long periods of time, then those selective pressures will eventually fix the response patterns in genetic material. This will occur through selection against any innate predispositions that hamper the response patterns and will proceed regardless of the patterns' origin. Even those patterns that were initially culturally determined will, given adequate time, become genetically transmitted through mediating dispositions. If an evolutionarily stable response strategy is universal, and has been universal for aeons, then nature—represented in whichever genetically determined predispositions promote its occurrence—must not only acquiesce but collude in its cross-generational transmission.

Admittedly, complex genetic effects may cause ultimate genetic compliance with environmentally transmitted response rules to be less than perfect or to take more time than might otherwise be expected. Highly aggressive women, for example, might fail to care for newborns, while men attracted to them might sire submissive daughters. Those heterozygous for particular genes (that is, who have only one copy of them) may be better adapted for certain behavior patterns than those who are homozygous (who have two copies), leaving the population with a proportion of poorly performing individuals. Adaptive traits may depend on many genes, leaving those with only one or a few of them selectively disadvantaged. In time, genetic selection should act to maximize the efficiency with which genes produce an evolutionarily stable response pattern. But for any given response rule, no guarantee exists that the most efficient adaptation has actually occurred. Sickle cell trait and anemia, of course, comprise the classic illustration of an adaptation, apparently to malaria, accomplished only with considerable genetic wastage. Among "deviant" behaviors, homosexuality in particular may result from inefficient genetic adaptation to an evolutionarily stable response rule, at least according to one sociobiologic theory (Chapter 15).

Nor is the capacity for genetic adaptation to environmentally determined response rules unlimited. Adaptations may occur in genetically determined talents, interests, preferences, and other easily modified characters that together comprise genetic predispositions, but not every selectively advantaged genetic outcome is achievable from human genes initially present. In the previous example, for instance, no competing female is likely to develop tusks, regardless of how useful these might be in intrasex competition. Genetic rudiments from which selective forces might eventually evolve tusks simply do not exist in the original female genes. Or if they do, other selective pressures, such as strength of the cervical vertebrae, might militate against their development. Similar remarks apply to development of strictly functional characters lacking in anatomic manifestations.

In spite of these caveats, universality—both contemporary and temporal—and evolutionary stability provide, when they jointly characterize a response rule, an indication of its likely genetic transmission. Extremely ancient response rules—those characteristic of nonhuman primates as well as of humans—are likely to be efficiently assimilated in the genes. Complex genetic effects may therefore be largely ignored, at least for psychologic purposes. Less ancient response rules admit the possibility of genetic wastage, manifested in a subpopulation of poorly adapted individuals, but are easily identified. Little confusion should therefore result. None of the evolutionarily stable response strategies discussed in later chapters is of such recent origin that the occurrence of significant genetic assimilation can be doubted. From their epigenetic model Lumsden and Wilson calculate that genetic assimilation may have occurred even in historical, much less prehistorical, periods (Lumsden and Wilson, 1981). Furthermore, none of these requires improbable mutations for fixation in human genetic material. Finally, the interactionist dictum must always be kept in mind: Insofar as response rules are genetically transmitted, their behavioral manifestations result from genetic activity occurring in the environment of adaptation. The genetic viewpoint is an heuristic device, not an excuse for ignoring environmental factors.

Two Important Consequences

An important consequence of the particular criteria chosen here for identification of genetically transmitted response rules is that they direct attention only to *social strategies*. Only social strategies, or response rules governing the interaction of individuals with each other, can be evolutionarily stable. Response rules governing the interaction of individuals with the nonresponding physical environment may be optimal, in that they achieve reproductive benefits at the least physiologic expense, and they may also be universal, but they can never be evolutionarily stable. Evolutionary stability requires that the strategic responses of the majority dictate selective pressures to each individual. This is possible only for strategies impinging on other persons—social strategies. Restricting attention to genetically transmitted social strategies would ordinarily be a drawback, except that strategies of this kind turn out to be the hierarchically superior response rules of greatest relevance to abnormal psychology. This will be demonstrated in later chapters. Here, however, it suffices to point out that the primacy of social life has been implicitly or explicitly acknowledged by virtually all students of human behavior (Appendix D). As a result, a system of abnormal psychology based on genetically transmitted social strategies is in the mainstream of modern psychologic science.

Second, if universality and evolutionary stability are used as criteria for probable genetic transmission of response rules, certain commonly encountered theories of abnormal behavior must be renounced. These theories, which comprise a large proportion of the extant sociobiologic literature on psychiatric topics, treat psychopathologic syndromes as manifestations of statistically deviant innate adaptive strategies with their own selective advantages. Tiger (1979a), for instance, speculates that depressed and manic individuals might, respectively, slow and accelerate the rate of social change within groups in a way that enhances group fitness. Though interactional effects of this sort may occur in some social groups, they do not seem sufficient basis for a theory of affective illness. Similar accounts have been offered of homosexuality (Chapter 15) and of schizophrenia.

In the latter cases, advantages to the group would have to offset the diminished fertility common to both disorders and the increased mortality consequent to schizophrenia (Gottesman and Shields, 1982). Other authors have seen potential sources of personal biologic advantage in abnormal behaviors. Depression in particular has long been thought of as a statistically deviant but nonetheless selectively advantaged behavior pattern (see, for example, Lewis, 1934). Theories of this kind accomplish in the genetic realm what interpersonal and behavioral theories sometimes accomplish in the psychologic: They equate psychopathologic clouds with their ostensible silver linings.

Both universality and evolutionary stability, however, restrict attention to social response rules evident among essentially all individuals. Therefore, a psychologic system based on response rules meeting those criteria cannot ascribe abnormal behaviors to deviant adaptive strategies, at least if they are to be genetically transmitted. Instead, psychopathologic syndromes must be treated as statistically abnormal manifestations of innate response strategies, which all individuals, both mentally healthy and ill, share in common. Just as congenital anomalies result from developmental miscarriage of innate anatomic structures shared in common by both healthy and deviant infants, so psychopathologic syndromes must result from exigencies of the same genetically transmitted social response strategies that organize normal mental life. Some clouds, in other words, have less of a silver lining and result more from developmental accidents.

A theory that looks for universal structures common to both normal and abnormal functioning will be especially congenial to Freudian analysts. Freud himself rooted psychopathologic theory in normal psychology and renounced special factors not operative in normal mental life. From the sociobiologic viewpoint, however, that unitary deep structures underlie both normal and abnormal psychology is neither a mandatory nor an obviously preferable hypothesis. Innate behavioral polymorphisms are known to occur in animals and may be even more likely among humans as the result of cultural coevolution (Lumsden and Wilson, 1981). Some polymorphous innate behaviors can be treated as multivalent unitary strategies, as is the case for response rules governing hostile interactions (Chapter 7), but a theoretical artifice of this kind may not always be plausible, particularly with respect to topics of psychologic interest. Ultimately, therefore, the power of a unitary approach to both normal and abnormal phenomena must be proven. Demonstration of deep structures common to both normal and abnormal behaviors, together with developmental accounts of each behavioral outcome, will be required for this purpose. This task is attempted in following chapters. Normal behavior is examined for evidence of hierarchically superordinate, genetically transmitted social strategies. Universality and evolutionary stability are used as criteria of likely genetic transmission. Social strategies defined in this manner are then applied to psychopathology. Just as their normal development accounts for healthy behavior, so their developmental miscarriage might be shown to account for mental illness. Before starting, however, a few more preliminaries are in order.

5

A Model of Proximate Causes

Genetically transmitted social strategies must be mediated by specific mental mechanisms. Attempts to relate strategies and mechanisms are really efforts to relate ultimate and proximate biologic causes. Acting together, four types of mental mechanism might produce adherence to genetically transmitted response rules.

Why a Mechanistic Model Is Necessary

To recapitulate, the genetic viewpoint characterizes modern ethology and, particularly, sociobiology. From this viewpoint, behavior is considered the product of genetic activity in a particular environment. This is an heuristic device, not a statement concerning sources of behavioral variation. Analytic units appropriate to the genetic viewpoint are response rules, which may be either genetically or environmentally transmitted and are usually hierarchically integrated. Broadest application of the genetic viewpoint requires that hierarchically superior response rules be genetically transmitted. Identification of hierarchically superior response rules should not prove difficult. Universality and evolutionary stability indicate likely genetic transmission. Response rules meeting these criteria are inevitably social and, by definition, are also widely distributed.

Although universal and evolutionarily stable social strategies may explicate both normal and abnormal behaviors, their immediate causes are the result of more elementary mental processes. Genetic activity may result in perceptual, affective, and other specific mechanisms, but it is unlikely to produce social strategies directly. Likewise, structures as abstract as social strategies are not likely to be represented in the human brain or in human mentation. Yet, if social strategies are abstractions, it needs to be shown that they are scientifically more palatable than ego strength, libido, and other hypothetical constructs that have given psychopathology a bad name. Hence, they must be systematically related to the measurable processes of which they are comprised, or rather, from which they emerge, as "patterns in nature" (Harre, 1979).

The present issue actually relates to *ultimate* and *proximate* biologic causes. In biology, ultimate causes are factors predisposing to the evolutionary selection of certain structural or functional features. For example, ultimate causes of gregarious behavior include the advantages conferred by aggregation and the high costs of solitary existence, both assessed in the environment of human adaptation. Because ultimate causes are the selective pressures leading to the evolution and maintenance of particular characters, ultimate causal explanations lend themselves to teleologic expression. Behaviors can be said to serve purposes embodied in selective pressures.

Proximate causes, by contrast, are the biologic-environmental mechanisms through which structural or functional characters are realized in the individual organism. For example, proximate causes of gregarious behavior might include the innate reinforcing properties of social interactions, which in turn are dependent on neuroendocrine mechanisms, and selective negative reinforcement of asocial tendencies during early development. Proximate causal explanations are expressed mechanistically.

Ultimate and proximate biologic causes can be studied without reference to the other. But the most fertile investigation of behavior in particular requires that each category of causal factor be accounted for (see, for example, Symons, 1979, p. 8). The study of proximate causal factors may especially suffer when ultimate causal considerations are ignored. Robinson (1979), for example, notes that brain-behavior studies have traditionally suffered from inadequate attention to the functional significance of behavioral measures. Lesion studies, for example, may be fatally flawed by inattention to behavioral ensembles of ultimate causal significance. By way of analogy, removing the tuner from a radio will have little effect on its function as a paperweight but will drastically effect its design-specific capacity to receive radio messages. The same point has been made regarding cognitive studies, which also proceed without much attention to ecologic validity (Neisser, 1982; Cole, et al., 1982).

Genetically transmitted response rules—behavioral patterns resulting from genetic activity—directly reflect previous selective pressures. Consequently, they are closely tied to ultimate causal explanatory schemes. Formed in adaptation to previous environmental exigencies, they are particularly well suited for the purposive inquiries that characterize much psychologic therapy. On the other hand, if anatomic, biochemical, or physiologic characteristics are used to elucidate behavior, then the inquiry must remain proximate causal, mechanistic, and, of course, nonteleological.

The problem of relating genetically transmitted response strategies to nervous and mental mechanisms is hereby redefined. It now becomes the problem of relating the units of an ultimate causal to the units of a proximate causal biologic analysis. Genetically transmitted response strategies, in other words, must be capable of proximate causal, mechanistic decomposition.

A Proposed Model

The remainder of this chapter indicates one way genetically transmitted response strategies may be reduced to proximate causal mechanisms sufficiently defined to become the objects of scientific study. It is important to note, however, that the issue of proximate biologic causation is an old one in psychiatric theory, although it is not traditionally stated in these terms. Just as Freud saw somatic drives as mediators between biology and behavior, so other theoreticians singled out other mental mechanisms through which human biology shapes behavior. Jung's concept of archetypes, specific images formed by evolution and influencing mental life, belongs in this category. So do the predetermined cognitive faculties from which modern "ego theorists" derive adaptive structures. Radical behaviorists attribute all behavior to a single process—that which modifies behavior according to reinforcement exigencies—which is also a biologic given.

The viewpoint adopted here assimilates these theories and others; it attributes proximate biologic causation to the activity of somatic drives, specific mental contents, innate cognitive faculties, or any other mental function predictably disposing the individual toward the response rule in question. Any mental process resulting in adherence to an advantageous response rule should be selected for, regardless of its specific classification (see Ewing's [1963] study of behavioral selection in *Drosophila*). Thus, mental mechanisms of many different kinds might play causal roles in human behavioral life. Some proximate mechanisms may be more advantageous, more rapidly evolved, or more flexible in unpredictable ways so that they become more important or subserve a wider variety of genetically transmitted response rules. This, however, is a matter of detail, not one of principle. In any event, the realization of response rules invariably requires the simultaneous activity of many different processes, not just a few.

If evolution has used a panoply of interacting mechanisms to achieve the behavioral patterns embodied in response rules, then guiding principles are all the more necessary for their post hoc disentanglement. Principles of this sort are provided by Pugh (1977), whose abstract analysis of naturally occurring control systems suggests a model for the proximate realization of genetically transmitted response rules. Pugh demonstrated that such systems, and even moderately complex man-made devices, cannot store sufficiently detailed response instructions to meet every possible exigency. Storing predetermined responses to more than a few such exigencies would require memory capabilities beyond what is physically practical. Pugh also argued, however, that control systems responding in a timely fashion cannot be preprogrammed to achieve any single superordinate goal, which, in the case of naturally occurring systems, would be survival or reproduction. For example, an organism preprogrammed only to maximize the chance of survival would be extraordinarily inefficient. Behaviors regularly associated with enhanced survival, such as seeking food or fleeing from predators, would have to be rethought by such an organism, which would quickly be replaced by organisms that took certain things for granted. These more efficient systems would not seek survival per se but, rather, less abstract goals associated with survival during the species' selective history.

Constrained by two opposing demands—one militating against preprogramming of specific responses and the other against employment of excessively general imperatives—naturally occurring control systems must take an intermediate form. To respond appropriately to complex environmental exigencies, organisms must employ response selection criteria more specific than ultimate behavioral imperatives (e.g., survival, reproduction) but still sufficiently general to provide guidance for every situation encountered. The criterion goals, and the possibility of their realization, may have either positive or negative valence for the organism. That is, they may be either sought after or avoided, and behavioral decisions will either maximize or minimize the probability of their realization. Pugh refers to those intermediate criterion goals as *innate values* and argues that estimates of their possible realization form the basis by which prospective behavioral choices are rapidly evaluated.

Dawkins (1976), too, makes a similar point: Behavioral programs dependent on innate stopping rules, or goal prescriptions that tell the organism when to cease activity, are superior in an unpredictable environment to programs dependent on action rules, or rigid behavioral prescriptions uninformed by adaptive goals. Time limits on goal achievement, however, require that stopping rules specify relatively simple goals. Stopping rules must also be hierarchically ordered so that the organism pursues specific goals in order of their adaptive significance. In effect, both Dawkins and Pugh argue that organisms must value certain environmental configurations, either negatively or positively, and must behave to achieve positively valued configurations and avoid negatively valued ones. The configurations must be sufficiently specific so that responses can be chosen rapidly, but sufficiently general to inform every decision.

Therefore, efficiency requires that environmental *appraisal processes*, to use Bowlby's (1969) term, play the central role in determining behavior of all but the simplest organisms. In turn, these imply the existence of *peripheral sensors* to detect valued environmental exigencies and of behavioral *subroutines* to generate adaptive responses. Other requirements for adaptive functioning in complex environments follow logically from these three. In particular, if a biologically valued configuration can assume varying forms with no common sensory component, a *data reduction* process is required to detect the configuration of biologic significance. This process will reduce various situations to their innately valued equivalents so that appropriate responses can be chosen. Obvious examples of the use of data reduction processes are those necessitated by human cultures. Cultures transform biologically equivalent configurations into many different sensory forms. Threat, for example, can be signified by gesturing, spear shaking, saber rattling, or gun toting, depending on the culture in which one lives. In addition, the identity of the person producing these signs also determines the degree of threat implied. The ability to recognize biologically equivalent threats in diverse acts by diverse persons—and to distill data in general—requires the accretion of cognitive models. Through these, information about the current situation can be reduced to critical elements, which can then be appraised in a culturally indeterminate fashion.

Similar flexibility is required on the output side too, since a stereotyped response repertoire will not suffice in complex environments. For example, to respond to threats with counter-aggression, individuals must learn biologically equivalent responses appropriate to their cultures. These may be fist fighting, spear throwing, sword fighting, or the use of firearms, depending on the society. Just as diverse environmental events must be reduced to one biologically critical situation, "threat," so one biologically appropriate response, "counter-aggression," must be expanded into diverse situationally appropriate acts. Knowing "what" and knowing "how" are equally necessary (see Mason, 1979).

Perceptual, data reduction, appraisal, and flexible response processes are merely the minimal number and kinds of mental mechanisms logically necessary to account for situationally adaptive responses in typical human environments. "Splitters" could no doubt list more, since the actual number of distinct steps between stimulus and response may be more a function of experimental ingenuity than of human physiology (see Robinson, 1979, p. 163). Nonetheless, with these four mechanisms in mind, a model can be made to show how mental processes result in adherence to genetically transmitted response rules: From perceptual input, cognitive models cull information about biologically critical exigencies. These are positively or negatively valued by innate appraisal processes. Response subroutines are rehearsed, and those promising optimization of future appraisal-based *utility functions* are activated. As used here, utility functions are overall numerical values assigned to particular situations and are composed from the combined output of two or more individual appraisal processes (Appendix E). From the continuous and serially integrated activity of perceptual mechanisms, cognitive models, appraisal processes, and tactical response subroutines emerge behaviors conforming to genetically transmitted social strategies.

Perceptual, cognitive, appraisal, and response subroutine mechanisms are discussed fully in Appendix E. Here, it is sufficient to note that the mental processes on which this model depends can be studied by objective means. Perceptual mechanisms subserving genetically transmitted social strategies have been thoroughly documented in both higher primates and humans. Cognitive models that serve to reduce complex sensory data have been the objects of psychologic research since Tolman (1932). This formulation of their role in mental functioning differs from most only in that it stresses reduction and transmission of new data to central decision-making processes. As demonstrated in Appendix E, innate appraisal processes relevant to genetically transmitted social strategies depend on neuroendocrine mechanisms and are subjectively experienced as affects. Tactical response subroutines are also easily defined.

Both elementary perceptual mechanisms and innate appraisal processes are built into the nervous system. Empirical evidence (Appendix E) demonstrates this to be true of perceptual mechanisms, and theoretical considerations (Pugh, 1977) require it to be true of innate appraisal processes. As discussed in later chapters, highly stereotyped affective valuations carry much of the burden for adherence to genetically transmitted response strategies. Both cognitive models and tactical response subroutines may also be stereotyped, either because of their representation in neural tissue or because of species-typical learning, but they are often idiosyncratic as well. Stereotypic cognitions are also discussed in Appendix E. Stereotypic subroutines include the "fixed action patterns" of classical ethology, the lower order somatic behaviors comprising sexual and other stereotyped interactions, and species-typical gestures.

Idiosyncratic models and subroutines are developed and maintained by specific mental mechanisms. Mechanisms leading to the accretion of cognitive models are varied and have been studied by "dissonance reduction" theorists (Festinger, 1957), "attribution" theorists (Kelley and Michela, 1980), and Piagetians (Phillips, 1975), among many others. Tactical response subroutines develop during juvenile play (Simpson, 1976), as the result of practice, and by observational learning. Observation is particularly important for potentially dangerous subroutines, when mistakes might be costly or hazardous (Bandura, 1979).

Readers interested in more detailed discussion of proximate causal mechanisms are referred to Appendix E. There the flaws of this model will be all too apparent. However, this framework, being minimally specific and consistent with Pugh's efficiency argument, still serves an heuristic function. By illustrating how diverse proximate mechanisms might produce adherence to genetically transmitted response strategies, it demonstrates the interrelation of descriptive and teleologic behavioral accounts. More sophisticated models of how proximate mechanisms combine to yield genetically transmitted response strategies should be based on research beyond the present purview.

II
Specific Social Strategies

6

Genetically Transmitted Social Strategies I

Infant-Caretaker Proximity Maintenance

Genetically transmitted social strategies serve to maintain proximity between infant and caretaker. Specific mechanisms, as well as responses to separation, are briefly described, using Bowlby's "attachment" framework. "Parental investment" is defined and applied to infant-caretaker conflicts, two of which are manifested in the realm of proximity maintenance. Infant-caretaker conflicts may have psychopathologic consequences.

Mutual and Specific Behavior

In considering genetically transmitted social strategies, the most logical starting points are those strategies that appear in the earliest days of life. These, of course, are social strategies governing the relationship of infant and caretaker. Prolonged childhood dependency sets primates in general, and humans in particular, apart from most other mammals (Mellen, 1981). As a result, dependent relationships comprise an essential key to unraveling certain unique facets of primate and human social life. Therefore, it is particularly fortunate that social strategies governing the infant-caretaker relationship have formed the subject of a most important psychologic study: *Attachment and Loss* by Bowlby. With this study, Bowlby reintroduced ethology into abnormal psychology and, in the process, irreversibly changed psychopathologic theory.

Essentially, the major social strategy described by modern observers of humans and animals, and applied by Bowlby to explicate psychopathology, consists in both infantile and maternal tendencies to maintain proximity to one another. Proximity, of course, is prerequisite to giving and receiving maternal care and protection, in which its selective advantages undoubtedly reside. These tendencies meet previously discussed criteria for categorization as genetically transmitted social strategies. Specific aspects of maternal care giving, moreover, fall under the heading of *Kin Altruism,* a social strategy that is the topic of a later chapter. Here, consideration is given only to proximity-seeking tendencies per se as they are elicited by maternal-infant distance, danger, sickness, or other discriminant cues.

Of the various aspects of these tendencies, the most important to note are mutuality and specificity. "Mutuality" refers to the two-sidedness of any attachment relationship. Both infant and caretaker participate in maintaining proximity. Not surprisingly, active responsibility falls to the caretaker in the early months. Relatively early, however, the infant selectively reinforces proximity maintenance and other altruistic acts and has at its command potent innate tactics (discussed later) for enforcing proximity maintenance from otherwise reluctant caretakers. As the infant matures, and before reaching the age of independent locomotion, he or she begins to assume more active responsibility for proximity maintenance. Thus, while in the first year of life proximity results largely from maternal behaviors, perhaps selectively shaped by infantile responses, in the second year the infant will crawl or toddle after the mother or simply refuse to let her go in the first place. "Specificity" refers to the discriminatory aspect of proximity maintenance. Caretakers act not to maintain proximity to any infant, but only to that infant identified as the object of their altruism. Similarly, even in the first year of life infants will not be satisfied by proximity to anyone, but will strive to achieve proximity to their own *attachment figure,* a preference that will last for many years.

Bowlby (1969) treats the specificity of attachment behaviors as a form of imprinting. Imprinting, first described in avian species, involves the rapid formation—during a limited phase of the life cycle—of preferences that thereafter remain relatively stable. Imprinted preferences, once formed, are of such peremptory force that they can only rarely be reversed or even replaced, except with the experience of severe trauma of a sort discussed in a later chapter. There is considerable evidence now that imprinted preferences to maintain proximity with and care for her own infant develop in the human mother within hours or days of birth. An important aspect of maternal attachment specificity, for example, consists in preferential responses to vocalizations of her own infant. Morsbach and Bunting (1979) found that twenty-two of twenty-seven mothers they studied had so learned their three- to eight-day-old infant's sounds that they could distinguish these from sounds of four other randomly chosen infants. As expected, if maternal attachment specificity develops very early, the events of the first few days postpartum have long-lasting repercussions on maternal behaviors. Klaus and co-workers (1972) found that first-time mothers who had more exposure to their newborn infants than is customary in most hospital obstetrics wards later maintained closer contact with their babies than mothers with less early exposure. Maternal-newborn contact beyond that typical in most hospitals may also reduce the probability of later child neglect (O'Connor, et al., 1977).

In contrast to maternal attachment specificity, infantile attachment specificity has provoked considerable controversy, at least in the psychiatric, if not ethologic, literature. Freud (1940), consistent with his attempt to derive social behavior from somatic impulses, hypothesized that infantile love for the mother results from her role as caretaker. As caretaker, she meets the infant's needs for nourishment, warmth, and sensory stimulation. Originally interested exclusively in these needs, the infant soon associates the mother with their alleviation. As a result, he or she desires the mother's presence, but only in response to pressing somatic needs. Only as the infant matures will he or she desire the mother's presence without regard to somatic discomfort. To refer to the ostensibly continuous love of the mother, independent of momentary somatic state, Hartmann (1952) used the term "object constancy." Unfortunately, object constancy had already seen service in quite a different context, so that its new use served to confuse two quite different ideas (Chapter 13). In any event, according to psychoanalytic theory, infantile attachment specificity develops through a stepwise process that would warm the heart of any learning theorist. Agreement of this kind, though, is less remarkable than it seems, since psychoanalysts and behaviorists alike share a common agenda: Construction of social behavior from rudimentary somatic reinforcers.

Unlike the Freudian theory of infantile attachment love, the ethologic approach taken by Bowlby argues that the infant, like his or her mother, is innately equipped to develop attachment preferences with or without intervening somatic rewards. Mediating reinforcements, according to the ethologic view, are of little importance in attachment imprinting, some manifestations of which antedate reinforcement histories altogether. DeCasper and Fifer (1980), for example, found that neonates prefer non-nutritive nipples that trigger recordings of their mother's voice rather than recordings of other women. This preference is evident on the first day of life, suggesting that its basis might be laid in auditory experiences occurring before birth. Even more convincing data come from experiments that dissociate somatic reinforcement and attachment figure. Harlow and Zimmerman (1959), for example, reported that infant rhesus monkeys raised with both cloth and wire surrogate mothers cling to the cloth surrogate when frightened, even if they obtain nourishment from the wire dummy. Fear-induced proximity maintenance is used here as a measure of infantile attachment specificity, which can be justified on both ethologic and sociobiologic grounds. Frightened infant monkeys also prefer unheated cloth dummies to a heating pad. Therefore, provision of neither food nor warmth determine identification of an attachment figure by infant rhesus monkeys. Instead, they choose their attachment figure on the basis of complex stimulus properties—including morphology and texture—that differentiate cloth surrogates from both wire surrogates and heating pads.

Proximate Causes

Given that proximity-maintaining social strategies are both mutual, in that they are manifested by both infant and caretaker, and highly specific, in that they respect the bounds of this social relationship, then through which proximate mechanisms are they actually manifested? Which are the eliciting cues, affective valuations, and innate or learned tactics acting in concert to maintain infant-caretaker proximity? First, cues eliciting maternal proximity-seeking behaviors are consistent with the protective and altruistic purposes for which proximity is selectively advantageous. For example, both nonhuman primate and human mothers seek proximity with their infants at times of alarm, in the presence of danger, or when rapid movement is required. Infants increase their own proximity-seeking behavior, which may consist in signaling, locomotion, or both, when alarmed, fatigued, in pain, ill, or in the presence of unfamiliar strangers. Childhood stranger anxiety, incidentally, has been the object of several psychologic theories, none of which take into account the real dangers posed by strangers to ancestral human infants. Another potent stimulus to both maternal and infant proximity seeking is separation itself, which explains the cyclical patterns of proximity maintenance evident following the development of infantile locomotion. When close, the infant has little need for proximity to the mother. Having wandered, though, he or she tries to rejoin her. Misinterpretation of this cyclical pattern is integral to Mahler's theory of separation-individuation, which is discussed later in this chapter.

Affectively experienced valuative processes also produce proximity seeking. From the maternal side, fear and anxiety from unplanned separations are only relieved by proximity to the infant. Signs of infantile distress elicit both subjective arousal and autonomic responses of a kind preparatory to adaptive behaviors (Donovan, et al., 1978). Positive feelings rewarding maternal proximity include security, relief, and affection, as well as the pleasure adults take from observing "cute" babies. Discriminant cues for cuteness probably include increased head size and facial foreshortening. Gardner and Wallach (1965) found that college students judged profiles more babyish as head shape was exaggerated even beyond normal limits. That cuteness is pleasurable is demonstrated by the popular market for cute pictures, posters, statuettes, dolls, and stuffed animals. All of these depict babylike animals or humans with more or less monstrously enlarged heads and small facial features. Their possession and enjoyment is popularly held to be the prerogative of women, precisely those who are most often called upon to function as infant caretakers. Whether males respond equally strongly to these objects, but fail to acknowledge it for cultural reasons, remains to be seen. Pleasurable responses to infantile security gestures such as smiles, cooing, babbling, and chuckling are equally powerful parental motivators, as any mother or father can testify.

For the infant, fear and anxiety are the foremost negatively valued motivators of proximity-seeking behaviors. Considered purely as affect, the so-called symbiotic longing—the desire for reunion with the all-encompassing mother (see Mahler, Pine, and Bergman, 1975)—may also belong in this category. Positively valued responses to proximity are experienced as feelings of security and safety and may also include the oceanic feeling (Fenichel, 1945) or sensation of universal union.

Although tactics subserving proximity maintenance have been mentioned, a more complete survey is justified. Maternal behaviors serving to maintain proximity to the infant include holding, carrying, following, and other obvious actions bringing mother and infant into contact. With older children, maternal calls, enforced by punishment for straying, also serve to maintain proximity. Somewhat more subtle are cognitive and perceptual habits characteristic of mothers of small children. These include curiousity about the child's whereabouts and the desire to maintain visual contact with the child. Infantile behaviors serving to maintain proximity to the mother are equally diverse. Crying, smiling, and cooing, among many other signals, have predictable effects on maternal behaviors. Another gesture predictably eliciting adult proximity is the raised arm, which is seen in both humans and nonhuman primates and is discussed by Bowlby (1969). Once a child is capable of locomotion, following, cuddling, and other active behaviors serve to increase proximity without adult intervention.

Three infantile proximity tactics—clinging, nonnutritive sucking, and attention seeking—deserve particular psychologic attention. Nonnutritive sucking occurs among primates of many species and consists of prolonged nonnutritive oral contact with the nipple (Bowlby, 1969). That clinging and nonnutritive sucking may be pleasurable in their own right is not at issue. Selectively advantageous behaviors of every type might in fact be pleasurable. However, clinging and the pursuit of oral contact also reinforce maternal-infant proximity. Infants who spend long periods clinging or at the breast have less opportunity to become separated from their mothers. Aside from their relevance to the theory of cutaneous or oral drives, propensities toward clinging and nonnutritive sucking also account for acquisition of transition objects, or objects cherished in place of the mother. In effect, behaviors predictably resulting in enhanced proximity to the mother in a natural environment may, outside that environment, be directed at objects other than the mother (Bowlby, 1969). Pacifiers, blankets, and teddy bears, among many other artifacts of civilized life, have sufficient morphologic and textural similarities to the mother's body to become the object of behaviors otherwise directed her way. The odor of well-used transition objects may also enhance their desirability to the child, as many mothers have discovered to their dismay. Not only is acquisition of transition objects more likely if the mother is absent or unavailable, but the intensity of behavior directed toward the transition object will fluctuate according to the same cues that stimulate or inhibit proximity seeking in general (Bowlby, 1969). Thus, fatigue, illness, or fear increase the child's desire to suck or cling to the transition object, as will temporary withdrawal of the object itself. Whether clinging and nonnutritive sucking in general, and transition objects in particular, are relevant to addictive and other psychologic disorders remains problematic, but at least the childhood phenomena can be placed without difficulty in an ethologic context.

Similar remarks pertain to childhood attention seeking. From the age at which they are first capable of locomotion, children periodically seek parental attention. They may call or return to the parent or show off to the parent their current activities or accomplishments. Superficially, the attention-seeking behavior of young children appears simply narcissistic (Chapter 15), particularly when it takes the form of apparent pleas for approval. But, just as clinging and nonnutritive sucking stand in subordinate relation to higher social goals, so does the infantile need for parental attention. Childhood narcissism, in other words, cannot be understood except in relation to its strategic setting. There it serves to engage the attention of powerful caretakers, whose interest in the child might otherwise transiently diminish. The tactical function of attention-seeking behavior is of particular importance in child psychology, where attachment insecurity and disordered self-esteem so frequently go hand-in-hand.

Response to Disruption

Under normal circumstances, infant and maternal perceptual, affective, and tactical processes are adequate to maintain proximity. But death, disease, psychopathology, and exigencies of adult life occasionally conspire to separate an infant from his or her attachment figure. The stereotypic infantile syndrome following disruption of proximity is well summarized by Bowlby (1969), who distinguishes three stages in its evolution. The first, or "Protest," stage consists of locomotory and signaling tactics normally serving to recover proximity, but now raised to a new pitch. Crying, screaming, and attempts to follow or find the attachment figure may persist for several days following disruption of proximity. During the second stage, "Despair," active tactical efforts to recover proximity cease, and behavior is marked by apathy, withdrawal, and lack of social interest. Social contact cannot be made, even though manifest behavioral evidence of attachment longings have ameliorated. Recovery of the attachment figure during this stage, unlike during the previous stage, does not elicit immediate joy, but instead occasions angry rejection. Only after a more or less lengthy period of anger will positive proximity-maintaining behaviors reemerge. The third stage, "Detachment," starts when infant and attachment figure have been separated for two weeks or more. During this stage, the apathetic and docile infant will manifest little or no emotional interest in temporary caretakers. Nor can the extreme emotional detachment be quickly reversed. The attachment figure, should she reappear, is likely to be met with long-lasting indifference. In extreme cases, and particularly among younger children, emotional detachment of this type may be followed by developmental failures and even by physical illness. Long-term consequences are likely. Studies of nonhuman primate infants deprived of their attachment figure will be discussed later, along with their implications for human psychopathology.

Considered as proximity-maintaining tactics, infantile behaviors following separation from the attachment figure are only partially explicable. The dramatic behaviors of the Protest stage are most easily understood, since they are transparent efforts to regain proximity. Behaviors characterizing the Despair stage, by contrast, are largely unintelligible. Conceivably, diminished responsiveness may have been selectively advantageous for ancestral primate infants temporarily separated from mature caretakers. Intense anger seen upon renewed contact with the attachment figure may serve to discourage future abandonments, as some have speculated, or may result from release of hostile feelings by attenuation of the attachment relationship (see, for instance, Reynolds, 1981). Frequently, infants reunited with their mothers—even after brief separations—will actually attempt to avoid them. Evidence points to the importance of anger in these cases, too, and suggests that avoidant behavior may be a way of ameliorating anger (see Main and Weston, 1982).

Even less sense can be made of behaviors characterizing Detachment. Why detached children make little or no attempt to regain attachment figures, and why some of them fall ill, remains entirely opaque, at least from an inclusive fitness viewpoint. Possibly, if infants separated for long periods in natural circumstances simply failed to survive in the course of primate evolution, behaviors now attendant upon prolonged separations could serve no tactical functions at all. If ancestral infants failed to survive prolonged separations, then no opportunity for evolution of adaptive tactics would have existed. The stereotypic behaviors seen in modern children suffering prolonged separations would then represent dysfunctional consequences of innate structures that only in other circumstances—in the presence of the attachment figure—act to promote inclusive fitness.

Although infants radically separated from all attachment figures may have inevitably died in the course of primate evolution, regardless of their behavioral response, infants might have lost individual attachment figures without necessarily perishing. Mothers, for example, might have died in the course of later pregnancies, leaving their previous offspring to be cared for by remaining kin. From an inclusive fitness point of view, loss of a single attachment figure, when others stand ready to act as caretaker, should not be followed by catastrophic reactions of the sort leading to permanent impairment. As noted previously, a central tenet of modern sociobiology is that individual behavior has been selected, at least in the environment of adaptation, to maximize inclusive fitness. This, of course, is just the representation of an individual's genetic material in future generations. Self-destructive reactions to loss when adaptive behaviors are actually available would seem inimical to maximizing that future representation. It is not surprising, then, that extremes of social detachment and consequent developmental failures are limited for the most part to children bereft of several or all attachment figures or to children whose environment precludes the development of attachment relationships in the first place. By contrast, those with surviving attachment relationships recover, at least superficially, from loss of even the principal caretaker.

Genetic Transmission

Do proximity-maintaining social strategies depend on genetic transmission, at least by the dual criteria submitted in a previous chapter? As to the first of these, universality, little doubt can exist. In the vast majority of known human cultures, a particular adult, usually the mother, remains in close and continuous proximity to a particular child, for whom she assumes a caretaking role. The adult-child association is highly specific and mutual, and its disruption is followed by behaviors originated by both adult and child that are intended to recover closeness. Even in those cultures, such as Israeli kibbutzim, in which for ideological or other reasons no particular adult attempts to maintain proximity with a particular child, proximity-maintaining social strategies are nonetheless in evidence. Communally raised children become attached to each other and to adults other than their biological parents (see Bettelheim, 1969), just as nonhuman primates may (see, for example, Bowden and McKinney, 1972).

The evolutionary stability of proximity-maintaining strategies also requires little comment. In fact, individuals who adhere to proximity-maintaining strategies are selectively advantaged regardless of whether their behavior pattern is ubiquitous or infrequent. Because proximity-maintaining strategies provide parents with access to their children for altruistic purposes, parents failing to actively maintain proximity to their own children, or indiscriminately maintaining proximity to children other than their own, will suffer a decreased capacity to aid their children through altruistic acts. Likewise, individuals genetically disinclined to respond to their children's attachment efforts, whether of the signaling or locomotory variety, will also suffer diminished inclusive fitness in comparison with individuals who do respond. In effect, parents who maintain proximity to their children to be ready to act altruistically whenever necessary will enhance their inclusive fitness, both in comparison with parents who are not altruistic and with those whose altruism is irregularly available. Similar considerations apply to infants and children. Children who wander from the very individuals who stand ready to provide altruistic aid when it is most needed will be selectively disadvantaged with respect to those children remaining in the orbit of a benevolent protector. Only late in childhood, when the child is more capable of fending for himself or herself, will the potential advantages of increased experience compensate for the risks of straying from the parent.

As for particular innate gestures subserving attachment, these too, once they have become ubiquitous, must be evolutionarily stable. Parents misinterpreting their children's cries of pain or fear, for example, will be severely penalized, as will children who produce signals or other behaviors unintelligible to their attachment figures. In addition, the possibility of receiving nonkin altruism (Chapter 11) makes it profitable for children to produce and for parents to understand signals common to all family lines, rather than idiosyncratic signals understood only by biologic parents. Intermarriage between family lines also militates in favor of universal signals.

Comparison with Bowlby

If proximity-maintaining strategies as a whole are both universal and evolutionarily stable, then they meet the criteria for likely genetic transmission. Neither in this conclusion nor in any particulars has the discussion thus far substantively deviated from Bowlby (1969). Yet, two important modifications of Bowlby's argument must be made before it can be fully integrated into a sociobiologic and ethologic framework. Dictated by theoretical considerations, these are required to account for phenomena central to psychologic interests. Other differences between Bowlby's and the present position, including the definition of innate behaviors, the distinction between strategy and tactical repertoire, and the place of affect, are of no real significance here.

The first important modification concerns the extent of attachment behaviors in normal life. Bowlby appears to argue that significant relationships throughout life are homologous to that between child and attachment figure. In this way, Bowlby appears much like Freud, who also sought in a single childhood relationship the Rosetta stone for later social life, or like Horney (1950), who attributed neurotic conflicts of all types to a single "basic anxiety," that of being alone and helpless in a hostile world. Other psychologic theorists have followed Bowlby in this respect and also assert that the mother-child attachment relationship is prototypic for later social interactions (see, for example, Hartog, 1980). In defense of Bowlby, and of those who follow him in this matter, homogeneity of social attachments is implicit even in some sophisticated ethologic studies, which occasionally treat all social bonds as if they were fundamentally alike (see, for example, Reynolds, 1981). From a sociobiologic point of view, however, homogeneity of social bonds cannot be taken for granted. Instead, particular categories of social relationships—and attachment as described by Bowlby is a social relationship, not a concrete connection as the word "attachment" seems to imply—must be analyzed in specific behavioral terms in order to determine their effects on inclusive fitness. Because behaviors comprising the maternal-infant attachment relationship differ from those comprising later social relationships, these cannot be treated as simply homologous. Infants, for example, do not characteristically mate their attachment figures, nor do adult mates usually maintain proximity in the fashion of child and mother. That certain behaviors characterize both types of relationship (see Weiss, 1982) should not be misconstrued, since these are mixed with other behaviors and employed to differing ends. Nor can mating, for example, be rationally considered "attachment with sex added," or the mother-child relationship might equally well be called "mating without sex," an obvious absurdity.

To emphasize the unique aspect of the infant-caretaker relationship described by Bowlby, the term "proximity maintenance" may be preferable to "attachment." Because avoidance of physical separation is what characterizes the relationship in question, "proximity maintenance" also describes the relationship without reifying it. The innate social strategies manifested in this relationship can be referred to as *proximity-maintaining strategies.* In this way they are easily distinguished from other social strategies described in later chapters.

The second, and by far the more important, modification of Bowlby's argument concerns his reliance on what has elsewhere been called *group selectionism* (see Irons, 1979). Among the theoretical foundations of Bowlby's work is the assumption that natural selection of behavioral traits occurs at the group level, an idea accepted by most ethologists until very recently. Groups whose gene pools are conducive to more adaptive behaviors, according to this view, drive less advanced groups to extinction. Although group extinction does occur in the animal world, and probably has occurred in the course of primate evolution as well, most ethologists and sociobiologists now believe that the major burden of primate behavioral evolution was borne by inclusive fitness differences occurring within groups (Irons, 1979). With due regard for the complexity of the issue (see Wilson, 1980), within-group, not between-group, competition is now thought to have been the major engine of behavioral selection within the primate line. Indeed, recognition of within-group competition, of individual rather than group level selection, provides the key to evolutionary explication of a wide variety of primate social behaviors, including virtually all behaviors of psychologic interest. It is among the major theoretical advances comprising modern sociobiology and has been influential as well in other biologic studies (see, for example, Lomnicki, 1982). Thus, not only does Bowlby's dependence on group selectionism limit his capacity to account for mental disorder, but it mires his theory in a behavioral biology no longer current.

The most serious limitation resulting from Bowlby's use of group selectionism is on his capacity to account for certain ubiquitous caretaker-child conflicts (see Hinde, 1982). If both adult and child seek an attachment relationship because it is, and has always been, advantageous to the group that young and old be bound together, then what are the origins of caretaker-child conflicts? From what source spring infantile attachment anxieties, which studies of caretaker-child conflict have shown to be pervasive in one degree or another? Conceivably, both conflict and anxiety may be accounted for through wholly psychologic mediation. The young, lacking in self-confidence, might consistently overestimate what they require from the attachment figure, while adults, lacking in patience, consistently underestimate infantile needs. Yet, to argue that a selectively advantageous social relationship is marred by psychologic factors like self-confidence and patience would seem to be mixing levels of explanation. Psychologic factors, after all, should reflect selective forces, if the thesis of this study is correct. By way of example, if harmony were of any value to the species, selection might have favored children with greater self-confidence or adults blessed with greater patience. Insofar as the caretaker-child relationship is inharmonious, specific inquiries must be made into the selective forces responsible for its inimical qualities.

Although he lacked the conceptual tools required for their explication, Bowlby nonetheless accurately described two classes of conflict between infant and attachment figure. In the first class belong those conflicts in which the attachment figure fails to provide adequate care, or is frankly inimical, and the infant responds by redoubling his or her own efforts to maintain the relationship. In relationships of this type, responsibility for maintaining proximity falls wholly on the infant. Bowlby (1969), for example, cites the increased following behavior of puppies and lambs and the increased clinging by infant monkeys in response to punishment. Human children, too, frequently cling to abusive parents (DeLozier, 1982). In the second class belong those conflicts in which the caretaker attempts to wean the infant from the attachment relationship before the infant is willing to give it up. Bowlby cites numerous conflicts of this type, both among nonhuman primates and humans, and concludes: "During the course of infancy and childhood in all higher primate species responsibility for maintaining proximity between mother and young shifts progressively from the mother to the young" (Bowlby, 1969, p. 243). The mother, in effect, becomes indifferent or hostile to proximity maintenance while the child still seeks it.

Parental Investment

Conflicts that are unintelligible from the viewpoint of group selection become intelligible when considered from the viewpoint of individual selection. Trivers (1978), in fact, has used the individual selection viewpoint, together with the concept of *Parental Investment,* to delineate two major types of parent-offspring conflict, which correspond closely to those noted by Bowlby. Parental investment, which must be counted among the most powerful of sociobiologic concepts, provides a specialized method of accounting for the inclusive fitness consequences of parental altruism toward real or potential offspring. Since proximity maintenance is for the purpose of parental altruism, conclusions concerning altruism apply as well to proximity maintenance. By definition, a parental investment is any investment, whether of time, effort, risk, or resources, that enhances the reproductive success of one particular filial heir at the reproductive expense of other real or potential offspring. Parental investment therefore signifies an invidious commitment; limited resources for parental altruism are devoted to one particular genetic descendant rather than to others. Parental investments begin, of course, before conception. Ovulation itself involves development of one follicle at the expense of others. A further parental investment occurs at implantation. By carrying a fetus, the mother gives it the opportunity to reproduce eventually. But she denies life, and therefore reproductive opportunity, to those potential heirs that may otherwise have been conceived during gestation. After birth, parental investments continue, though now in seemingly more volitional forms. By nursing, the mother nourishes the newborn child. But, since ovulation may halt during lactation, she decreases the probability of conceiving new life. Metabolic and other demands of neonatal care, moreover, may steal time and effort from older children, whose future reproductive success may consequently be diminished. The father too, insofar as he provides for the newborn, may have less to give to older children. Throughout infancy, childhood, and adolescence, every calorie of energy, minute of time, and iota of risk devoted to the maturing individual, if it comes at the expense of real or potential others, may represent a parental investment.

Like capital investments, parental investments can be summarized in cost-benefit terms, but the real cost-benefit ratio of any given parental investment cannot be calculated, except postdictively. Incremental enhancements of future reproductive success depend for their realization on too many unknown factors to be fully predictable. Costs, some of which are borne by offspring who do not exist at the time a decision must be made, are doubly impossible to accurately foresee. Fortunately, however, due to the effects of natural selection on parental willingness to make investments that have been advantageous in past generations, cost-benefit ratios need not be calculated anew for each parent and child. Clearly, for example, protecting the young from predation has always had a statistically advantageous cost-benefit ratio. Although protection may have made no difference for some youngsters, who may have perished later anyway, or due to parental injury may have resulted in excessive costs to other real or potential heirs, for the average parent-child pair protection must have been a high-yield parental investment. Parents predisposed to make this investment would, on the whole, have furthered their own inclusive fitness more than oppositely predisposed parents, and the predispositon, insofar as it was genetically founded, would have spread quickly through ancestral gene pools. Thus, the eagerness with which modern parents make certain parental investments provides an index of the average cost-benefit ratios similar investments must have yielded in past ages.

Parental Investment and Conflict of the First Type

Regarding the first parent-infant conflict, which results when the parent fails to provide the level of attention and nurturance demanded by the infant, a simple translation into the terms of parental investment is possible. In effect, the infant demands a higher rate of parental investment than the parent is willing to provide. It is likely that benefits accruing from parental investments vary according to the rate at which parental investments are made. At very low rates of parental investment—when the parent fails to provide much in the way of daily care for the infant—the infant's probable reproductive success is no doubt low. Given sufficiently little care, the infant will either perish altogether or become maturationally

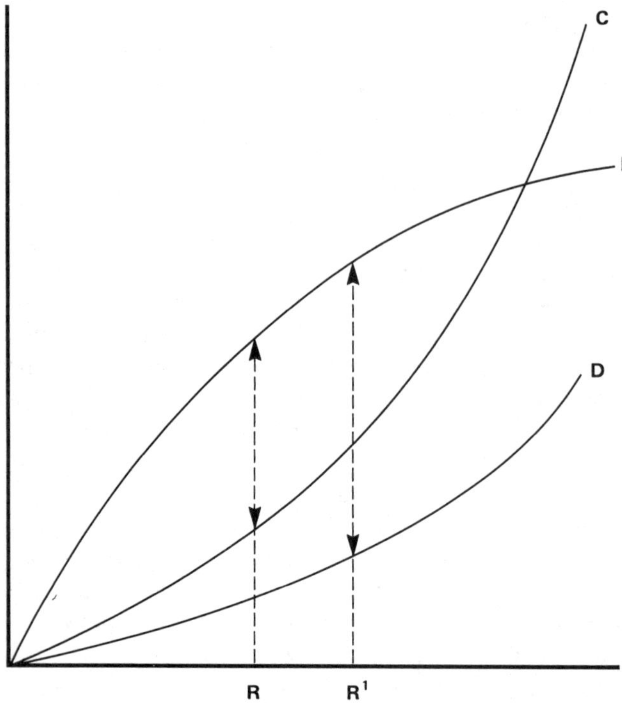

Figure 1. Inclusive fitness benefits (curve **B**) and costs (curve **C**) as functions of parental investment rate (horizontal axis). Curve **D** depicts a multiplicatively depreciated cost function.

retarded. At somewhat higher rates of parental investment, the infant's probable reproductive success will rapidly improve, but may still be suboptimal. Optimal or nearly optimal future reproductive success for a given infant may result only from very high rates of parental investment. Beyond that point, however, a higher rate of parental investment will cause little or no further enhancement of probable reproductive success. The curvilinear relation between rate of parental investment and probable reproductive success of a given infant is illustrated by curve B in Figure 1, which is adopted from Trivers (1978). It can be expressed mathematically by saying that I_b, the incremental change in benefits resulting from increases in parental investment rates, steadily diminishes as the absolute magnitude of those rates becomes larger.

Not only is likely benefit a function of the rate of parental investment, but so is probable cost. However, instead of rapidly increasing to a maximum level, as is the case for benefit, cost probably increases only gradually with rate of parental investment. Only at very high rates of parental investment would cost rapidly accelerate. By way of illustration, at very low rates of parental investment—corresponding to a state of relative neglect—few resources are withdrawn from other real or potential offspring to benefit the neglected child. Even at intermediate rates of parental investment the resources devoted to the child in question are likely to be sufficiently small—at least compared to those at the parents' command—that other offspring are deprived of relatively little potential aid. Only when the rate of parental investment becomes very high—when the parents devote nearly all their resources to a particular infant—does the parents' capacity to invest in other offspring become sharply limited. At this point the costs of further parental investments increase dramatically. The relation between rate of parental investment and probable cost, expressed in terms of diminished reproductive success of nonbeneficiary offspring, is illustrated by curve C in Figure 1. It too can be expressed mathematically, in this case by saying that I_c, the incremental change in cost resulting from changes in parental investment rates, becomes steadily larger as the absolute magnitude of those rates increases.

Since the maximum inclusive fitness to parental genes results from maximizing the total reproductive success of all offspring, the rate of parental investment devoted to a particular offspring should maximize the difference between benefit and cost. This is the rate of ongoing parental investment that results in the greatest number of second generation filial descendants from all real or potential first generation offspring. In Figure 1, the rate of parental investment marked R is that leading to the greatest difference between benefit and cost functions (curves B and C). Insofar as parents act to maximize their own inclusive fitness—and a central tenet of sociobiology is that parents living in an environment resembling the one to which they are adapted will do just that—they should choose to make parental investments in particular offspring at the rate R.

Readers familiar with elementary calculus will recognize that the rate R represents the point where an incremental change in benefits, I_b, is always counterbalanced by an equal incremental change in costs, I_c, for small increments or decrements in parental investment rates. In other words, at the rate R

(1) $$I_b = I_c$$

for small changes in rate.

However, the infant is unlikely to be fully satisified with the rate of investment, R, maximizing parental inclusive fitness. In order to maximize inclusive fitness of his or her own genes, the infant must assume a rather different view of his or her worth relative to that of potential or real siblings. From the parents' point of view a unit of reproductive benefit conferred on one child is of the same value as a unit of reproductive cost incurred at the expense of another. This is because both children share with the parent an equal proportion of his or her genes. From the child's point of view a unit of reproductive benefit received is worth two units of reproductive cost incurred at a full sibling's expense. This is because even a full sibling carries only half the beneficiary's genes. Reproductive costs incurred by half-siblings, who carry one quarter the beneficiary's genes, are discounted by a further factor of two. One unit of benefit received would just balance four units of cost incurred at the expense of a half-sibling. In effect, the child, in order to maximize inclusive fitness of his or her own genes, must depreciate the cost function of any given rate of parental investment—dividing by a factor appropriate to the degree of sibling relatedness—and then seek a rate of parental investment that maximizes the difference between benefit and depreciated cost. Curve D in Figure 1 illustrates the depreciated cost function as it appears to the child. As illustrated in Figure 1, the rate of parental investment (R') that maximizes the difference between benefit and depreciated cost (curve D) will always be greater than the rate that maximizes the difference between benefit and cost as they appear to the parent. The child, in order to maximize inclusive fitness of his or her own genes, must seek to receive a rate of parental investment greater than the rate that maximizes inclusive fitness of parental genes. The discrepancy between these two rates, in fact, is the source of the first type of parent-infant conflict, which, although manifested in most extreme form when the parent prefers a very low rate of parental investment, is actually ubiquitous. It is now also obvious that conflict of this type depends on divergence between genetic interests of parent and child, which is why it cannot be understood within a group selectionist framework, which emphasizes only what parent and child share in common.

If necessary, that upward shifts in preferred rates of parental investment follow from multiplicative depreciations of the cost function can be mathematically deduced from equation 1 and from the fact that I_b and I_c are decreasing and increasing functions, respectively, of the absolute rate of parental investment. That is, the second derivatives of the benefit and cost functions with respect to rates of parental investment are always negative and positive, respectively. However, this is a problem in elementary calculus that is beyond the scope of this discussion. Depreciating the cost function as it appears to the parent effectively diminishes I_c for any given rate of parental investment. This means that equation 1 will no longer hold at the rate R. In order to find the new rate of parental investment, R', at which equation 1 is again true, I_b must be decreased and I_c increased until they are again equal. Necessary changes in both I_b and I_c will only occur with increased rates of parental investment. The same argument applies to multiplication of the benefit function.

An individual acting throughout life to maximize his or her own inclusive fitness would therefore seek different ends as child and parent. As a child, such an individual would seek a rate of parental investment higher than that offered to his or her own future children. Yet, these children too should demand a higher rate of parental investment than their parents willingly offer, so that the pattern of conflict repeats itself. Other cross-generational conflicts are maintained because the same individuals take both sides at different stages of the lifespan, a process all too easily confused with defensive introjection.

What are the tactics used by children to increase the rate of parental investments they receive? Obviously, since parental altruism cannot be coerced, these must cause parents to prefer a higher rate of investment than they would otherwise choose. The key to altering parental preferences, however, lies in the fact that both the benefit and cost functions as they appear to the parent are situation-specific. Cost functions, for example, depend for their rate of increase largely on parental resources. Parents controlling more physical and social resources can increase parental investments in any one child at less cost to other children than is the case for parents with fewer resources under their control. As shown previously, when the cost function is depreciated, preferred rates of parental investment should rise. Contrariwise, parental impoverishment will increase the cost function, reducing preferred rates of parental investment. Turnbull's (1973) description of child neglect among starving villagers testifies to the real effects multiplying the cost function has on human parental investment rates. Age and parity affect the cost function as it appears to parents in a fashion similar to resource control. Younger parents, because they are more capable of having future offspring, may be less willing to invest exclusively in living ones. Similarly, the more living siblings there are, particularly if any of them are sick, endangered, or immature, the less parents will be willing to direct excessively high rates of parental investment toward any given child.

While the cost function is largely influenced by parental characteristics—resource control, age, and parity, for example—the benefit function as it appears to parents is more influenced by characteristics of the beneficiary. By way of illustration, rates of parental investment ordinarily considered excessive, because they would result in little further increment in reproductive success, might yield considerably more incremental benefits when directed toward a sick child. In effect, illness might increase the benefits resulting from enhanced rates of parental investment. Multiplication of the benefit function has the same effect on parental investment preferences as depreciation of the cost function. Conversely, if a child is irremediably ill, rates of parental investment that otherwise yield considerable incremental reproductive benefits might actually become fruitless. The benefit function is depreciated, which has the same effect as multiplication of the cost function. Child endangerment should have the same biphasic effect: only insofar as the child can be aided will excessive rates of parental investment continue to yield additional benefits. Immaturity, too, can increase the benefit function. Young children, being more dependent on parental care, can likely profit from rates of parental investment that would yield few incremental benefits if directed toward an older child.

Returning to the tactics children may use to increase their parents' preferred investment rates, it is clear that the benefit function as it appears to parents is more easily manipulated than the corresponding cost function. The latter is dependent on parental and, to a limited extent, sibling characteristics outside the control of any given child. Even before the parental benefit function can be manipulated, however, the child must make himself or herself available for reception of parental investments. The child, that is, must counteract any parental tendency toward withdrawal. Insofar as the child's efforts to maintain proximity signify immaturity or need to the parent, redoubled proximity efforts alone—these being, after all, the narrowly construed subjects of this chapter—may suffice to manipulate the parental benefit function in the desired direction. The fact that young of many species increase their own proximity-seeking behaviors in response to failing rates of parental investment is now well documented. Puppies and lambs, for example, follow punitive attachment figures more persistently than they follow altruistic ones, and infant monkeys cling more tenaciously in the face of ill-treatment (Bowlby, 1969). Human infants, too, may cling to abusive parents (DeLozier, 1982).

If enhanced proximity seeking alone fails to improve rates of parental investment, however, more specific attempts may be made to manipulate the parental benefit function. The child may feign illness, fear, or immaturity in the hope of increasing the rates of parental attention he or she receives. The parents, to allocate investments to maximize their own inclusive fitness, should be on the alert for mimicry of this sort and may even be motivated to punish it as a means of deterring dishonest children. Even if the child forgoes frank mimicry, however, he or she should remain only too eager to alert the parent, by proximity seeking, gestures, and signals, whenever illness, immaturity, or external danger might justify to the parent increased rates of parental investment.

Those who know children are aware that interactions very much like those described here are frequent occurrences between parent and child. Human children are ever eager to inform their parents of new situations that justify higher rates of investment. Illness or injury elicit stereotyped signals including moaning, screams, cries, and, if the child is old enough, verbal complaints, which effectively alter the parental benefit function. Faced with environmental exigencies to which they cannot respond or that appear threatening to them, children will follow and cling to their attachment figure and indicate in a variety of other ways their subjective distress. In addition, youngsters not receiving what they consider an adequate share of parental attention frequently feign illness, mimic immaturity, or confabulate dangers in order to obtain what they are missing. As expected, parents observe their children for malingering, regression, and lying, and punish infractions mildly in order to deter them. Parents and children, in other words, engage in an unceasing and easily observed struggle over rates of parental investment consistent with their differing inclusive fitness interests and mediated largely through the benefit function as it appears to the parent.

Tactics used in childhood to increase the rate of parental investment frequently reappear in the behavior of disturbed adults. Dependent persons in particular may mimic either physical or psychological illness, present themselves as incompetent or immature, or exaggerate the extent of anticipated difficulties in the hope of receiving special assistance. Also, patients prone to malingering, regression, or exaggeration in order to obtain special attention frequently show other evidence of their preoccupation with early attachment experiences. In psychotherapy, tactics of this sort frequently emerge following disappointments in the therapist, who is thought to be insufficiently interested in the patient's well-being. In dependent adults, enhanced proximity seeking to punitive attachment figures, together with observational learning (see Bandura, 1973), may contribute to the clinical phenomenon known as "identification with the aggressor."

Parental Investment and Conflict of the Second Type

Concerning the second type of parent-infant conflict mentioned by Bowlby, it should be readily apparent that it is merely a special case of the conflict already analyzed, that over rate of parental investment. As the infant matures, the benefit and cost functions as they appear to the parent justify a lower and lower rate of parental investment (Trivers, 1978). Eventually, the high rate of parental investment characterizing early childhood must diminish, although in species characterized by *kin altruism* (Chapter 11) parental behavior may remain somewhat beneficent throughout the child's life. The maturing child, whose inclusive fitness interests coincide only partially with his or her parents', may transiently prefer that parental investments continue at their previous high rates. Manifested in the realm of proximity maintenance, the conflict between parent and maturing child presents itself as the shift in responsibility noted by Bowlby, but it can also be observed in disagreements over specific parental favors. Considering first the benefit function as it appears to the parent, the effects of the beneficiary's advancing age are obvious. Parental investments in a healthy newborn may salvage from otherwise certain loss its entire reproductive life. The same efforts expended on behalf of an older child may marginally enhance its future reproductive success, but cannot yield benefits incrementally equivalent to those attainable earlier in the child's life. Expended on behalf of an even older child, equivalent parental investments may have no definite impact at all on reproductive success. Therefore, increasing age effectively depreciates the benefit function, which has the same effects as multiplication of the cost function. But the cost function too may increase since the older child is more likely to have younger siblings, which increases the cost of parental investments on his or her behalf.

The parent, in order to maximize his or her own inclusive fitness, must terminate a given level of parental care when the incremental benefits expected from it no longer exceed its predicted incremental costs. Therefore, age-related changes in benefit and cost functions as they appear to the parent will lead him or her to terminate the high level of parental care characterizing the earliest stage of the parent-infant relationship. Since the child, however, discounts the cost function by a factor dependent on his or her genetic relationship to potential or real siblings, he or she should continue to desire the same high level of parental care long after the parent becomes unwilling to continue it. From the parents' point of view, the child seems to demand continued high rates of parental investment long after their incremental benefit and cost differences no longer justify them. Until maturity further reduces the incremental benefits, as they appear to the child, of high rates of parental investment, parent and offspring will be in conflict. Only after the marginal benefit and cost differences as they appear to both parents and offspring are in agreement will they concur in diminished rates of parental investment. Even then, the extent of the diminution called for will likely be a source of further conflict.

The precise age at which parent-child conflict of the second type occurs, its severity, and alternative sources of care taking available to the child all depend on cultural factors. Conflict of this type may be more severe in modern than in primitive societies (see Konner, 1982).

Tactics and countertactics used by parent and child in conflicts over termination of high rates of parental investment are the same as those employed in conflicts of the first kind. No difference in tactics is to be expected, given that one conflict is a special case of the other. The child will hasten to inform the parent of factors adjusting the benefit and cost functions in his or her favor or may mimic those factors in the ways already described.

Parent-child conflicts at the end of the early attachment period, when rates of parental investment diminish sharply from their previous high levels, have interested many psychologic theorists. Perhaps the best known of these is Mahler, whose work with Pine and Bergman (1975) has been widely circulated among mental health professionals. Unfortunately, Mahler, Pine, and Bergman make few distinctions between observed behaviors and hypothetical constructs or between facts and psychoanalytic theories. They also ignore cultural factors. What may be useful in Mahler, Pine, and Bergman's work are their descriptions of the so-called "practicing" and "rapprochement" phases, which seem to correspond to fluctuating states reached in parent-child conflicts at the end of the early attachment period. Together, they comprise the "separation-individuation" crisis, which normal children are said to eventually master. During the practicing phase, for instance, the infant becomes increasingly independent from his or her mother. He or she ventures away from the mother, secure in the belief that she will continue to be vigilant. Having sensed, however, that the mother will permit greater distance than feels secure, the infant enters the rapprochement phase. Rushing back to the mother, he or she attempts, using a variety of means, to insure her continued love. Between practicing and rapprochement, in other words, the infant loses faith in maternal constancy. The ever-concerned mother of the practicing phase becomes someone to be wooed. Failures of infantile reassurance during the rapprochement phase are said by Mahler and co-workers to result in adult psychopathology, particularly borderline personalities (Mahler, 1971). These will be treated in a later chapter in somewhat similar terms, although in the language of ethology and sociobiology rather than object relations theory. It may reflect the basic incompatibility of psychoanalytic object relations and an ethologic view that Mahler, Pine, and Bergman failed to cite either of Bowlby's first two volumes on attachment, which were in print before their own study was published and covered many of the same topics.

Yet a third type of infant-caretaker conflict—that over altruistic or egocentric acts between siblings—is also explicable in inclusive fitness terms (Trivers, 1978). Because it falls outside the purview of infant-caretaker proximity maintenance, it is discussed in Appendix F. Material in Appendix F illustrates the view of ethical ideology presented in Chapter 3 and also complements information presented in Chapter 9.

Finally, before leaving the topic of parent-child conflicts, mention should be made of their implications for identical twins. Insofar as they are able to judge genetic relatedness, identical twins should neither discount parental investment costs incurred at the other's expense nor reproductive benefits directed the other's way. As a result, identical twins might experience, on the basis of their inclusive fitness interests, less in the way of parent-child conflict than that typical of merely fraternal siblings. All this is complicated, however, by difficulties of ascertainment and by simultaneous birth, which creates different resource-sharing exigencies from the very beginning. Whether special psychologic mechanisms could have evolved to regulate relationships between parents and the relatively few identical twins who might be born and survive in a primitive environment is also problematic. Nonetheless, the family relationships of identical twins, like sibling interactions in general, deserve further study from a combined ethologic and psychologic viewpoint.

7

Genetically Transmitted Social Strategies II

Rules of Hostility

The inclusive fitness consequences of potentially hostile interactions lead to certain response strategies. These include "hawk," "dove," and "retaliator" strategies. "Payoff matrices" are used to evaluate inclusive fitness consequences of particular strategies as well as to assess evolutionary stability. "Resource holding power" may be related to subjective self-esteem.

The Problem of Hostility

Although infant-caretaker proximity seeking is conflict ridden, its overall theme is one of cooperation. Both parent and child desire that the child survive, and both possess complementary behavioral, gestural, and affective traits ensuring that outcome. By contrast, many of the genetically transmitted social strategies discussed in later chapters are competitive to the core. Rather than share a common goal, participants in interactions of this sort seek ends incompatible with each other's inclusive fitness interests. Instead of feeling mutual affection, participants are more likely to feel mutual hostility. To understand these strategies, one must first be introduced to the sociobiologic theory of within-species contests. This has been elegantly reviewed by J. Maynard Smith (1978a), whose arguments will be summarized in this chapter. Those interested in a more extensive treatment of within-species contests should read Maynard Smith (1982).

Before proceeding, however, it is worth mentioning the difficulties posed by within-species fighting for group selectionist theories of behavioral evolution and some popularized responses to those difficulties. As the reader will recall, group selectionist theories attribute behavioral selection to extinction of whole groups. Although well-controlled hostility can be explicated in group selection terms—it might, for example, be best for the group that males fight for dominance, ensuring the leadership of the most competent—they become more difficult to explain in terms of group interest, as soon as hostilities get out of hand and result in serious injury. It would seem that group interests could always be better served, for example, by nonlethal violence, rather than by violence that kills or disables.

Since most lay biologists, as it turns out, belong in the camp of group selectionists, popular films and literature have addressed this question and have proposed two contrasting intellectual solutions to it. One of these is to emphasize the ostensibly cultural origin of dysfunctional violence. Nature, according to this view, does not produce the type of violence inexplicable in group selection terms; it is the result of the cultural perversion of human nature. Thus, clashing deer, elk, gorillas, or baboons, among many other animals, are portrayed as commonsensical, symbolic fighters, whose tangles terminate without serious injury once their purposes have been accomplished. Only men and women, culturally fallen from animal grace, continue battles to the point of death and maiming. Murder, mayhem, and war, according to this view, are no more the natural product of human nature than semiconductors, automobiles, and space stations, but result instead from its subjugation to the cultural machine. This viewpoint, in one respect the polar opposite of Freudian social theory, is less plausible than it seems at first glance. Even if humanity did hold a patent on lethal violence, which it does not, and even if that patent were cultural, for which no evidence exists, it would still be necessary to ask why a basically peaceful animal stands so ready to adopt murderous ways. Nor would it offer any realistic means of ameliorating human violence, since a return to the state of nature is no longer possible.

A second popularized resolution of the problem posed by dysfunctional violence is to treat it as a natural, but accidental, by-product of other traits for which biologic advantages are more obvious. In particular, evolution of human murderousness has been laid at the feet of big game hunting, which ostensibly requires a readiness to shed blood of all kinds. The protohuman group, according to this view, may have tolerated an occasional murder in order to eat meat. Like the cultural theory of violence, the by-product theory also enjoys a wide following. This is in spite of the fact that it makes even less sense than the cultural theory. Men and women, for example, distinguish humans and nonhumans for a wide variety of purposes; why they should fail to do so for violent purposes is not at all clear. Physiologic studies show little connection between predatory and inter-individual aggression (Konner, 1982). Nor are the subjective experiences accompanying hunting similar to those accompanying murder. And if it was good for the group to eat meat, then the meat-eating group which successfully banned murder should have been even more successful, according to a group selectionist view, and should have replaced meat-eating groups who killed each other.

An Inclusive Fitness Solution

In contrast with the more popular solutions, the scientific response to the problem posed by within-species violence has been to hasten the demise of group selectionist theory. As described in Chapter 6, group selectionist theories, because they stress that which individuals have in common, cannot explicate situations in which behavior is determined by divergence of selective interests. Also, once the blindfold of group selectionist theory is dropped, within-species violence appears in its full scope and magnitude. Animals, as it turns out, actually do harm their own kind whenever doing so predictably enhances inclusive fitness. Typical lion prides, for example, consist of two adult males, seven adult females, and young of both sexes (Bertram, 1976). Immature males leave the pride before reaching maturity and, pairing up, may attempt to take over another pride by driving away the adult males. If they succeed, they are likely to kill cubs fathered by the males they have defeated. Although clearly incompatible with the numerically measured interests of the group or species, infanticide by newly regnant males—because it renews the fertility of otherwise lactating females—serves the killers' own inclusive fitness interests. Similar behaviors occur among hanuman langurs, black and white colobus monkeys, and hamadryas baboons (Clutton-Brock and Harvey, 1976).

If within-species violence can be used to promote inclusive fitness, then inclusive fitness, and not group or species welfare, must ultimately regulate the willingness to employ violence in particular situations. This follows from the basic tenet of sociobiology: Behavior has evolved to maximize inclusive fitness in the environment of adaptation. If inclusive fitness considerations regulate violence, then the inclusive fitness consequences of various levels of violence, and of various methods of within-species fighting, will prove to have widespread psychologic ramifications manifested in any sort of competitive or potentially competitive interchange. It is precisely these consequences J. Maynard Smith (1978a) has elegantly summarized and that are the topic for much of this chapter.

Basically, Maynard Smith explored the payoff matrices resulting from alternative combat strategies used in within-species *contests.* A contest, according to Maynard Smith, is any dyadic social interaction in which the two participants would rank the possible outcomes in different orders of preference. Combat strategies are specifications of behavioral responses to particular contest exigencies. They may be pure, in which case given behaviors are invariably associated with given elicitors, or they may be mixed. Mixed strategies are probability schedules giving the likelihood of particular behaviors in response to particular exigencies. The *payoff matrix* for a contest specifies the inclusive fitness result for every possible permutation of strategic choices. Thus, using Maynard Smith's nomenclature, the expected payoff for an individual using strategy I against an opponent following strategy J is $E_j(I)$, where E indicates its expected, or probabilistic, quality. If the contest is such as to allow each of two participants a choice between strategies I and J, the complete set of possible outcomes (for individual A) is specified by the payoff matrix:

(1)

		B's choice	
		I	J
A's choice	I	$E_i(I)$	$E_j(I)$
	J	$E_i(J)$	$E_j(J)$

Suppose that in a given population of potential contestants, p is the probability that an individual will employ strategy I in the above contest and $q = 1-p$ is the probability that an individual will employ strategy J. The average payoff, $P(I)$, to the individual using strategy I will then become:

(1.1) $$P(I) = pE_i(I) + qE_j(I)$$

Similarly, the average payoff to an individual using strategy J will become:

(1.2) $$P(J) = pE_i(J) + qE_j(J).$$

Recall that an evolutionarily stable strategy is one that, once having become ubiquitous in a population, cannot be dislodged by mutant strategies resulting from genetic change. In light of equations 1.1 and 1.2, this means that strategy I is evolutionarily stable if, for any alternative minority strategy J, $P(I)$ is greater than $P(J)$. In other words,

$$pE_i(I) + qE_j(I) > pE_i(J) + qE_j(J) \tag{1.3}$$

whenever p approaches one. Therefore, the notion of evolutionary stability can be related to the entries in payoff matrices describing the outcomes of social contests.

But what if two strategies, I and J, coexist in a state of equilibrium? For two strategies to coexist in the same population in a state of equilibrium, the benefits resulting from one strategy must equal those resulting from the other. In other words, $P(I)$ must equal $P(J)$. When the full algebraic expressions for these terms are substituted and rearranged,

$$p/q = (E_j(J) - E_j(I))/(E_i(I) - E_i(J)) \tag{1.4}$$

where p and q are the frequencies with which individuals use strategies I and J, respectively. In other words, the two strategies exist in equilibrium at relative frequencies determined by their payoff matrix.

This result may be interpreted in two ways. Each individual may employ strategies I and J, p and q percent of the time, respectively. I and J will then comprise a mixed strategy, which may or may not be evolutionarily stable with respect to other mutant strategies. Alternatively, p percent of the population may always use strategy I, while q percent of the population may always use strategy J. I and J will then be pure strategies, which may or may not be evolutionarily stable with respect to each other and to mutants, were they to become sufficiently dominant.

Maynard Smith applied these considerations to elucidate intragroup violence. In particular, he asked how hostile interactions might affect inclusive fitness and how inclusive fitness considerations might regulate the occurrence and intensity of violent conflict. He first defined two hypothetical alternative strategies to be used in hostile interactions. The first, or *hawk,* strategy is to escalate the intensity of violence until injured or until the opponent has retreated. The second, or *dove,* strategy is to threaten violence, but to retreat if the opponent escalates, thereby avoiding injury.

If the benefit of victory is V, the cost of being wounded is W, and the time cost of a lengthy standoff between doves is T, then the complete payoff matrix for contests using either or both of the two strategies will be:

(2)

		B's choice	
		Hawk	Dove
A's choice	Hawk	$0.5\,(V - W)$	V
	Dove	0	$0.5\,V - T$

The entries of this matrix can be deduced from definitions of the two alternative strategies. One of two fighting hawks, for example, must suffer the first wound and retreat, leaving the other victorious. Therefore, the expected payoff is to be victorious half the time and to be wounded half the time, or $0.5(V - W)$, where the minus sign indicates that W represents cost, not benefit.

If p is the probability that an opponent will be a hawk and q the probability that he or she will be a dove, then the inclusive fitness result of using the hawk strategy will be:

(2.1) $$0.5p(V - W) + qV.$$

Results obtained using the dove strategy will be:

(2.2) $$q(0.5V-T).$$

If V, the benefit of victory, is greater than W, the cost of being wounded, then

(2.3) $$0.5p(V - W) + qV > q(0.5V - T)$$

for all possible values of p and q. In other words, if the cost of being wounded is less than the benefit of victory, hawk is an evolutionarily stable strategy with respect to dove. Any doves in a population will quickly be driven to extinction by their more belligerent fellows. If, however, the cost of being wounded is greater than the benefit of victory, a similar analysis reveals that neither hawk nor dove strategies are evolutionarily stable with respect to each other. In fact, it turns out to be better to be a dove if most everyone else is a hawk, and to be a hawk if most everyone else is a dove. As a result, hawk and dove strategies would coexist in the population in relative frequencies determined by the magnitudes of V, W, and T given in matrix 2.

Actually, Maynard Smith defined yet a third violent strategy, the *retaliator.* The retaliator uses a hawk strategy when matched against a hawk and a dove strategy when matched against a dove. Basically, the retaliator does not attack first but escalates his or her own violence to match an opponent's. A somewhat more complex analysis akin to those demonstrated above reveals that the retaliator strategy has significant advantages with respect to both hawk and dove strategies. In fact, a population consisting initially of individuals using all three strategies will, insofar as the choice is genetically influenced, evolve to a population employing only the retaliator strategy. In this population, the retaliator strategy would be evolutionarily stable with respect to mutant hawks. It would not be evolutionarily stable with respect to mutant doves, who, in the absence of hawks, are actually using the same strategy. Therefore, retaliatory use of violence, together with some empty threats, should be especially salient in animal conflicts.

Resource Holding Power

Unfortunately, this analysis does not tell the full selective story. If it did, and since only hawks can induce retaliators to fight, violent conflicts could not occur except as the consequence of genetic disequilibrium. At least the more stable human breeding populations might then be markedly more peaceful than they actually seem to be. The analysis, however, fails to account for social cognitions and instead treats potential combatants as mere gamblers, rather than as shrewd game players. Considering hawks and retaliators, for example, it is clear that they could substantially improve their average payoff by taking note of their opponent's size and power and by retreating—like doves—from those likely to wound them. If individuals employing this cognitively modified strategy were of average size, they would still be victorious in half their confrontations. By fleeing from larger hawks, however, they could reduce the average cost of violent encounters below $0.5W$, the random level. Hawks and retaliators enhancing their average payoff in this way would have an inclusive fitness advantage with respect to others employing the same strategies blindly. Therefore, insofar as they depend on genetic substrates, tendencies to estimate fighting abilities and to use compared estimates as the basis of strategic choice should replace tendencies to engage in uninformed combat strategies (see Parker, 1982).

For the comparison of fighting abilities, Parker (1978) coined a measure called *resource holding power.* Its estimation, he noted, is not at all straightforward. In fact, potential combatants stand only to gain by convincing opponents that they have more of it than they actually have, inducing some of them to flee rather than fight. Bared canines, lowered antlers, and piloerection, among other agonistic displays, are all used by animals to exaggerate their resource holding power. In the human world, displays of resource holding power are more often culturally sanctioned and less often involve exhibitions of physical strength. Exaggerated display of resource holding power may be followed by what Parker calls *conventional fighting.* Conventional fighting provides for further mutual testing of relative resource holding power without incurring the risks of severe injury intrinsic to all-out combat. Insofar as it prevents all-out combat, nonlethal display combat is beneficial to both parties. Only in the case of great disparities in resource holding power—neither party having anything to gain from a preliminary contest—would it cease to be mutually advantageous.

Unbridled and potentially lethal combat will usually follow conventional fighting only if both parties remain convinced that they each hold a sufficient advantage in resource holding power so that victory is relatively assured and the probability of injury small. Natural selection has no doubt favored a highly conservative attitude toward injuries, so that even relatively improbable serious injuries may suffice to deter escalation of nonessential conflicts. By contrast, individuals should be willing to escalate against an apparently superior opponent only when the benefits of victory seem so vital that highly probable injuries are of no account beside them.

Studies of rhesus monkeys raised on low-protein diets demonstrate how the value of victory can influence tolerance for risks. In competition for food access, but not for other resources, protein-deprived monkeys will dominate monkeys raised with more adequate diets (Wise and Zimmerman, 1973). Particular failures of the concept of dominance, which predicts that priority access to resources of many different kinds should coincide (Clutton-Brock and Harvey, 1976), may well be explicable on this basis. A less than perfect correlation between access to several different resources would be expected if resources varied somewhat in their relative value to competing individuals, and if these were sufficiently similar in their resource holding power that changes in contest strategies could result from differences in perceived benefits.

In general, then, choice of strategies in potentially violent interactions should be based on mutual exchange of information. Each individual should try to exaggerate an impression of strength on the other while realistically comparing his or her own and the other's fighting abilities. Ritual displays and nonlethal display contests further this information exchange and are mutually advantageous to potential combatants. Only when preliminary displays lead both to believe in their own superiority, or if contested resources are so vital to one or the other that extraordinary risks are tolerated, will more dangerous combat actually occur. Otherwise, an individual determining that an opponent is more powerful should use a dove strategy, while an individual determining that he or she has the greater power should use a hawk strategy. In the absence of adequate information, potential combatants may maximize inclusive fitness by using retaliator strategies. The tendency to use dove strategies in similar situations would not be disadvantageous unless individuals using hawk strategies under those circumstances also existed in the population. *Uninformed hawks,* though, are selectively disadvantaged with respect to retaliators, and should eventually disappear unless other aspects of their trait compensate for the inclusive fitness disadvantage in uninformed combat.

Genetic Transmission

The extent to which humans adhere to these broad prescriptions is so obvious as to require little comment. Efforts to appear powerful in contest situations, and to size up one's opponent without being bluffed, are widely acknowledged prerequisites to actual hostilities. In the absence of adequate information, a wait-and-see attitude equivalent to the retaliator strategy would be universally recommended. Individuals foolish enough to attack those about whom they have no information in the first place—individuals who employ a hawk strategy when uninformed—are considered reckless, courageous, or suicidal, but in any event are universally recognized as being out of the ordinary. The impulse to appease those likely to inflict serious injury and the temptation to dominate those weaker than oneself are also broadly appreciated. Certain exceptions to these rules—cases in which Davids attack Goliaths without apparent concern for injury—can generally be attributed to the very high value placed on victory, the absence of which may be subjectively worse than being wounded. In others of these cases, religious or ideologic beliefs have distorted perception of the real power relationship. Instances in which Goliaths flee from Davids are attributable to these same factors, now working in reverse.

If the rules regulating hostile interactions maximize inclusive fitness in a state of nature, then the same may be said for civilized society. Even in technologic societies, which no doubt limit the efficacy of other previously significant selective pressures, those who disregard the strategies governing potentially violent interactions undoubtedly suffer greater morbidity and reduced reproductive success in comparison with those who adhere to them. In fact, in any major American city, it would be easy to get killed by forgetting them.

In light of their universality and evolutionary stability, response rules regulating hostile interactions are likely to depend on genetic transmission. Unlike other strategies of this type, however, strategies regulating hostility are never manifested in isolation. Instead, they govern behavior in a variety of contests, the actual occurrences of which are determined by other social strategies. By defining contested resources, these other strategies pit individuals against each other in the first place. In the following chapters these other genetically transmitted social strategies are further described, both separately and in their interaction with rules governing violence. Here, however, it suffices to point out that hostility regulating social strategies are of psychologic interest in their own right, independent of the particular contests in which they function.

Self-esteem and Resource Holding Power

An important component of these strategies is the tendency to monitor and compare one's own resource holding power to that of potential antagonists. Among the sources of information useful for estimating resource holding power, outcomes of previous contests may be most widely employed.

Other things being equal, individuals who have successfully escalated conflicts in the past should be more ready to escalate current conflicts beyond the display stage. Individuals with previous histories of defeat, by contrast, should be less ready to escalate contests, even against somewhat inferior opponents. That this prediction is generally true has been demonstrated for both human and nonhuman subjects (Kahn, 1951; Patterson, et al., 1967; Caplan, 1970) and may be of considerable psychologic importance.

Among humans, however, assessment of resource holding power is vastly more complex than among nonhumans, so that previous successes or failures tell only part of the story. Social position—including authority, prestige, wealth, and birthright—together with other complex interrelated factors serve to determine the outcome of human contests far more than simple physical prowess. Human contests are typically social, and physical force may be used only when social means of conflict-resolution have failed. Even fighting ability cannot be easily assessed, since skill, experience, and potential alliances are more crucial to human violence than mere strength. Wounds, moreover, may be social as well as somatic, and may be borne by kin or allies rather than by oneself. Ideologies confound perceptions of resource holding power and have real effects on it mediated through motivational changes. They may also affect the willingness to incur loss. In the human case, therefore, evaluation and comparison of resource holding power requires the consideration of physical, political, social, and ideologic factors encompassing the whole of an individual's experience of him or her self and of others.

The clinical variable most resembling this broader, more human concept of resource holding power—because it is frequently seen to be based on the same variety of factors—is self-esteem. Not only past victories and defeats, but physical prowess, authority, prestige, wealth, birthright, friendships, and moral factors influence self-esteem in the same fashion and with the same valences as they influence resource holding power. Just as, for self-esteem, defects in one area may be compensated for by accomplishments in another, so, for resource holding power, weakness in one area may be overbalanced by other strengths. Though clinically manifested self-esteem is undoubtedly multidimensional, at least one of its elements may be resource holding power, as defined by the theory of interpersonal conflict applied to human beings.

In a related discussion, Barkow (1980) argues that human self-conceptions arise from internal representations of individual characteristics affecting fitness. Even though a compound, resource holding power is certainly such a character. As a behavioral determinant, Barkow considers self-conception an emergent property not fully predictable from the representations on which it is based. In a similar fashion, the full characteristics of self-esteem are only partly explicable in terms of resource holding power. In a later chapter, the relation of resource holding power and subjectively experienced self-esteem, for which indirect support is found in both psychologic literature and clinical experience, will be further explored. First, though, it is necessary to examine specific contests from which hostilities may arise.

8

Genetically Transmitted Social Strategies III

Sexual Competition

As the result of differences in the minimum parental investment each parent must make in any one child, male and female inclusive fitness interests diverge. To maximize their inclusive fitness, males must compete for female reproductive capacity. Females, on the other hand, must compete for good male genes and for male parental investments. The consequences of each kind of competition are easily enumerated and are psychologically significant.

The Law of Sexual Selection and Male Parental Investment

That males and females must mate to achieve any degree of reproductive success is obvious. Less obvious, however, are the circumstances in which, and the partner with whom, mating should occur to maximize reproductive success, as well as the fact that these elements differ substantially for males and females. Because mating choice and circumstance are responsible for many of the conflicts described in the previous chapter, the principles of mate and circumstance selection for both males and females will be discussed here. First, however, the source of discrepancies between preferred male and female mating behaviors must be investigated.

Consider a hypothetical, reproductively closed population of breeding males and females. A moment's consideration should convince the reader that the total number of offspring mothered by females in such a population must equal the total number of offspring fathered by males. If there are equal numbers of males and females, therefore, the average number of offspring will be the same for the two sexes. However, although the average number of offspring for the two sexes is and must always be the same, the degree of individual variation in number of offspring might potentially differ greatly between the sexes. As it turns out, a key factor in determining the degree of reproductive variation is the minimum parental investment required from parents of each sex. For mammalian males, this minimum is the time and energy required for sexual intercourse, a paltry investment indeed. For mammalian females, by contrast, this minimum is the time and energy of intercourse, pregnancy, lactation, and more or less prolonged maternal care, depending on the species. Due to the enormous minimum investment required of mammalian females, individual variation in mammalian female reproductive success is sharply limited by an upper bound to the number of possible offspring. By contrast, the number of offspring potentially sired by a given male is, practically speaking, unlimited. Since the average male reproductive success is fixed by that of females, however, extraordinary reproductive success of one male must be balanced by the reproductive failure of one or more other males. Mammalian males, therefore, must compete with each other for their share of the offspring mothered by the pool of available females.

In any species, members of the sex with the smallest minimum parental investment per offspring (Trivers, 1978a), or with the greatest reproductive potential (Clutton-Brock and Harvey, 1976), compete with each other for the opportunity to mate with members of the opposite sex. This is an important sociobiologic principle, that is sometimes referred to as the *law of sexual selection*. The intensity of sexual selection pressure, which in most species takes the form of competition between males, is easily quantified (see, for example, Wiley, 1973; LeBoeuf, 1974) and is sufficiently great to have been a major factor in behavioral evolution. Readers will recognize in the law of sexual selection another manifestation of the central tenet of sociobiology, that individuals will behave in such a way as to maximize their inclusive fitness.

Not only will discrepancies in male and female reproductive potential result in male competition for mating, but the intensity of that competition will vary with the potential magnitude of male reproductive variation.

Factors increasing male reproductive variation will exacerbate male sexual competition (Clutton-Brock and Harvey, 1976). Thus, polygamous mating systems, resource monopolization, shorter male life spans, highly concentrated breeding seasons, or geographically restricted mating arenas will all result in more intense male competition for a share of female reproductive capacity. Factors working to reduce male reproductive variation, such as highly dispersed resources, longer life spans, and temporally and geographically random breeding opportunities, will all serve to mitigate male competition.

If the law of sexual selection dictates that mammalian males must compete for mating opportunities, then what can be said of mammalian females? Although access to the opposite sex largely determines reproductive success of the mammalian male, reproductive success of the mammalian female is relatively independent of sexual access. A female with only sporadic access to fertile males might nonetheless bear as many offspring as she is capable of rearing, and in fact might ultimately bear greater numbers of viable offspring than a sexually more active female. Excessively frequent conceptions, for example, might only result in miscarriages and consequent damage to maternal health. Because males compete to mate with even the least attractive female, she is likely to obtain that minimum number of sexual contacts needed to optimize the number of live births. What, then, are the limiting factors on female reproductive fitness?

As it turns out, there are one or two such factors, depending on whether the species in question bears precocious or immature young. In species bearing precocious young, parental investments required to optimize an offspring's reproductive success are largely made by the end of gestation or shortly afterward. There is little the females of such species need from the male, except his genes. The quality of those genes, insofar as they affect the reproductive success of her offspring, will affect the female's own inclusive fitness for better or worse. Therefore, females of these species will choose their mates in order to obtain the best male genes. Generally, the genes most likely to enhance the reproductive success of male offspring will maximize their mother's inclusive fitness, since these are the offspring with the greatest reproductive potential. Since these genes are associated with successful competition with other males for reproductive opportunities, females bearing precocious young should choose their mates largely on the basis of proven ability to compete for their sexual favors. Since sexually dominant males, however, will find it advantageous to mate as many females as possible, it is unlikely that a preference for males of this type will lead to conflicts with other females. Hence, in species bearing precocious young, female attempts to maximize reproductive fitness should result in little or no conflict with others of the same gender.

In species bearing immature young the situation is very different. Since parental investments do not terminate with or shortly after birth, females of these species may obtain from the male not only his genes, but also parental investments in the offspring he has sired. In rare species, male parental investments comprise most or all parental care (Knowlton, 1982). Insofar as male parental investments enhance the future reproductive success of her offspring, they also contribute to the female's own inclusive fitness. Not only do male parental investments provide young with resources only a male might offer, but they also free some of the female's own resources, which can then be devoted to other real or potential offspring. Their cost, furthermore, is largely borne by offspring the male might potentially father by other females, rather than by others of her own young. Contrariwise, a given female's failure to obtain male parental investments on behalf of her own offspring frees them for use on behalf of the male's offspring by other females. Thus, male parental investment is essential to maximize female inclusive fitness in species bearing immature young, and the female's pursuit of male investment intrinsically involves competition with others of her own sex.

As described in a previous chapter, male competition for sexual access and female choice of competitively successful males should be evolutionarily stable complementary strategies. This is the case regardless of whether male sexual competition and female sexual choice are direct or are mediated by male accumulation of resources requisite to parental investment.

Because humans are characterized both by immature young and by sexual disparities in reproductive potential, male and female competition for sexual access and parental investment, respectively, provide the twin bases on which human sexual psychology can be firmly built. To perceive the form of that psychology, one need only consider the implications of underlying competitive exigencies, which will now be examined for each sex separately. In what follows, various statements will be made concerning male and female behaviors in our and other societies. Certainly, specific male and female social roles are highly flexible and culturally variable and should be made to conform with the higher ideal of equal opportunity. Yet, to be stable, sexual roles must also be consistent with the biologic preferences of the more powerful members of at least one sex, or with their underlying gender-specific social strategies. Because sexual roles are in some sense ethical demands, this is consistent with the position previously taken with respect to ethical ideologies (Chapter 3). It runs counter to the notion—promoted by certain contemporary social theorists—that sexual roles are arbitrary demand systems with no basis at all in gender-specific biology (see, for example, Pleck, 1981).

Female Sexual Strategies

First, if females must compete for male parental investment, then the males they prefer must be those who control resources. Although priority access to resources among males is not perfectly correlated (Chapter 7), there is enough agreement that males capable of greater child support efforts can be easily identified in any given culture. The complication, of course, is that representations of human male social power vary widely from culture to culture, so that there is no invariant attribute to which women, in maximizing their own inclusive fitness, are uniformly attracted. Instead, women in every locale are generally attracted to those males whose real or symbolic power is locally acknowledged, whether these be bank presidents in New York City or headsmen in tribal villages. Because a number of women are likely to be interested in a single powerful man, competition for his attention will exist among women. That competition is usually decided on the basis of physical and psychologic attractiveness, although female efforts to directly obliterate competition are not unknown.

One consequence of the female preference for powerful men is particularly noteworthy. Because human males accumulate social power only in mid life, young women are frequently attracted to men older than themselves. In the female preference for older men, Freud saw an attempt to recreate the infantile infatuation with the father, the powerful older man of family life. In fact, however, to treat these adult preferences as the result of infantile experiences may be putting the cart before the horse. It is equally plausible to argue that a girl's childhood infatuation with her father is colored by her emerging sexual preference for powerful men, a preference that will take on adaptive significance only following puberty. Once sexualized, the relationship with the father may reemerge to affect her relationships with other powerful men, but these are nonetheless not motivated by it.

In preferring powerful men who happen to be older, and in competing for their attention, however, the woman has only half-solved the problem of obtaining parental investments. This is because the male's ability to make substantial parental investments is of no use to the female unless he is actually willing to commit his resources to her children. Therefore, those men sufficiently attractive to a woman to be seriously considered must be further screened for signs that they will reliably make the parental investments on which her inclusive fitness depends. Now the difficult part, from the female's point of view, is that males will inevitably attempt to mimic those signs of reliability in order to mate, which is the single highest priority on their own fitness agenda. Having mated, and perhaps impregnated the female, these successful mimics could then choose to make no parental investments whatsoever. Paternal refusal to provide care would have little adverse effect on the father's inclusive fitness, given the small investment he has made and the ease with which he can father other children, but would leave the heavily committed mother at a significant fitness disadvantage.

The female response to the threat of male abandonment must be to require increasingly stringent and time-consuming tests of reliability before allowing the male to mate with her. This is as true of nonhuman monogamous species as of human beings (Breuer, 1982). If all females require male suitors to expend considerable time and resources in courtship, then in effect they have raised the minimum male parental investment, decreasing the likelihood of future abandonment. Signs of loyalty, which, for human males, differ greatly from culture to culture, must be scrupulously examined for evidence of insincerity. Not only should the woman require evidence of the male's commitment to her, she should also require evidence of his disinterest in other women. If the male suitor is courting other women, he might also be telling them that he intends to stay with them and their children, vitiating the reliability of his messages to any female. Also, unless the male is so powerful that he can simultaneously provide for an unlimited number of children, the offspring he might sire by various women might compete with each other for parental investments, an undesirable state of affairs from the female point of view.

Once pregnant, a woman has wagered a large portion of her lifetime reproductive potential on the judgment she made in accepting male advances. Although there is little the mother or mother-to-be can do to directly enforce fidelity from the physically more powerful male, there are certain options at her disposal. First, she may choose to ignore male infidelity that is, by cultural convention, limited to sexual intercourse. As long as there is no danger that the male might form an emotional commitment to another woman, or to her children, sexual infidelity per se poses no inclusive fitness threat to the female except that mediated by venereally transmitted disease. In the absence of culturally imposed conventions, however, sexual infidelity may lead to actual abandonment, and therefore poses a considerable threat. Second, since the inclusive fitness of her own male kin depends in part upon provision of care for her children, they may be willing, when called upon, to enforce some degree of fidelity from her wandering mate. Third, she herself may punish any woman who attempts to lure away the male with whom she has already mated. The threat of punishment may discourage other women from becoming interlopers; at the same time it reduces the straying male's options. Fourth, she may continue to compete with other women, but now for her own mate's attention. However, compared to its earlier version, female competition with potential interlopers will be vastly more complicated, since male jealousy and the so-called *Coolidge effect* (described at the end of this chapter) will both play vital roles. All of these options, of course, are pursued in various cultures, some of which particularly encourage one or more of them rather than others.

Although the broad outlines of female mating preferences in many cultures follow more or less directly from the strategic need to compete for male parental investment, which in turn is a consequence of bearing extremely immature young, there are other female sexual characteristics that are not clearly explained by the inclusive fitness point of view. A few of these are unique to human beings and are discussed fully in Appendix G.

Male Sexual Strategies

Turning now to the male sex, several obvious points can be made. To begin with, as an obvious result of his competition for female reproductive capacity, the human male must be ready to mate whenever the opportunity occurs. Male readiness for sexual activity is all the more remarkable when compared with that of the female, whose inclusive fitness would be severely compromised by casual sexual intercourse. Since, however, the minimum parental investment required of the male is trivial, promiscuous sexual relations never decrease his inclusive fitness. Male inclusive fitness can only be increased by the possibility that casually sired children may reach reproductive maturity without paternal aid. Male readiness to mate whenever the opportunity occurs should be manifested both psychologically and physiologically: not only should the male be highly motivated to obtain whatever sexual opportunities come his way, he should become sexually aroused as the result of minimal stimuli—such as female nakedness—signaling the possibility of intercourse.

Little doubt can exist concerning the relative sexual alertness of men and women. With respect to both sexual appetite and readiness to become aroused, the average man and woman differ dramatically (see Mellen, 1981 for review). Symons (1979) makes several important observations consistent with this difference. First, whereas female nakedness is generally understood by men as a sexually arousing invitation, the nakedness of strange males is interpreted by women not as sexually arousing, but as threatening. Second, men make an effort to view the naked female body, while women are less aroused by simple male nudity than by stimuli suggesting a loving erotic relationship. Thus, reams of pornography are purchased by heterosexual or homosexual men. Most pornography ostensibly addressed to heterosexual or homosexual women is actually purchased by homosexual or heterosexual men, respectively. Along the same lines, male homosexuals, like their heterosexual counterparts, seek out casual sexual encounters; homosexual women, like their heterosexual counterparts, form sexually faithful long-term relationships.

Differences in male and female readiness for sexual arousal, and in the nature of the stimuli most arousing to each sex, may be of considerable importance in understanding childhood sexual experiences. In particular, precisely what constitutes an arousing view of parental and sibling sexuality may differ between the sexes even before puberty. If so, male children may be more aroused by parental or sibling nudity, while female children may be more aroused by displays of parental affection. The arousing psychologic content even of so-called primal scenes—or views of parental intercourse—may be utterly different for children of opposite sexes.

Stoller (1976, 1979), noting the split between arousal and affection in the male sex, has argued that the sexual excitement typical of most males is intrinsically hostile towards women. If the capacity for arousal without either affection or commitment signifies hostility, then Stoller is of course correct. If the sole criterion for hostility, however, is the absence of affection, then many other interactions may also be deemed hostile, including most of the purely instrumental interactions that make up a substantial part of daily life. Used in this fashion, hostility no longer has any meaning, except to signify the absence of what, after all, occurs only rarely in adult life. By contrast, inclusive fitness considerations clarify the real roots of male-female arousal differences without using pejorative terms.

Opportunities to mate, however, are likely to come the male's way only if he has successfully competed with other males for control of those resources requisite to parental investments. Regardless of how various groups represent this control, or organize male competition, the struggle between males may rest on a foundation of potential violence. As noted in the previous chapter, violent conflicts should occur only when the inclusive fitness benefits of victory exceed the likely costs of losses incurred. This may frequently be the case for male sexual competition. A male failing in conventional ways to obtain a share of resources adequate to make parental investments, and therefore to attract a mate, has lost all possibility of reproductive success. He may have little to lose by escalating to unconventional or violent competition. Females, by contrast, may still reproduce regardless of the outcome of their competition with other females and for that reason are less likely to compete violently. That male sexual competition will frequently rest on the capacity for individual or joint violence has both physiologic and psychologic implications. First, this is the basis of sexual dimorphism, or difference in male and female size and form, which is most marked in species characterized by large disparities in reproductive potential, and therefore by intense male competition. Energetic and other constraints limit the degree to which male combat-related structures can profitably evolve, or sexual dimorphism would no doubt be even greater than it is today. Second, the readiness to engage in violence, and participation in organized violence, are as sexually disparate as bodily form. The social order of essentially all human groups, whether primitive or technologically advanced, rural or industrial, is protected from dissatisfied males largely by the threat of superior violence. In advanced societies, for example, those who fail to control resources are prevented from violent escalation only by the threat of organized force. For the most part, those who escalate anyway are male, rather than female. In primitive societies lacking organized police forces, as many as one quarter of males may die as the result of murder and warfare (Symons, 1979). By comparison, female fatalities from intragroup violence are rare.

Even Maccoby and Jacklin (1974), who consider most sex-related behavioral differences illusory, agree that males and females differ significantly in their readiness for aggression. In nonhuman primates, readiness for aggression may depend in part on circulating levels of male sex hormones (Rose, Holaday, and Bernstein, 1971; Rose, Gordon, and Bernstein, 1971). In humans, male sex hormone levels have been shown to increase following wrestling victories (Elias, 1981).

Among the violent crimes undertaken by competitively unsuccessful males in our own society, none is more directly expressive of the underlying inclusive fitness exigencies than sexual assault. It is a peculiar measure of how far sexual drives have fallen from their Freudian heyday that even rapists are now widely thought to be driven by nonsexual motives. Hostility, for example, is commonly said to motivate rape, and the rapist is said to seek his victim's degradation, rather than sexual pleasure per se. Alternatively, sexually assaultive males are said to be following a culturally dictated masculine role that places a high value on male sexual conquests. These lines of argument, as Symons (1979) points out, partly rely on the testimony of convicted rapists, who presumably have some ax to grind in purging their crimes of sexual significance. Parole boards, for the most part, view sexual motives as more intractable than hostile or narcissistic ones. Undoubtedly, most rapists are sufficiently sadistic that degradation of the female is prerequisite to their sexual pleasure (see Chapter 15) and sufficiently insecure as to need sexual conquests. But the abstraction of sexual motives from rape obscures the way in which it differs from aggravated assault, for example, or from other forms of exhibitionism. The rapist not only assaults and "conquers," but he annuls female sexual choice. In this way he takes from his victim that which she would prefer to give to someone else, or to no one at all, but certainly not to him. This "theft" is as primary to rape as any of the sadistic and exhibitionistic attitudes with which it is performed (see Alexander, 1979).

Fortunately, however, violence is not the primary male propensity. Given the opportunity, normal men will compete in culturally appropriate ways with others of their sex, a tendency that is at least more salient than its female counterpart. Although various societies symbolize it in differing ways, men everywhere compete for control of useful resources. It is all too easy to forget that in competing for prestige, leadership, power, or wealth, men are also competing to attract women. But males successful in the competitive strivings of everyday life are universally those capable of attracting the most, or at least the more, desirable sexual partners. A social system that failed to associate male competitive success and sexual access would be be highly unstable: Both the most powerful males and the majority of females would likely hasten to discard such a system, if not explicitly, then through systematic cheating.

Although the recent development of effective contraception, and its relatively greater use by economically successful individuals, has somewhat obscured the relation, quantitative evidence nonetheless testifies to the general correlation of social and reproductive success for males in any given society. Even in Western society, an inverse correlation exists between income level and childlessness (Kunz, et al., 1973), an observation that prompted Tiger (1979a) to suggest that members of our society "convert" money into children. Irons (1979a) found that social and reproductive success were positively correlated in the nonindustrial societies he studied, in part because of decreased mortality among the children of successful parents, but also due to differences in birth rates. So great is the male reproductive variation in primitive societies most like the probable environment of human adaptation, and so highly correlated are social and reproductive success, that occasional groups of successful males may literally dominate the genetic composition of later generations. The famous Yąnomamö leader Shinbone, for example, had forty-three children of his own and one hundred nieces and nephews by paternal siblings (Chagnon, 1979). In Yąnomamö society, male social and reproductive success are nearly identical (Chagnon, 1979). Yąnomamö males, in fact, devote much of their time to undisguised fights over women (Chagnon, 1979a). The outcomes of these fights, like those over other resources, depend largely on the ability to forge working alliances with other males, these alliances being the real working capital of Yąnomamö life.

The association of male resource competition with sexual access, which results from inclusive fitness exigencies faced by the two sexes, has been turned upside down by psychoanalytic theory. Failing to appreciate the implications of Darwin's argument, Freud imagined that the sexual aspects of adult male competition result from misplaced infantile competition with the father. Yet, males who fail to sexualize conventional competition with other men are biologically implausible. Previous generations of men content to compete for rewards not including sexual access, if they ever existed, would have been rapidly replaced by males who also demanded sexual opportunities as the reward for achievement of whatever passed for power and prestige in their societies. Therefore, it is far less plausible that adult males reveal their infantile side by competing for women than that boys reveal their adult side by competing with their fathers for female family members. It is no more infantile to desire another man's woman than to desire his home, his money, or his position in society.

Men whose position in society is such that it provides for sexual choice must express sexual preferences. Given the underlying competition for female reproductive capacity, male sexual preferences should discriminate in favor of females with the greatest reproductive capacity. These are women near the beginning of their reproductive careers. They are also the women who appear healthy. Other than youth, perhaps the only universal criterion of feminine sexual attractiveness is a clear complexion. Like youth, a complexion free of scars, pallor, or discoloration has no doubt reliably indicated robustness, and therefore good reproductive potential, throughout human history.

Other signs of health, and therefore of sexual attractiveness, are locally or temporally circumscribed. Numerous observers, for example, have noted that the male preference for overweight women coincided in European history with the depredations of tuberculosis. Plumpness, as opposed to emaciation, was a reliable sign of freedom from this all too common disease. Likewise, the "Venus of Willendorf," the oldest extant representation of the human form, depicts an extraordinarily obese woman. In this respect it typifies an artistic preference persisting throughout Neolithic times (Bruch, 1973). In areas of the world, where hunger has been recently experienced, such as among certain African tribes, overweight women are today considered sexually more desirable than their slim sisters. In wealthier societies, slender women are currently most sought after, and their heftier sisters are forced to torture themselves with diet and exercise if they wish to enjoy masculine attentions. In these populations, in contrast to the Neolithic and modern African societies, slimness may signify a more active behavior pattern—at least among those not patently ill—and therefore better health than is implied by plumpness.

However, factors other than the reproductive capacity of any one woman also enter into masculine sexual choices. First, and most obviously, a man capable of making parental investments in the children of two or more women will wish to have more than one mate. Males, in fact, will wish to have as many mates as they can obtain, each with the maximal reproductive capacity. But the capacity of some men to monopolize sufficient resources to make simultaneous parental investments in more than one family, and therefore to attract more than one female, means that other men must be deprived of resources entirely. In human societies, polygamy is therefore associated with extreme social inequalities, easily monopolized forms of wealth, and high levels of crime by discontented males (Bacon, Child, and Barry, 1963).

Actually, polygamy may be self-promoting, at least in preagricultural, hunter-gatherer societies. Because women in these societies gather dietary staples, wives themselves are economic resources with which men can attract more mates (Breuer, 1982). Women joining a large harem are better assured of a steady food supply—particularly when they themselves are unable to gather—than either single wives or members of smaller harems. This motivation for joining a harem is enhanced by the fact that multiple wives are frequently sisters (Murdock, 1949) and therefore more willing to support each other.

Second, insofar as the male intends to make parental investments in his future offspring, he must mate women likely to be sexually faithful. Others might cuckold him, leading him to make parental investments in other than his own offspring and thus decreasing his inclusive fitness. Symons (1979) suggests that the resulting attentiveness to potential female infidelity leads men to dichotomously classify women according to their sexual reliability. Certainly, the classification of women as either "madonnas" or "whores" is frequently noted in psychotherapy with male patients.

Among the signs of likely female fidelity might be a madonna-like disinterest in sexual relations, so that sexual disinterest would come to be prized in women with whom men have more than casual liaisons. Psychoanalysts (see Freud, 1912) interpret the distinction men make between sexually pure (marriageable) and sexually tainted (potentially seduced) females as evidence for splitting of affection and sexuality rooted in the Oedipal conflict. Once again, attention to inclusive fitness considerations is essential for a more complete view.

That the madonna-whore complex subserves male sexual jealousy, and the fear of cuckolding, implies that those men for whom it is most salient are likely to be sexually insecure. Uncertainty concerning their own attractiveness leads these men to be more than normally preoccupied with female fidelity or its ostensible absence. However, sexual insecurity and Oedipal neuroses are the subjects of a later chapter.

A third consideration for male sexual preference, one culturally more restricted than reproductive potential and perceived fidelity, are the female's male kin. Like preferences for sexually faithful women in good reproductive health, this too is explicable in inclusive fitness terms. In many societies, fathers and matrilateral brothers of mated females contribute substantially to the rearing of her children, in the first instance because these are grandchildren and in the second because they are predictably related uterine kin. "Matrilateral" and "uterine," of course, refer to their descent from the same female parent. In societies in which *paternity confidence*—the male's certainty that his mate's offspring are also his own—is low, males may more advantageously invest in uterine kin than in children by their own mates (Appendix I). These societies are also the only ones in which a female need not choose mates on the basis of their capacity for parental investments, since those investments would be directed to other than her own children anyway (see Chagnon and Irons, 1979). Child-rearing aid by grandfathers and matrilateral brothers may consist in reciprocal alliances with husbands of their daughters and sisters, or may consist in full responsibility for food, shelter, and education, depending upon cultural mores. Males in such a society would enhance their own inclusive fitness by preferring mates whose male kin are capable of greater investments in their future children. In fact, among primitive peoples potential alliances with matrilateral kin of wives-to-be significantly dictate marriage patterns, particularly of the bilateral cross-cousin type (Chagnon, 1979a).

In more advanced societies, the male will desire to marry into land-owning or wealthy families.

Once having settled on a woman of his choice, the human male must convince her or her kin of his willingness and capacity to make parental investments in her offspring. The only exceptions, of course, are those societies noted above in which fathers and matrilateral brothers take sole responsibility for aiding their daughters and sisters in child rearing. Although the tokens of courtship vary widely from culture to culture, in every case they notify women of male affection, reliability, and steadfastness. The courting male, through these tokens, portrays his aim as relational, rather than merely sexual. Oftentimes, he merely mimics those expressions of affection that he knows females require before dispensing sexual favors. However, he is susceptible as well to actually forming the intentions he occasionally mimics, and he will then desire a long-term relationship. What this indicates, of course, is that males willing to make parental investments in at least some of their children have had greater inclusive fitness than those who leave all of their children in the lurch, so that the corresponding tendencies have been effectively selected for.

Long-term Relationships

The long-term sexual and child-rearing relationship resulting from reciprocal male and female choices is delimited in most societies by one or another form of wedding ceremony. Typically, wedding customs more or less explicitly trade paternity confidence for male parental investment (Irons, 1979b). In many societies, the male will also formally contract to restrict his own sexual activity—his mate's is restricted as a condition of paternity confidence—which further ensures that his parental investments will be limited to his wife's offspring. Of the simplifications that have earned ethology a bad name among students of human behavior, perhaps none is so egregious as the one that compares human marriage to pair bonding in nonhuman animals. Human marriage can only be understood as a condensation of multiple male and female social interests, both sexual and nonsexual, in particular, culturally determined environments. Marriage, for example, serves to protect male and female reproductive interests—the context in which it is encountered here, to reduce same-sex competition within groups, to delimit kinship relations for altruistic and incest-avoidance purposes, and to provide natural alliances leading to formation of larger social groups (Chapter 10). A complex cultural institution serving all these social functions cannot be compared to formation of isolated heterosexual pairs in other species (Symons, 1979), nor to the pairing of gregarious species lacking one or more human social strategies. Nor can the variety and complexity of human marriage customs be explicated without considering each of their many social functions in each of many cultural environments (see Chagnon and Irons, 1979).

Once in a long-term sexual and child-rearing relationship, the human male becomes more or less preoccupied with fidelity. First, he wishes to ensure his mate's chastity, a desire that no doubt follows from the inclusive fitness penalties that are accrued by cuckolds. Second, he lusts after other women, with whom he may even surreptitiously cheat. This tendency, too, no doubt follows from inclusive fitness considerations, in this case the advantage to the male of casually sired offspring. The male's tendency to look for additional fertile fields in which to sow casual and uncommitted reproductive investments has been known in recent years as the *Coolidge effect,* after the president of that name (Symons, 1979). That male jealousy and the Coolidge effect are more than cultural artifacts is apparent from the study of nonhuman males for whom similar inclusive fitness considerations apply. Males of other monogamous species also frequently cheat (Breuer, 1982), and, like men, are quick to be jealous of their female mates (Barash, 1977).

Significantly, discrepant male perceptions of male and female infidelity are also embodied in male dictates on these subjects, incorporated in the laws and customs with which men have tried to control female behavior. Even as they excuse their own indiscretions, males of many cultures are remarkably intolerant of female infidelity. With devices, Draconian laws, and personal violence men have attempted to prevent or deter women from cuckolding them, which is felt to be a personal betrayal far more serious than that implied by their own faithlessness. Even in modern times, murder has been considered justifiable if it is occasioned by male sexual jealousy. Nor is polyandry, or institutionalized wife-sharing, generally as acceptable to human males as polygamy is (Murdock, 1949). In fact, the few human societies in which polyandry occurs prove the central part played by parental investment in masculine sexual jealousy. In Ceylon or

Tibet, for example, males participating in polyandrous marriages are generally so poor that they would be unable to support a family on their own (Yalman, 1971; Crook, 1980). Sharing female reproductive potential with other males is therefore the only chance to reproduce that these multiple husbands have. Even so, the husbands in polyandrous Ceylonese or Tibetan marriages are frequently brothers, so that children born to the female in these arrangements are at least nieces and nephews of the males who jointly contribute to their upbringing (see also Maynard Smith's [1978b] discussion of Tribonyx trios).

Finally, that certain long-term relationships lead to infanticide, though it seemingly contradicts the inclusive fitness viewpoint, is nonetheless sociobiologically intelligible. Infanticide, and its interrelation with male and female mating patterns, is discussed briefly in Appendix H.

Because sexual patterns of the human male and female are universally consistent with competitions for female reproductive capacity and male parental investment, respectively, and because these are evolutionarily stable social strategies, male and female sexual patterns likely depend on genetic transmission. More evidence relevant to this is found in Chapter 15. Here, however, the way lies open to the Oedipal conflict, and thus to the heart of Freudian theory.

9

Genetically Transmitted Social Strategies IV

Oedipus Rex Revisited

Kinship complicates the inclusive fitness effects of sexual competition and mating. When competitors are genetically related, the inclusive fitness difference between victory and defeat is smaller than when competitors are unrelated. Genetically inbred matings will penalize both participants and those who are kin to them. To prevent sibling incest, ethical strictures may supplement the "Westermarck effect."

Father-Son Sexual Competition

In the previous chapter, male and female sexual choices were described from an inclusive fitness viewpoint. Human males compete for female reproductive capacity; human females compete for male parental investment. A wide range of gender-typical sexual propensities are consistent with these underlying social strategies. No account was taken, however, for the effects of kinship—either between competing or mating individuals—on sexual choices, in spite of the fact that kinship complicates the inclusive fitness results of both competition and sexual intercourse for both males and females. Even though the inclusive fitness complications introduced by kinship are numerically small, the propinquity of kin throughout human prehistory ensures their selective efficacy and therefore their contemporary behavioral significance. Fortunately, effects of kinship on sexual choice are easily deduced from a few simple principles. Because clinical experience most consistently points to the importance of father-son sexual competition and male incest wishes, these topics will be analyzed first. Mechanisms that act to prevent inbreeding will be described next, followed by a few remarks on the female viewpoint.

To begin with, if two competing males are father and son, the inclusive fitness difference between victory and defeat will be narrowed for both of them. Consider the case of unrelated competitors. If a given male is victorious, and impregnates the female for whose reproductive capacity he has successfully competed, he will gain $0.5 - C$ inclusive fitness units. This follows from the genetic relatedness of father and child, 0.5, and accounts for the cost to the victorious male of whatever parental investments, C, he makes on its behalf. Should the same male be defeated, he stands to gain essentially nothing. In fact, because the victor is bound to share some of his genes, especially if they both belong to a small group (see Chapter 10), he will gain some benefit from the victor's child. Here, however, we will ignore that. Therefore, the inclusive fitness advantage of victory, as opposed to defeat, in sexual competition with an unrelated male will be:

(1) $$(0.5 - C) - 0 = 0.5 - C.$$

In other words, the advantage of sexually outcompeting an unrelated male will be that of having a child, minus whatever costs there are in actually raising it.

Now consider the case of father and son (or, with appropriate modifications, of uncle and nephew, as discussed by Malinowski [1927]). The inclusive fitness benefit obtained by the victor will again be $0.5 - C$. However, because father and son share half each other's genes, the same male, should he be defeated, will still gain substantial benefits. Because the victor's child carries one quarter of his genes, these will be $0.25 - 0.5C$, where $0.5C$ is the cost of paternal investments depreciated by the degree of genetic relationship with the victor, who must actually bear them. In other words, the loser will still gain half as many inclusive fitness units as the victor, if the two men are father and son. From this it follows that the inclusive fitness advantage of victory, as opposed to defeat, in sexual competition with either one's father or son will be:

(2) $$(0.5 - C) - (0.25 - 0.5C) = 0.25 - 0.5C$$

or half the advantage from sexually outcompeting an unrelated male.

Therefore, insofar as competitive motivation has evolved to coincide with inclusive fitness benefits, motivation for sexual competition between father and son may be relatively dampened. In effect, kin altruism, or the tendency to promote reproductive interests of individuals carrying the same genes (Chapter 10), should ameliorate competitive motives integral to male sexual strategies. The residual selective pressure in favor of sexual competition between father and son, $0.25 - 0.5C$, may be especially strong, though, in species characterized by little or no male parental investments. In these species, C has little modifying effect on the advantage of unbridled competition. In fact, studies of nonhuman primates, for whom male parental investments are minimal, seem to support this notion (Fox, 1980). For example, young chimpanzee males live with their mothers until five or six years of age. At that time they begin working their way up through the ranks of older males in order to participate in the largely promiscuous matings with females in heat. Apparently, older males compete blindly with the young newcomers, whose paternity they may not even know, and younger males fight back with equal lack of discrimination. Since male parental investments are minimal among chimpanzees, the inclusive fitness gain from sexual victory over one's own father or son is still sufficiently large, 0.25, to justify relatively serious hostility. Male baboons, who also contribute little in the way of parental investments, carry hostility between father and son even further. Forcibly expelled from the troop, young male baboons are forced to live on the periphery. There they suffer very high mortality, both from predation and from savage attacks by dominant males. Even of those who survive, many will nonetheless fail to mate in their troops of origin. If there were inclusive fitness advantages to dominant males in sparing their own male offspring, then means might have evolved for their recognition and promotion. Instead, however, baboon fathers wage war on their sons just as against unrelated younger males, and baboon sons battle back with equal lack of discrimination.

Men, of course, make enormous parental investments, so that $0.25 - 0.5C$, the inclusive fitness advantage to sexually defeating one's own father or son, is correspondingly diminished. Also, many other factors likely attenuate the advantages of sexual competition between human father and son. These include the great age disparity between human fathers and their sexually mature sons so that fathers may be less well equipped to raise children than are their grown sons, the potential predictability of the son's reproductive success (Appendix H), and the importance of kinship groups to human social endeavours (Appendix I). When all these factors are taken into account, inclusive fitness consequences may even favor altruism; fathers in particular may benefit by ensuring their sons sexual access. Nonetheless, elements of father-son sexual competition are visible in human social arrangements, and under certain circumstances may be quite significant. Fox (1980), for example, notes that male initiation rites serve in many societies to exclude young men from the group of breeding males to which their own fathers belong. In some cultures, dangerous initiation feats not infrequently result in death or permanent disability, and those who fail in them and survive must either leave the group or renounce their manhood. Fearsome initiation rites particularly characterize those societies in which young men stay with their mothers until adolescence and are less common in cultures that gradually assimilate young men into the male group (Whiting, et al., 1958). In this respect, human initiation rites appear similar to the trials suffered by young chimpanzees or baboons who have outgrown maternal protection.

Evidence for the male-competitive meaning of initiation rites is also found in the relative rarity of female initiation and in the frequent employment—as part of male rites—of circumcision, subincision, or other forms of symbolic genital mutilation. Female genital mutilation, when it is practiced, may be characteristically aimed at reducing sexual pleasure and, by implication, enhancing female faithfulness. Females, in any event, are seldom required to risk their lives and health as a condition of breeding, even if jealous males hope they will get no pleasure from it. The fact that dominant men with powers of selective cultural retention in primitive societies have chosen to retain fierce initiation rites that ensnare their own sons equally with other males is very significant. It illustrates the ambivalence of the father-son relationship when it concerns sexual matters. If the son's sexual failure was wholly unacceptable to most fathers in these societies, initiation rites ending in injury, death, or banishment would have long since disappeared.

However, it is in mental, rather than strictly cultural, life that father-son sexual competition is most frequently evident. In mental life, father-son sexual competition is manifested in Oedipal fantasies, which Freud first discovered and which countless psychoanalytically informed treatments have effectively confirmed. Disavowed father-son sexual competition is encountered so ubiquitously in psychotherapeutic treatment that most analytically trained psychotherapists consider it universal among men raised in nuclear families. The discussion above, however, suggests that its intensity may depend significantly on both cultural factors and social class. For example, members of the lowest social classes, or of impoverished societies, find that successfully raising children is associated with very large costs to both male and female parent (see also Sloman's [1983] model of family functioning). Thus, *C* is correspondingly large, and father-son sexual competition should be relatively muted. Members of the highest social class in any society find that raising children is associated with very little cost, but father-son sexual competition may nonetheless be muted due to the predictability of the son's reproductive success and the father's consequent stake in promoting it (Appendix H). It is in the middle class of any society that the various relevant factors may be most conducive to father-son sexual competition, at least in fantasied form. It is of some interest that most psychoanalyzed male patients come from precisely the middle-class backgrounds in which father-son sexual competition might be most intense, and that the psychoanalytic movement coincided with the rise of middle-class society, the masculine psychology of which it has accurately captured. Finances, of course, account perfectly well for the preponderance of middle-class patients, but something more than ability to pay may also be at work. Freud, too, came from a middle-class background, as have most of his followers. Class differences in the intensity of Oedipal fantasies, if they actually occur, may also explain the relative failure of psychoanalytically oriented treatment with members of the lower classes (see Sloane, et al., 1975). Whether males raised in the highest social class benefit from Oedipal interpretations to the extent expected in middle-class males is, and most likely will remain, a matter of speculation,.given the small numbers of such individuals.

As mentioned previously, classical psychoanalytic theory treats father-son conflict as the origin of later male sexual competition. In this respect, it is probably wrong. The theory developed here suggests that competition with the father does not cause adult sexual competition, which would likely occur in the father's complete absence. Instead, competition with the father provides those cognitive and emotional experiences on which later competitive attitudes are founded. It is as prototype, not cause, that father-son sexual competition is psychologically significant, and it is as prototype that it deserves psychotherapeutic attention.

Male Incest Avoidance

Inclusive fitness analyses also shed light on male incest wishes. These suggest that, although young boys may want to marry their mothers and sisters, mature males probably have other ideas in mind. Although they may use the reproductive potential of female family members to further their own reproductive success, for inclusive fitness reasons adult males should prefer using it in nonincestuous ways. This is because products of inbred matings are less likely to be viable, and more likely to be reproductive failures, than products of matings between genetically unrelated individuals (for another reason, see Thompson, 1982). That males prefer to trade reproductive potential of related for that of unrelated women is corroborated by Levi-Strauss (1969), who argued that male control and exchange of female kin for mating purposes lies at the heart of human society and culture. According to Levi-Strauss, the male urge to exchange "own" for "other" females results in kinship systems and exogamy rules. Though kinship systems and exogamy rules vary somewhat from culture to culture, no society is without them entirely (Fox, 1980). Although less salient in more advanced societies—many of which have replaced direct trades with monetary and other payments for brides (Daly and Wilson, 1979)—exchange of females between powerful males is typical of primitive societies. Younger females in particular may be traded either to obtain more wives for their fathers or to obtain mates for their brothers (see Chagnon, 1979a; Fox, 1979). In many primitive societies, women are virtually all that males do trade.

However, while kinship and exogamy rules reflect a male preference for nonincestuous use of female reproductive potential, they also serve unrelated functions. These cause cultural kinship and genetic relatedness to be only partially coincident. That culturally marriageable and unmarriageable partners are not always genetically distinct has been used by some to deny altogether the incest-avoidance function of kinship systems. This conclusion, though, is largely unwarranted (see Appendix I). Exogamy rules undoubtedly do serve—among other important functions—to minimize the number of genetically inbred matings.

The Westermarck Effect and the Incest Taboo

But if kinship systems and their associated exogamy rules reflect aversions to genetically inbred marriages, then what clues are used to recognize genetic relatedness in the first place? So-called *recognition genes,* which might allow highly related individuals to directly spot each other, are thought to be highly improbable for technical reasons (see Alexander and Borgia, 1978; Irons, 1979c). A more likely clue to genetic relatedness, which is also psychologically more interesting, is childhood propinquity. That is, since parental investment strategies require that siblings be raised in close proximity to each other, individuals who avoided sexual contact with those with whom they had grown up would be effectively prevented from at least some inbred matings. An aversion to sexual relations with former childhood companions would prevent sibling incest and would encourage selective retention of exogamy rules forbidding its occurrence.

That childhood propinquity dampens adult sexual interest was proposed by Edward Westermarck, who, in the 1920s, compiled a classic tome on marriage patterns. It is now known as the *Westermarck effect.* Westermarck's hypothesis was largely forgotten following Freud's demonstration of repressed sexual desire directed at siblings and other family members, which superficially contradicts it, but has been resurrected in modified form by modern students of behavioral biology. Fox (1980) and Shepher (1983), for example, argue that suppression of adult sexual interest depends not only on propinquity, but on physical-sexual childhood contact, most likely before the age of six. Deviations from the Westermarck effect, Fox and Shepher argue, occur only in societies that prevent physical contact between children raised in otherwise close propinquity. This was the case, for instance, in late nineteenth century Vienna, and would account for Freud's discovery of repressed incestuous feelings. The bulk of recent evidence in favor of this revised version of the Westermarck hypothesis comes from the study of traditional Chinese marriages and from follow-up studies of children raised on Israeli kibbutzim, some of whom are allowed considerable childhood sexual contact and are actually encouraged to marry each other as adults. Several of the Israeli studies are summarized by Fox (1980) and Shepher (1983). Spiro, for example, found that children raised together in a communal children's group did not marry or have sexual intercourse with each other as adults, nor did they express sexual interests in those with whom they had been raised. Shepher found that of 2769 kibbutz marriages, not one was between individuals who had been continuously raised together before the age of six years. Talman, who studied three Israeli kibbutzim, also found an absence of sexual activity between adults raised in the same childhood peer groups. In China, the practice of rearing together children who would one day marry has been shown to decrease marital success and sexual satisfaction, in comparison with marriages between individuals raised in separate households (Wolf, 1966, 1968).

Conceivably, childhood propinquity and sexual contact also curb later sexual interests between same-gender homosexual relatives, who usually avoid sexual contact with each other in the same way opposite-gender heterosexual relatives do (Mellen, 1981; Myers, 1982).

In animals, sexual imprinting during development, and avoidance of sexual activity with those on whom imprinting had occurred, has been described for many species (Hill, 1974; Bateson, 1982) and is likely homologous with the Westermarck effect.

Inbred matings are selectively disadvantageous not only to participants, but to their relatives as well. In the case of sibling incest, parents of the incestuous couple will be penalized by having potentially defective grandchildren. Therefore, it serves the inclusive fitness interests of parents to discourage genetically inbred matings between their children, should the Westermarck effect fail to curb sexual interest. Among the tactics they use, punitive aggression might play a large role, as might ethical mores. In general, those with the power of selective cultural retention should mold ethical mores to discourage whichever genetically inbred matings remain attractive to other family members.

That parents shape ethical mores to prevent sibling incest in cultures where the Westermarck effect cannot be relied on is demonstrated by Fox (1980). He notes that the degree of childhood sexual contact and the severity of taboos against later sibling incest are inversely related for a number of cultures. In societies that allow extensive sexual contact between children, parents presumably need few ideologic strictures to prevent later incestuous matings between their offspring. In societies in which sibling sexual interest is not attenuated by the Westermarck effect, parents selectively retain Draconian strictures, with an accompanying ideology, serving to protect their own inclusive fitness interests. Among these latter societies, of course, was that in which Freud's patients originated. The conflict these patients experienced between incestuous wish and social stricture was not, as Freud thought, a clash between biology and culture. Instead, it represented the clash of culturally exaggerated sibling incest wishes with parental inclusive fitness interests embodied in the regnant ideology. Once again, an apparent clash between biology and culture turns out to be a clash between individuals.

But if the Westermarck effect, supplemented when necessary by parental ideology, serves to largely prevent sibling incest, what equivalent mechanisms exist to discourage cross-generational inbred matings? Once again, the inclusive fitness interests of nonparticipants produce pressures in favor of ethical strictures, but these may be relatively less effective than in the case of sibling incest. At least mother-son matings may be less likely, when the son is actually mature, due to the male preference for younger—and therefore, reproductively more capable—women. However, that very factor might also encourage father-daughter matings. One potential mechanism for the suppression of cross-generational sexual interest within the nuclear family is particularly intriguing from a psychologic point of view. Since parents and children participate in mutually beneficial attachment strategies, suppression of sexual interest as part and parcel of attachment behaviors would effectively serve to reduce desire for both mother-son and father-daughter matings. Because older children are subsidiary attachment figures for their younger siblings, the same mechanism might discourage matings between siblings with significant age discrepancies. In advancing a related hypothesis, Fox (1980) speculated that nursing relationships might dampen later sexual interest in the same manner as childhood physical intimacy.

Although the relationship between attachment and later sexual interest is speculative, several clinical phenomena suggest the value of further research in this vein. First, evidence from countless psychoanalyses suggests that childhood sexual interest in the opposite sex parent first manifests itself only after proximity maintenance ties to major and minor attachment figures begin to loosen. Thus, the period from three to six years, following the weaning conflicts described in a previous chapter, see the first flowering of incestuous sexual interest for both boys and girls. Second, clinical experience with certain pathologically dependent marital relationships shows that sexual interest is commonly suppressed, at least in the more dependent partner. Men with passive-dependent attitudes toward their wives, for example, frequently demonstrate little in the way of sexual appetite. Although situations of this sort are plausibly interpreted in classical Oedipal terms—as suppression of sexual interest in a neurotically perceived mother figure—an inverse relationship between attachment-type behaviors and sexual interest could equally well account for them.

Finally, an inverse relationship of this sort might also explain certain behaviors typical of the hysterical personality. Hysterical patients maintain a characteristically ambiguous relationship with their own sexuality, using it to attract wished-for attention while disavowing sexual interest. At the same time they are notably dependent. So-called "oral hysterics" (Marmor, 1954), for example, are markedly similar to passive-dependent or borderline personality types whose psychopathology will later be shown to result from attachment exigencies. Female hysterics frequently make older men, eligible as father-figures, the targets of their sexualized appeals. Although the hysteric's behavior, like that of the passive-dependent husband, can be plausibly interpreted in Oedipal terms, an inverse relationship between attachment behaviors and sexual interest could also reasonably account for them. The female hysteric, for example, might be construed as a passive-dependent personality whose life and thought are dominated by excessively salient attachment needs, and who uses male sexual interest to attract fatherly attachment figures upon whom she can then rely. Being dominated by attachment concerns, however, the female hysteric actually feels little or no sexual interest in the men with whom she flirts, nor—because falsely intentioned sexual come-ons are largely disapproved—is she willing to avow the uses to which she puts her sexuality.

A Few Remarks on the Female Point of View

The effects of kinship on sexual competition and interest have been treated thus far largely from a male point of view. This is due to the clinical importance of male sexual attitudes toward family members and to the more variable role played by the same attitudes in female psychology. Also, female reproductive potential is more easily quantified than male parental investments, so that it was easier to begin with male competition. As promised earlier, though, a few remarks will now be addressed to the female point of view.

First, like men, women should want to avoid inbred matings. Their preference in this regard should be even stronger than that of the male. The male may easily terminate parental investments in abnormal offspring, whereas females, by the time an abnormality becomes apparent, have already committed significant parental resources. Females, moreover, should object to inbred matings between other family members and should attempt to prevent these in the same way as males.

Second, just as men may want to nonincestuously use the reproductive capacities of female family members, so women may want to use the parental investments of male family members. They may accomplish this through avuncular and sisterhood traditions (see Chagnon and Irons [1979] for examples), just as men use alliances and sexual control.

Third, just as sexual competition between unrelated females is muted in comparison with that between unrelated males, so sexual competition between related females is likely minor in comparison with that between related males. Necessarily large parental investments, in conjunction with diminished fertility of older females, undoubtedly tip the inclusive fitness balance decisively in favor of sexual altruism, at least between mother and daughter. Just as for males, however, the fantasies of young girls and the behaviors of mature women may not coincide. Girls, who are largely incapable of judging the father's real standing in the world of adult men, may see their fathers as especially desirable mates. Insofar as they see him as one-of-a-kind, this may contribute to their envy of the mother. In later life, by contrast, more accurate judgment of the father's real standing may attenuate these feelings, at least compared with the feelings sons of the same age have toward their fathers. In general, Freud and later analysts have failed to convincingly demonstrate a role for familial sexual competition in female psychology equal to the powerful and consistent role it plays in male psychology.

10

Genetically Transmitted Social Strategies V

Ingroups and Cognitive Conformity

Group behaviors likely depend on genetically transmitted social strategies. These govern formation of "ingroups," who direct hostility toward "outgroup" members and dictate conformity with consensual world views. Psychologic theories may have obfuscated both the significance of group relations and the nature of consensual authority.

Two Related Strategies

In previous chapters social strategies have been described that lead an individual to seek or avoid particular interactions with other specific persons. These persons are selected on the basis of their personal characteristics or because of chance factors. Here, however, a different type of social strategy is described, one that predisposes an individual to maintain or avoid contact with groups of people. The persons comprising a group with which an individual maintains contact will inevitably be those with whom he or she has specific interactions of a sexual, competitive, dependent, or nurturing kind. Nonetheless, it is possible to argue that an individual's relationship to a group as a whole is not determined by the sum of his or her interactions with persons in the group, and that social strategies exist that predispose men and women to perceive social aggregates as unitary bodies. They either seek them out or avoid them, according to previous experience. A corollary to this argument, which is developed further later in this chapter, is that tendencies to aggregate are neither dependent on nor dictated by the need for specific individuals, nor are xenophobic tendencies the result of previous bad experiences with strange persons. Instead, orientation toward and away from groups depends on information processing structures equal in stature to those structures determining individual relationships. Like individual relationships, relations between individual and group meet the criteria previously discussed for likely genetic transmission.

This argument, of course, contradicts one implicit in psychoanalytic theory: That needs for personal relationships wholly determine affiliative behavior. Specific needs no doubt do determine personal relationships, yet group affiliations at least are likely more than their sum. Indeed, instances in which an individual's group affiliation is at odds with more personal relationships are the subjects of considerable artistic and ethical interest. *Romeo and Juliet,* for example, is the story of such a dilemma. In recent years many interesting social-psychologic experiments have pitted individual relationships against affiliative tendencies in order to study their interaction (see, for example, Sherif, 1966).

To be fair, however, not only psychoanalysts have viewed group structure as being built from the bottom up. The belief that group affiliative tendencies are entirely derivative dates at least from the eighteenth century, when it was espoused by Jeremy Bentham (see Bock, 1980), and is found as well in post-Freudian ethology. Kummer (1979), for example, argues that dyadic interactions alone account in principle for group phenomena. Actually, Kummer's point is probably correct, at least when applied to lower species. Unlike primate social arrangements, some of these may actually be constructed along Freudian lines. Individual sheep in a natural flock, for example, show little regard for the group as a whole. Instead, each merely stays in proximity to the ewe on which it is imprinted. The leader of the flock is the "head mother" to which second generation ewes are themselves attached (Audy, 1980). Other ethologists, though, have noted that at least human group processes depend on social categorization mechanisms qualitatively distinct from those mechanisms governing face to face interactions (see, for example, Tajfel, 1979), a position consistent with their control by conceptually independent social strategies. Freud himself was hard pressed to explain discontinuities evident between personal and group relationships. Thus, he considered it a "mystery" that individually acquired morality could be "obliterated" in the service of collective hatred, leaving only those primitive tendencies long since suppressed in interpersonal relationships (Freud, 1915). If collective behaviors were merely the sum of personal relationships, the same moral structures should be evident in both.

What distinct patterns—above and beyond personal relationships—are regularly seen in the individual's response to the social group? Actually, two distinct response patterns, so closely intertwined that each is necessary to the other, can be usefully discussed. The first of these is the tendency to draw distinctions between individuals belonging or not belonging to one's social group and to direct hostile behavior toward the latter. Toward the former, by contrast, are expressed cooperative and friendly impulses, and hostile feelings are attenuated. Thus, cooperative enterprises tend to occur within group boundaries, while hostilities are generally waged across them. The second response pattern, inextricably bound up with the first, is the tendency to believe the same things as others in the group with which one identifies oneself. Thus, individuals tend to accept as valid world views associated with their social group. Generally, coordination of world views between group members is accomplished indirectly. Certain group members, designated as "authorities," act as exemplars of consensual world views and in this role correct the beliefs of others to better approximate the consensual. The authority, therefore, acts as a cognitive template, and in this role aligns individual world views to the consensual one he or she carries.

Ingroup, Outgroup Distinctions

Common knowledge testifies to the universality of the first of these group-related social strategies. Although various cultures manifest differing degrees of hostility toward strangers, few societies exist in which strangers can freely meld without some invidious distinction being drawn. Barriers of appearance, dress, and language effectively prevent rapid assimilation across group lines. Even within larger social units various signs, including badges, uniforms, vocabulary, dialect, and idiosyncratic accents, are employed by subgroups to maintain their own distinctiveness (Tajfel, 1979). Many societies or subgroups go so far as to deny outgroup members full human status. In these groups, the societal designation often coincides with the term for human being (Berger and Luckman, 1966). Myths of superiority are less extreme results of the same tendency. Some societies even encourage the killing of ostensibly nonhuman outgroup members; at the same time they forbid killing within the group. Dehumanization in general is a common disinhibiting device for aggressive tendencies (Bandura, 1979), particularly those that cross group lines, and to indicate its role, formation of mutually hostile groups has sometimes been called "pseudospeciation" (Campbell, 1978).

Additionally, distinctions between ingroup and outgroup members are drawn by societies of every technologic and economic stripe: They are neither the product of civilization nor the stepchild of economic organization. Even hunter-gatherer tribes distinguish their own members from individuals belonging to other tribes, and conflicts with the latter are much more likely to end in violence than conflicts limited to the ingroup. Chagnon (1979a) presents evidence that hunter-gatherer tribes split to maximize genetic relatedness between ingroup members. The average pair of ingroup members in one such tribe, for example, were only slightly less genetically related than first cousins. In this way, *kin altruistic* and ingroup strategies coincide in these primitive communities. Significantly, dental evidence indicates genetic relatedness between ten protohumans who apparently perished as a group three million years ago (Tiger, 1979a), suggesting that protohuman social groups were also highly related.

This occurrence in hunter-gatherer tribes suggests that ingroup, outgroup distinctions go far back in human history (Wilson, 1978a). For this reason, Tinbergen (1976) argues that human social behavior is adapted to closed ingroups composed of mutually familiar members inimical to strangers. Actually, since hominid groups in the Plio-Pleistocene eras probably consisted of no more than fifty individuals, close relationships between members were virtually inevitable (Mellen, 1981). If hostility to strangers also characterized these groups, then a phenomenon akin to what psychotherapists call "splitting," by which individuals are partitioned into dichotomous and prejudicial categories with little consideration for the fine details of their behavior, has characterized humanity from its earliest recognizable beginnings.

Outgroup-directed violence also characterizes some nonhuman primates, although not to the degree evident among homo sapiens. Chimpanzees may occasionally kill animals from other troops, or animals attempting to leave their troop of origin (Goodall, 1979), and violent encounters have been described between groups of rhesus monkeys. Introduction of strange individuals to groups of macaque monkeys results in "scapegoating" and even death (Reynolds, 1981). Also, like human groups, groups of nonhuman primates are composed of highly related individuals and split to preserve genetic kinship (Chepko-Sade, 1979).

The distinction between ingroup and outgroup members is not only ubiquitous, both ethnographically and historically, but it is also central to the common sense notion of affectively significant, volitionally maintained groups. These groups, which must be distinguished from socially random aggregations based on common characteristics, affectively trivial associations such as school classes, instrumental associations such as commercial societies, and, finally, family and kinship associations, are inevitably characterized both by greater ingroup harmony and by the preferential placement of hostility outside the group. An affectively significant volitional group that discriminated against its own members is essentially unthinkable, since by definition the centripetal social forces disrupting the group would be greater than those forces leading to harmonious intercourse. Groups of this kind may be more or less ethnocentric, but the gradient of probable hostility must always favor its occurrence outside, rather than inside, the group.

If invidious distinctions between ingroup and outgroup members are ubiquitous, they are also likely to be evolutionarily stable. As indicated in a previous chapter, ubiquitous, evolutionarily stable social strategies probably depend on genetically transmitted propensities. In this regard, it is essential to consider the human environment of adaptation, which differs considerably from that of most modern men and women.

Symons (1979) points out that intelligent hominids with advanced tool cultures have existed for over one million years, a time span in comparison to which the ten-thousand-year history of agricultural civilization is indeed brief. Preagricultural hominids lived by hunting and gathering, presumably in small groups. Therefore, it is likely that group-related social strategies are adapted to the small social units appropriate to a hunting and gathering existence, rather than to the large social aggregates of agricultural or industrial society. Not only do the social groups to which individuals cohere today differ from those in the human environment of adaptation, but the alternatives to group coherence also differ. The isolate life in an age of hunter-gatherers is likely to have been utterly different from the isolate life today. Keeping these factors in mind, it is apparent that affiliative tendencies in the human environment of adaptation must have conferred significant selective advantages.

Among these advantages, for example, would have been the benefits of common defense against predation and of common hunting of large animals. Even passive togetherness decreases the probability of a given individual falling victim to a predator (Hamilton, 1978), and out of a passively advantaged group the tendency to engage in common defense could evolve. Not only does group affiliation confer protection from predators, but in some species physical location at the center of a group may provide more security (see, for example, Kruuk, 1964). Alexander and coworkers (1979) consider predation a prime selective force responsible for the evolution of primate grouping tendencies, and, judging by australopithecine finds (see Mellen, 1981), predation must have remained an important force through at least early hominid evolution. More recently, intergroup warfare may have supplanted nonhuman predation as a selective force leading to larger group sizes (Alexander, 1979). As for hunting, group forays enlarge the range of possible prey disproportionately to the increase in pooled needs. Even the largest animals were presumably hunted by organized protohominid bands (Mellen, 1981). Fox (1980), in fact, credits social organization with allowing early hominids to occupy an ecologic niche—that of the "big carnivore"—-unoccupied in East Africa two million years ago.

Other advantages, especially greater reproductive and learning opportunities, may also favor group over solitary lifestyles.

The major drawbacks to group living are that it makes each individual more conspicuous to potential predators and that it exposes him or her to greater intraspecies competition for food and other resources (Clutton-Brock and Harvey, 1978). With respect to the first of these, cryptic (that is, camouflaged) species tend to be solitary, as are sick or birthing individuals of other species. The latter cannot flee with the group, so that their inclusive fitness interests may be better served in some cases by temporarily absenting themselves. The intense competitions for female reproductive capacity and for male parental investments likely to occur within groups have already been described. Clutton-Brock and Harvey (1978) treat the formation of social groups as a compromise between competing advantages and disadvantages. For instance, terrestrial species—for whom the danger of predation is increased and cryptic defenses are impractical—form larger groups than species living under less vulnerable circumstances. Aggregation of resources, such as food supplies, also favors formation of larger groups than would be possible if group members were forced to compete for highly dispersed, and therefore scarce, resources.

The selective advantages of affiliation, however, fail to completely explain hostility toward outgroup members. Obviously, once members of other groups had become hostile toward strangers, then an aversion to outsiders would be evolutionarily stable. But what advantages accrued from outgroup hostility in the first place? One possibility is that outgroup hostility served to protect resources in the ingroup's home range (Clutton-Brock and Harvey, 1978). Members of a group hostile to other groups might prosper by protecting resources from outside intrusions. In fact, however, the degree of territoriality of primate groups varies widely from species to species. Some primate species exclude strangers from their home range, while others freely tolerate them. In general, species with the largest home ranges, which are correspondingly more difficult to defend, tend to be the least territorial. Females, of course, are a special kind of resource and might advantageously be sequestered from strange males. Thus, not only is territoriality more intense among males (Clutton-Brock and Harvey, 1978), but male hostility is directed mostly toward male rather than female outgroup members. Though females of higher primate species may cross group lines for mating purposes, males of the same species would meet violent opposition from male members of any group they attempted to infiltrate. In general, primate males seem to consider female outgroup members as potential sexual resources, while male outgroup members are seen as dire enemies.

Since the tendency to allocate hostile behaviors according to invidious ingroup, outgroup distinctions is both ubiquitous and evolutionarily stable, its occurrence probably depends on genetically transmitted propensities. Lorenz (1960), Wilson (1975), and Lumsden and

Wilson (1981) make much the same point. Lumsden and Wilson, for instance, argue that the tendency to "dichotomize" others into ingroups and outgroups results from innate, genetically determined, epigenetic rules.

Recently, some of the observations made above with respect to human groups have proven intelligible in terms of *mutualism theory* (Maynard Smith, 1982a; Wrangham, 1982). Mutualistic interactions are cooperative behaviors that produce immediate benefits for all participants, in comparison to their prospects should they act alone. Mutualistic interactions can be subdivided into *interfering* and *noninterfering* types, depending on their effects on other individuals (Wrangham, 1982). Interfering mutualistic interactions benefit participants, but prevent other individuals from cooperating to gain the same advantage. Thus, if two or more individuals cooperate to monopolize food supplies, their success will prevent other coalitions from doing the same thing. Noninterfering mutualistic interactions benefit participants but have no effect on others. Thus, if two or more individuals cooperate to build a shelter, their success should not prevent other coalitions from doing the same thing, unless building materials or sites are in very short supply. Suppose that individual *I* can choose as a mutualistic partner either individual *J* or individual *K*, and that the benefits of cooperation—as opposed to solitary action—are B_c. Then the inclusive fitness advantage accruing to individual *I* from cooperating in a noninterfering way with either *J* or *K* is always

$$(1) \qquad B_c(1 + R(ij) + R(ik)),$$

where *R(ij)* and *R(ik)* are *I*'s degree of genetic relationship with *J* and *K*, respectively (see Wrangham, 1982, for this and following equations). *R(ij)* and *R(ik)* depreciate benefits obtained by *J* and *K*, according to the proportion of genes they share with *I*. This assumes, of course, that due to the noninterfering nature of the mutualistic interaction, both individuals *J* and *K* will eventually gain the benefits of acting in a successful coalition, regardless of which of the two is chosen as a partner by *I*. Since the benefit of choosing *J* or *K* is always the same, individual I should be indifferent to whom he cooperates with, at least insofar as they are equally effective participants.

Now, however, assume that the mutualistic interaction is such that it will prevent the formation of other successful coalitions and that the benefits from acting alone are negligible. The inclusive fitness advantage accruing to individual *I* from cooperating with *J* will be

(2) $$B_c(1 + R(ij)).$$

The advantage from cooperating with individual *K* will be

(3) $$B_c(1 + R(ik)),$$

which will not equal equation 2 unless *R(ij)* and *R(ik)* are identical. Consequently, in the case of interfering mutualism, individual *I* will be best served by choosing his partner, *J* or *K*, according to which is more closely related. Mutualistic groups that act to interfere with formation of other successful coalitions—that is, competitive or interfering mutualistic groups—should therefore be composed of closely related kin. As noted above, mutually hostile groups of closely related individuals typify primitive human social arrangements.

Cognitive Conformity

Similar remarks also apply to the second group-related response pattern. Not only has no society lacking belief systems been described, but how such a group might function is quite inconceivable. All societies, moreover, possess a division of knowledge according to which certain individuals are recognized as the exemplars of the consensual view of particular subjects (see Berger and Luckman, 1966). The social division of consensual knowledge, according to Berger and Luckman, is part and parcel of social role division in its most elementary form. These exemplars continually adapt the relevant world views of other group members to conform with their own, which are accorded normative status in whatever subject matter the division of knowledge has deemed them authorities. In some societies, notions of truth and authority are not even clearly delineated (see D'Azevedo, 1982). In this way, authorities promote the coherence of group thinking and of group beliefs concerning important issues. Both the manner of designation of authorities, and the degree to which authority is circumscribed or diffused, differ greatly from culture to culture, and particularly between technologically primitive and advanced societies. Nonetheless, the basic phenomenon remains the same: Individuals designated as possessing normative world views communicate those views to other group members, who stand more ready to incorporate them than views—often factually superior—that lack the consensual imprint.

Transmission of "world views" by transiently designated "authorities" also occurs among animals. Thus, group-living species dependent on coordinated action possess the means for informed individuals to communicate environmental maps—sufficient to locate food, shelter, or other valuable resources—to other individuals who recognize their special status (see Menzel, 1975; Griffin, 1981; Breuer, 1982). However, because these means are gestural and representational, they are severely limited in the range of models they can successfully convey. The extent to which acquired world views can be coordinated, therefore, is correspondingly limited. On the other hand, freed from these limitations by productive, combinatorial linguistic codes, human cognitive consensus—together with the notion of authority on which it depends—extends into every realm of common group interest. It is small wonder, then, that behavioral scientists from many disciplines now agree that human cognition in particular is an essentially social process. Berger and Luckman, for example, argued that specific models of reality are inseparable from group social life, and that particular social forms demand acceptance of particular consensual world views as a condition of individual participation. Trevarthen (1979) argued that the notion of the isolated human seeker after truth must eventually be supplanted by theories that treat cognitive functions as ancillary to social functioning. In recent years, various experimental paradigms have been used to demonstrate this same point. Approximately two thirds, for example, of a random sample of normal subjects will inflict on other persons what they have reason to believe is severe pain, if that is requested of them by an ostensibly knowledgeable authority figure (Milgram, 1963). Likewise, the probability that an individual will aid someone in distress is decreased in the company of unresponding bystanders (Latane and Darley, 1968). Apparently, ethical judgments are most often made according to the social demands of the moment, rather than according to invariant internalized standards. The same is true of less abstract cognitions. Subjects will modify correct judgments of objective physical parameters in order to conform to what they believe is a majority opinion (Asch, 1956). The fluidity of "objective" judgments is particularly notable if the apparent majority is unanimous. There are, apparently, no facts so "hard" as to be uninfluenced by social conformity.

If the social division of knowledge is responsible for perception of authority, then authority itself—and its correct delineation—is obviously of great psychologic importance. Unfortunately, numerous confusing metaphors, at least some of them selfishly motivated (see Sennett, 1981, for examples), have obscured the real roots of social authority. Two of these, in particular, deserve attention here. First, both psychologic theorists and neurotics have all too often likened cognitive authority to the parental role. Psychologic theorists have been overanxious to find childhood bases for every adult relationship. Neurotics, although without a theoretical ax to grind, misperceive the present in terms of past experiences. Certainly, parents are authority figures to their children. They convey to their children consensually approved world views that the children are expected to adopt and that also legitimize parental dominance. Nonetheless, relations with adult authority figures subserve group functions for the most part different from the functions subserved by parent-child interactions and are dependent on differing proximate mechanisms (see Chapter 14). Considering the means by which consensual knowledge is divided, for example, it becomes apparent that adult authority is vastly more complex than the authority parents assume with respect to their children.

Second, authority is frequently likened to simple power. Yet, power refers to the real interpersonal dominance of certain individuals, while authority refers to an ascribed right to be dominant. This right, in turn, is felt to result from consensually superior knowledge or consensually validated world views. These views allow the authoritative individual to make decisions consensually more respected than those of less authoritative persons. For that reason, societies most often delegate authority and social power simultaneously, a tendency perfected, however, only in democracies. Only in the democratic society is consensus methodically measured and power delegated to coincide with the results. Yet, even hereditary rulers are thought by at least some of their subjects to possess—either genetically or by divine right—the capacity for superior wisdom in governance. The same is true for designated powers: Policemen are assumed to know the law, judges to know jurisprudence, physicians to know medicine. Powerful individuals lacking cognitive authority are widely considered imposters. Policemen ignorant of the law, judges unfamiliar with jurisprudence, or physicians unacquainted with medical science are all considered wrongly placed. On the other hand, individuals lacking power but possessing consensual authority are widely felt to be dispossessed.

If acceptance of consensual world views divided among authority figures is ubiquitous in human societies, then what can be said of its selective advantages? Once again, establishing evolutionary stability would indicate likely dependence on genetically transmitted propensities, as Wilson (1975) suggests is the case. First, advantages to the individual from group cognitive coherence are numerous. The success of common hunting, defense, or other socially coordinated behaviors depends on some minimal number of common beliefs shared among group members (Reynolds, 1981). Each participant in a group hunt, for instance, must possess approximately the same impression of terrain, weaponry, prey, and roles within the hunt. The same is true of participants in common defense. An individual failing to adopt group cognitive models necessary to these activities would be at best useless and at worst a danger to himself and others. Serious failure of cognitive conformity might impede the transmission of vital traditional information, create discordant reinforcers for those who must otherwise work together, and—since cognitive authority and social power normally coincide—promote leadership struggles within the group. Adoption of consensual views may also serve to suppress internally generated dysfunctional ideas that might otherwise disorganize behavior. The very notion of rational thought, a generally acknowledged prerequisite to behavioral organization, is closely connected if not coincident with that of demonstrability (see Goody, 1978). The importance of cognitive conformity to individual adaptation is the topic of a later chapter.

Discussing advantages to consensual world views, Tiger (1979a) goes so far as to argue that achievement of cognitive consensus, including "common responses" to "common symbols," is the major adaptive function of human behavioral plasticity. Insofar as it treats reduced rather than enhanced variation as selectively advantageous, Tiger's argument reverses certain widely held prejudices concerning the functions of behavioral plasticity. Lumsden and Wilson (1981) also conclude that conformity is highly adaptive. The tendency for uniform enculturation within groups of highly related individuals, according to Lumsden and Wilson, not only accelerates genetic assimilation of adaptive cultural practices, but it also leads to selection of conformity-promoting genotypes. Insofar as world views are cultural artifacts, tendencies toward cognitive consensus would therefore be highly adaptive in their own right.

In addition, conformity may also deflect potential hostility. Cognitively deviant individuals may be shunned due to their relative uselessness in group endeavors, and because behavioral differences secondary to aberrant world views mark them as foreign. Hostile behaviors normally suppressed within the ingroup are thereby released. In this latter respect, the functions of familiarity in small groups may be served in large groups by conformity (Bischof, 1978). Because proximate mechanisms responsible for assimilation of pragmatically essential or inessential cognitive models are likely identical, rejection of ingroup cognitive deviants may occur regardless of the actual heresy involved. Intense and indiscriminate rejection of this sort would further penalize those less inclined toward consensual thinking and might ensure the evolutionary stability of cognitive conformity. That intellectual nonconformity, without regard for its pragmatic importance, releases hostility in human groups is demonstrated in the history of human persecution. Berger and Luckman (1966) point out, moreover, that stable consensual world views contain "nihilating" devices specifically aimed at detoxifying deviant cognitions. By voiding the inferential content of deviant viewpoints, and by placing them squarely in the consensual framework, formal devices of this type reduce cognitive dissonance for the true believer. They also justify persecuting the disbeliever. "Mental illness" appears to be such a device in Soviet society, and there are some who believe it plays that role in our society as well (Szasz, 1961). That even individuals find each other likeable and intelligent according to their perceived agreement on certain basic issues has also been demonstrated in the psychology laboratory (Byrne, 1969).

Given inclusive fitness penalties for even mild degrees of nonconformity, how is intellectual creativity maintained in human communities? Obviously, some direct or indirect benefits must accrue from those proximate mechanisms responsible for otherwise penalized nonconformist thought. Both *reciprocal altruism* (Chapter 11) and sexual competition, for instance, may favor intellectual capacities predisposing to innovation, even as innovation itself is penalized through group-related social strategies. Group selection, too, may have acted to ameliorate the intellectual rigidity resulting from within-group social strategies. Societies demonstrating the most extreme degrees of cognitive consensus may be technologically backward in any age, so that war and intergroup resource competition have favored groups less hostile to intellectual dissent. Intellectual creativity and its relation to psychopathology are discussed further in a later chapter.

Psychological Implications

Psychopathologic syndromes likely related to group-level social strategies include schizotypal and paranoid personality disorders (Chapter 14). Also, at least one form of loneliness is plausibly viewed as the subjective experience of an appraisal process enforcing group affiliation. Audy (1980), for instance, found that social isolation interpreted as extrusion from a social group was particularly likely to trigger loneliness, which explains the absence of a simple relationship between aloneness and loneliness (Sermat, 1980; Rubenstein and Shaver, 1980). Consistent with this notion, though written from an attachment theory framework, is Weiss' (1982) remark that loneliness appears as "separation distress without an object." Other conditions commonly encountered in clinical practice have as one of their manifestations the subjective need to "melt away" in an anonymous crowd, failure in which leads to loneliness or anxiety or sometimes to both. Certain passive personalities, for example, assume the coloration of whatever crowd is at hand, as if sheer anonymity was their goal. Existential psychologists in particular have noted that the need for excessive conformity may stifle self-development (see May, 1958).

For still other individuals, those with authoritarian personalities (Adorno, et al., 1950), it is the xenophobic component of the ingroup, outgroup strategy that is most salient. Authoritarian personalities, in fact, may be those hypothesized by Tajfel (1979), who require that sharp distinctions be drawn between ingroup and outgroup and who inappropriately perceive social interactions as relevant to intergroup, rather than interindividual, issues.

Group-related social strategies, insofar as they define the conditions of guilt-free violence, also shed light on the psychopathology of military forces. In particular, since ingroup cohesion and clear ingroup, outgroup boundaries are required to neutralize the factors normally inhibiting personal violence, wars in which either of these conditions fail to be met might occasion a high incidence of psychologic disorders. Both of these factors, for example, might contribute to the high frequency of psychologic disorders in Viet Nam war veterans (see Keane and Fairbank, 1983). Vietnamese guerrillas mingled freely with and were indistinguishable from Vietnamese allies, so that in-group, outgroup boundaries were frequently invisible. On returning home, American veterans also encountered a society unable—through ingroup cohesion—to neutralize the affective consequences of violence. In fact, returning soldiers were frequently treated contemptuously and bore the burden of accusations normally reserved for ingroup murderers.

Just as the soldier's psychology depends on group-related social strategies, so does the occurrence of war in the first place. Hence, the propensity to direct hostility toward perceived outgroup members undoubtedly contributes to racial, ethnic, and nationalistic violence and to their frequency throughout human history. Similarly, tendencies toward cognitive consensus within the ingroup contribute to the possibility of mass delusions leading to war. Were men and women innately inclined to judge outgroup members individually, or to seek truth rather than merely consensus, human social arrangements would pose far less danger to human survival than they presently do. Amelioration of the dangers to human welfare inherent in unchanneled group-related social strategies is urgently required since the advent of nuclear technology.

Finally, mention should be made of the modern, and not so modern, tendency to join certain nontraditional societal subgroups. In one of the rare psychiatric studies explicitly based on sociobiologic theories, Galanter (1978) cast some light on ingroup membership, belief, and outgroup hostility, and on their potential relation to modern cult phenomena. One hundred and nineteen members of a religious cult gave retrospective and current estimates of subjective distress, the first being for the two month period before joining the cult, and the second for the two month period after joining. On the basis of these estimates, Galanter argued that neurotic distress results from disaffiliation with larger-than-family groups, and that membership in the cult relieved that distress by remedying the state of disaffiliation. Although factors of self-selection, attribution, and response bias weaken his conclusions with regard to neurotic suffering, this and other studies by Galanter (1983, 1983a; Galanter and Buckley, 1978; Galanter, et al., 1979) vividly illustrate the psychologic power of group affiliation. One finding deserves particular attention: The best predictor of reported relief after cult membership was stated distrust of nonmembers! Those who reported the greatest distrust of nonmembers also reported the least willingness to accept their beliefs compared to those of members, consistent with the importance of ingroup cognitive consensus, a point also noted by Galanter.

Significantly, at least one survey of EST graduates also suggests that powerful affective responses to EST training are associated with continuing organizational contact and with invidious attitudes toward those outside the EST family (see Finkelstein, et al., 1982). Both of these findings suggest the importance of group-related social strategies to perceived results of EST training. From an ethologic and sociobiologic viewpoint, large-group training and cult experiences provide valuable areas for future research.

11

Genetically Transmitted Social Strategies VI

Altruism

Two social strategies govern altruism. "Kin selection" requires that altruistic acts benefit individuals carrying the same genes as the altruist. "Reciprocal altruism" requires that altruistic acts be directed toward those likely to be altruistic themselves. Selective pressures consequent to kin and reciprocal altruism may have played important roles in human cognitive evolution.

The Problem of Altruism

As in the case of affiliative tendencies, psychopathologic theorists have treated altruistic tendencies as entirely derivative. The selfish impulses assumed to comprise primary human motives are, according to these theorists, twisted by conflict and defense mechanisms into their opposite. When fully examined, altruism is said to bear the imprint of its motivational sources. Also as for affiliative tendencies, an ethologic and sociobiologic framework must take a contradictory approach. Altruistic tendencies, in fact, must be considered as primary to the human endowment as selfish ones. Their development does not necessarily depend on the transformation of egocentric motives, or on the action of intrapsychic defenses, which they actually antedate (Rheingold and Hay, 1978). Those cases in which altruism does function as a mask for unconscious egocentrism reveal little of its true nature. The hand, for example, may be used to shade the eye. Yet, no one would dream of accounting for its structure in opthalmologic terms.

While altruism cannot be understood as merely derivative, the selective forces accounting for its separate evolution merit special attention. In what follows, we will discuss only what Wilson (1980) calls strong altruism. Other altruistic tendencies resemble "mutualism" and are best treated under different headings (Chapter 10).

First, selection of altruistic behaviors may not always be accounted for in terms of the altruist's reproductive success. From a biologic viewpoint, in fact, altruism involves the sacrifice of some of one's own reproductive potential in order to increase that of others (Bertram, 1982). Most often the sacrifice is minimal: A matter of time and resources that could be otherwise employed. In these cases, it is easy to imagine that a small sacrifice in effort or safety might be repaid by a larger, perhaps indirect, benefit of the altruistic act itself (see, for example, Trivers, 1971). Avian warning calls, for instance, not only save fellow birds; they also discourage predators, who are likely to leave an area where they are unable to catch prey. Thus, the "alarmist" bird makes himself safe by saving the lives of others. In other cases, though, the sacrifice is relatively large, and indirect benefits may or may not be apparent. Biologic explanations for this type of altruism, unless it results from miscalculation, must depend for their logical structure on either the crucial distinction between reproductive potential and inclusive fitness or on hidden benefits less obvious than those usually considered.

Second, evolution of altruistic behaviors cannot be accounted for in terms of group selection. Because altruistic behaviors benefit other individuals in the social group, and in fact are essential to the operation of any social unit, it is easy to conclude that beneficial effects on group functioning might be responsible for selection of altruistic tendencies. Darwin (1859) himself reached this conclusion in considering the social insects. In fact, though, if altruistic behaviors are disadvantageous to the genes promoting them, then other genes arising in a group of altruistic individuals would rapidly proliferate. The proliferation of genes failing to promote altruism would further increase the disadvantages accruing to those that did promote it, reducing their frequency even more. Eventually, when sufficiently few individuals in the group were altruistic, the group would stop functioning completely. All the genes, both those that did and did not promote altruism, would then likely perish together. Therefore, genes that promote altruistic behaviors must be advantaged with respect to those that do not, regardless of their beneficial effects on group function.

Objections to sociobiology's treatment of "altruism" result in part from its use of the term. This seems to omit the necessarily intentional aspect of "altruism" in its common usage (Stent, 1978). Thus, sociobiologically "altruistic" acts may be performed without knowledge of or regard for their consequences, or may be intentionally generous, and it is only in the latter form that they seem to require specific psychologic explanations. Yet, sociobiology's failure to draw that distinction merely reflects the limits of the discipline. Fitness consequences follow biologically altruistic acts regardless of whether or not their proximate causation involves conscious intention, a matter better left to proximate causal psychologic science.

Other objections, though, concern the hypothesized association of good deeds with selective advantage. Even those who feel untroubled by psychoanalytic theories consider selective theories of altruism excessively cynical. Selfish gain, they argue, should not be sought in altruistic acts. It is true that one sociobiologic theory of altruism emphasizes the banal fact that people prefer to do favors for those who have been and will be nice to them. Yet, it is misreading that argument to think that altruism must be alloyed with egocentrism. Rather, the *reciprocal altruism* theory describes the situational restrictions on purely altruistic tendencies that are required if they are to enhance gene fitness. Underestimation of the truly altruistic, conditioned by psychoanalytic doctrine and superficially proven by the neurotic tendency to hide baseness behind good deeds, is an Achilles heel for modern psychopathology (see Wallach and Wallach, 1983), for which much-reviled sociobiologic theories actually provide a welcome tonic.

Kin Selection

As it turns out, there are actually just two situations in which genes promoting altruism of the type discussed here may become selectively advantaged. Their explication in the last two decades (Hamilton, 1964; Trivers, 1971) provided the key theoretical insights on which modern sociobiology is based. The first of these, which was adumbrated by Fisher (1930) and Haldane (1932) half a century ago, occurs when altruistic acts confer reproductive benefits on kin. If reproductive benefits to kin, devalued according to the degree of genetic relatedness, outweigh reproductive costs incurred by the altruist, then altruism will act to enhance the inclusive fitness of genes promoting it. This is the theory of *kin selection*. In general, if C is the expected loss of reproductive potential incurred by the altruist, B is the expected benefit in reproductive potential accruing to the recipient, and k is the degree of genetic kinship (ranging from 0, or no kinship, to 1, or perfect genetic identity) between altruist and recipient, then altruistic acts satisfying the relation:

$$kB > C \tag{1}$$

will enhance the inclusive fitness of those genes promoting them. Altruistic acts failing to satisfy this relation may, by contrast, severely penalize the genes promoting them, depending on the degree to which C exceeds kB.

Equation 1 does more than simply specify a set of circumstances. It also specifies an evolutionarily stable social strategy. Organisms capable of carrying out or withholding altruistic acts according to whether or not they will likely satisfy equation 1 would enhance the inclusive fitness of their own genes. In a population of kin altruists, mutant individuals might differ from normal individuals in one of two selectively disadvantaged ways. They might fail to carry out altruistic acts for which equation 1 holds true, or they might carry out altruistic acts for which equation 1 is not true. In either case, obvious inclusive fitness penalties will be incurred.

Yet, to perform or withhold altruistic acts according to whether or not they are likely to satisfy equation 1 requires that three separate terms be taken into account. First, an individual following that strategy must parcel out charitable acts according to the likely reproductive benefit, B, accruing to the potential recipient. This reproductive benefit is determined not only by the nature of the altruistic act itself, but by characteristics of the potential recipient, particularly his or her remaining reproductive potential. Thus, not only should either hopeless or trivial situations elicit fewer altruistic acts, but elderly or ill recipients should also tend to be discriminated against by altruists following a kin selection strategy. Nor would kin altruists necessarily think about these contingencies, which might instead be embodied in the evolved discriminative cues for altruism. A child in distress may simply arouse more intense altruistic impulses than an elderly person in the same predicament.

Second, an individual following a kin selection strategy must parcel out altruistic acts according to the degree of genetic relatedness, k, he or she shares with potential recipients. Not only must kin be distinguished from unrelated individuals, but the former must be graded according to their genetic similarity. If k is 0.5, as it is between first-degree relatives, the likely benefit to the recipient need only be twice the likely cost to the altruist in order for equation 1 to be satisfied. If k is 0.25, however, as it is between second-degree relatives, then the necessary ratio of benefit to cost becomes at least fourfold. First-degree relatives, of course, include parents, siblings, and children; second-degree relatives include grandparents, half-siblings, and grandchildren (see Chapter 9). More distant relatives, since they share even a lower proportion of genes, require even higher benefit-to-cost ratios to justify altruistic acts. As is the case for estimates of benefit, kinship estimates made for altruistic purposes may quite unconsciously be embodied in evolved discriminative cues. For example, small social groups in hunter-gatherer societies are highly related (Chapter 10), so that tendencies to restrict altruism to the ingroup also restrict it to highly related kin. Parental investment tendencies might further restrict altruism to the most highly related members of the ingroup, as might tendencies to adopt kinship systems contingent upon paternity confidence (Appendix I). Juvenile propinquity—which plays a likely role in the avoidance of inbreeding (Chapter 9)—is yet another potential cue to probable genetic relatedness (Kummer, 1978).

Finally, the kin selection strategy specified in equation 1 requires that altruistic acts be parceled out according to the likely cost, C, incurred by the benefactor. Cost, similar to benefit, is a function not only of the altruistic act itself but also of the individual performing it. In particular, personally diminished reproductive prospects may be associated with decreased costs to the potential altruist. No deliberate consideration of likely costs need be postulated, however. Discriminative cues for altruistic behaviors may account for likely costs just as they might for benefits and kinship. Fear of injury alone would discourage altruistic acts with the greatest possible costs, as might anticipated future pleasures, or concern for young dependents. The potential shift of altruistic tendencies in postreproductive life—based on diminished probable costs—is discussed in Appendix G.

That a kin selection strategy ubiquitously guides much of human altruism can hardly be doubted. Individuals in all societies distinguish kin from nonkin and stand more ready to direct their charity toward the former. The role of particular kinship systems in guiding altruistic efforts is discussed in Appendix I. Among kin, children are particularly favored beneficiaries, while the old are frequently discriminated against. Should serious shortfalls strike, the old are frequently the first to voluntarily do without. Regardless of beneficiary, favors entailing great risks are made only when great benefits might ensue. A culture in which kin were discriminated against, one in which individuals stood less ready to aid a distressed child than a distressed adult, one in which the very young were encouraged to starve themselves for the benefit of geriatric group members, or one in which lives were willingly risked for whimsical rather than serious purposes, is highly unusual, if such a culture exists at all.

Being both ubiquitous and evolutionarily stable, it is likely that kin selection strategies guiding altruistic behaviors depend for their occurrence on genetically transmitted propensities. At least some of these may be the discriminative cues already described, which embody assessments of benefit, cost, and kinship. Others may consist of parenting and group social strategies or nonsocial preferences such as the desire to avoid personal injury.

Reciprocal Altruism

The second situation in which willing sacrifice of reproductive potential might enhance gene fitness is that defined by *reciprocal altruism* theory, which was mentioned earlier. Reciprocal altruism theory explains those altruistic behaviors not conforming to kin selection theory, either because the recipient is not kin or because the devalued benefit is insufficient to genetically justify the cost. Reciprocal altruism theory essentially argues that nonkin directed acts of charity will enhance the inclusive fitness of genes promoting them if and only if they are directed toward beneficiaries likely—on the basis of previous altruistic history—to later requite them (Trivers, 1971). Since benefits greatly exceed cost for most acts of charity—consider, for example, the disproportion between having been rescued and having thrown a rope—an altruist's expectation that he or she will be the beneficiary of future altruistic acts at times of potential need will likely outweigh the transient cost of helping another. Even favors resulting in severe costs may still fit the reciprocal altruism formula, if the altruist's kin may benefit from its future repayment. Although kinship considerations greatly complicate the reciprocal altruism strategy, and the proximate mechanisms necessary to realize it, reciprocal altruism operative between kinship alliances may be a crucial factor in many human societies. Like the kin selection strategy, a reciprocal altruism strategy for allocation of altruistic acts is likely to be evolutionarily stable, at least in a population of nondispersing, mutually dependent individuals capable of learning each others' behavioral history. Having proven himself egotistical, for example, a mutant living in a population of reciprocal altruists would soon be deprived of altruistic benefits. On the average, these would have greatly exceeded the cost of those altruistic acts he himself refused to perform, resulting in a net loss of inclusive fitness.

Equation 1, which describes altruistic acts meeting the criteria of kin selection theory, can be modified to account also for reciprocal altruism. The resulting general formula is

$$kB + R > C + kP, \quad (2)$$

where the new terms, R and P, denote the likely benefits and costs of anticipated reciprocal favors, respectively. Altruistic acts for which equation 2 holds true will enhance the inclusive fitness of genes promoting them (Irons, 1979). Altruistic acts for which equation 2 fails to hold may decrease considerably the inclusive fitness of genes promoting them, depending on the degree to which the right-hand terms exceed those on the left. Anticipated costs of reciprocal favors, like the benefits expected from the altruistic act itself, are depreciated according to the number of genes the altruist shares with the recipient who must later bear them.

Equation 2, unlike its simpler predecessor, can even account for altruistic behaviors occurring between individuals from different species. In such instances, the coefficient of relatedness, k, is close to zero, so that equation 2 simplifies to:

$$R > C. \quad (3)$$

This, of course, is just another way of saying that the anticipated reciprocal benefits, R, exceed the immediate cost, C, incurred by the altruist. Cleaning symbioses among fish, for example, are explicable in these terms (Trivers, 1971). Patterns of mutual support among unrelated nonhuman primates are also explicable in purely reciprocal terms (Packer, 1978) and vary as well in the ways predicted by equation 3. Thus, during periods of resource shortage, when C in equation 3 becomes larger, rhesus monkeys refrain from purely reciprocal altruism and direct their favors instead to those with the highest degrees of genetic relatedness (Loy, 1970). Among baboons, unrelated animals sufficiently dominant to be useful allies—those capable of returning the greatest reciprocal favors, R—are more likely to be aided by inferior animals anxious to secure their future goodwill (Packer, 1978).

Just as kin selection strategies require that certain variables be effectively anticipated, so reciprocal altruism strategies require that reciprocal benefits be more or less predictable. The difficulty of predicting reciprocal benefits, however, has been likened to the problem posed by the so-called "prisoner's dilemma," a two-person exchange popularized by game theorists (see Trivers, 1971). Both the strengths and weaknesses of this analogy illustrate important facets of reciprocal altruism. Essentially, the prisoner's dilemma pits two opponents, each blinded to and unable to influence the other's play, in a nonzero sum game. For both players, the optimal reward in this game comes from mutual cooperation, the greatest penalty from efforts to cooperate with an unfaithful partner. Thus, players must either settle for a suboptimal outcome or risk everything on the other's intent to cooperate. This is also said to be the choice faced by the potential reciprocal altruist. In choosing to be altruistic, he or she risks reproductive potential on the recipient's willingness to reciprocate. But the absence of altruism, on the other hand, consigns both altruist and potential recipient to a suboptimal outcome.

In fact, however, reciprocal altruism and the prisoner's dilemma differ in crucial respects. Neither partner in an altruistic exchange is completely blinded with respect to the other nor wholly without means for influencing the other's behavior. For this reason, a more accurate analogy illustrating the complexity of reciprocal altruism treats the altruistic exchange as a transaction in inclusive fitness "currency." The greatest good to both potential altruist and recipient comes from a continual process of loaning and repaying this currency. In this sense, reciprocal altruism is really a form of mutualism (Chapter 10), in which costs and benefits for the cooperating partners are no longer simultaneous. But in spite of this mutual interest, the momentary creditor (or altruist) is always at the mercy of the momentary debtor (or recipient), who can stop playing the game precisely when the other is most disadvantaged. Yet the creditor, should he or she fail to "make a loan" when called upon, resigns both players to a suboptimal outcome, in which both lack credit for emergencies. Unlike in the prisoner's dilemma, however, estimates might be made of the "credit-worthiness" of potential recipients, and means might be found for enforcing repayment of loans already made.

If information concerning the other's intentions and the capacity to influence these are in fact needed to avoid the prisoner's dilemma, then organisms allocating altruistic acts according to a reciprocal altruism strategy must acquire both information and influence. In particular, potential altruists must look for evidence that potential recipients are willing to requite favors. Potential recipients, in turn, might attempt to display that evidence to those on whom they depend for future favors. If they have failed to behave altruistically in the past, they must convince potential benefactors that their lapse was temporary, and that they can be relied on to reciprocate future favors. Intentions to reciprocate may also be mimicked, so that potential altruists might profit by being suspicious. Altruists failing to receive reciprocal benefits might reap long-term rewards from punishing ungrateful recipients—or at least those who fail to provide convincing evidence of their return to reciprocal altruism. Expectation of probable punishment for failure to reciprocate might change the payoff matrix for potential recipients, inducing them to requite obligations they would otherwise shirk and discouraging them from signaling false intentions. In short, the need for information and influence fostered by reciprocal altruism should lead to the development of specific signals, defenses against mimicry, and punitive impulses, without which potential altruists find themselves in a prisoners' dilemma. Together with the tendency to deny favors to those who have been untrustworthy, these signals, defenses, and punitive impulses comprise the essential proximate mechanisms needed to successfully pursue a reciprocal altruism strategy.

Tendencies to allocate favors to those who have been and will likely continue to be altruistic are deeply entrenched in human behaviors (see Gouldner, 1960). The society in which altruistic acts between unrelated individuals imply no obligation whatsoever, or in which individuals are as eager to please those who have neglected them as those who have treated them generously, is hardly conceivable. A society in which kind acts were repaid, not with kindness, but with total indifference, would be more a subject for science fiction than for human ethnography. Nor is it clear how such a society could sustain personal interactions, group activities, or cooperative endeavors of any kind. As for the signals, defenses, and punitive impulses required to prevent reciprocal altruism from becoming a prisoners' dilemma, these too are prominent in the behavior of individuals from all cultures. Hopeful recipients everywhere are anxious to appear altruistic themselves, and every society has means by which remorse may be communicated following occasional lapses. These means, however, are the subject of scrutiny and doubt. Ostracism and moralistic aggression regularly occur in human groups of every kind, when individuals are judged not to have taken opportunities to repay altruistic debts.

Being both evolutionarily stable and ubiquitous, altruistic strategies for allocation of favors are likely dependent on genetically transmitted propensities. Significantly, clinical evidence also suggests that specific brain mechanisms underlie many of the processes on which reciprocal altruism depends (Jenner, 1978). Mania, which can be both elicited and treated pharmacologically, is often accompanied by extraordinary generosity toward those whom the manic believes are his or her friends. Severe depression, by contrast, is commonly accompanied by feelings of remorse, often for lapses so picayune as to escape normal attention. Suspicion of altruistic motives forms an essential component of paranoid disorders, which also reflect neurochemical processes, and moralistic aggression is frequently prominent in patients with inferior temporal lobe seizure foci (Blumer and Benson, 1975). Affective and paranoid disorders are subjects of later chapters.

Finally, mention should be made of the important role played in human cognitive evolution by the demands of reciprocal altruism strategies. Cognitive requirements for successful exploitation of reciprocal alliances—particularly when these are compounded by kin selection strategies—are prodigious. They include long-term memory capacities, discriminative capacities requisite to detection of mimicry, capacities to weigh predicted benefits and costs, and many other social cognitive abilities. Sanctions against nonaltruistic group members also require specific cognitive capacities, which are notably lacking in nonhuman primates (Kummer, 1978). Selective benefits from exploitation of reciprocal altruism may well have contributed to the remarkable increase in human cerebral volume that occurred during the Pleistocene (Trivers, 1971). The fact that human cognitive capacities evolved to subserve social strategies is of great psychologic interest, as discussed briefly in Appendix D.

III
Mental Disorders

12
Proximate Causal Syndromes

Certain mental disorders are best characterized in proximate causal terms. Organic brain lesions disrupt proximate mental mechanisms in such a way as to cause diffuse dysfunction of genetically transmitted social strategies. Syndromes in this category include organic brain syndromes, psychosis, and autism. The relation between psychosis and underlying nonpsychotic psychopathology remains obscure.

Organic Brain Syndromes and Psychoses

Ultimate and proximate biologic causes are usefully distinguished. As demonstrated in later chapters, certain abnormal behavior patterns are quite efficiently described using ultimate causal, or social strategic, concepts. Foundations for these descriptions have been laid in previous chapters. Other syndromes, though, are better described in proximate causal, or purely mechanistic, terms. Disorders consequent to localized brain lesions are typical of those best characterized in proximate causal terms. Not that brain lesions fail to result in social disability, but, rather, that the social strategic impairments are so diffuse as to defy neat description. The same disability is far more easily described in terms of mental processes—affect, attention, memory, and planning—impaired following destruction of central nervous tissue. Descriptions of this type, moreover, have been perfected by neuropsychologists, who have also developed powerful tests for characterization of information-processing impairments following circumscribed brain lesions.

Psychosis, too, is probably best characterized in proximate causal terms. An extraordinary amount of evidence, a small portion of which will be described here, testifies to the fact that psychosis manifests a central nervous system dysfunction, or lesion, equivalent in principle to those resulting from trauma, infection, tumor, or metabolic imbalance and leading to dysfunction of many social strategies. Psychosis differs from other organic brain syndromes, of course, because it produces a characteristic pattern of proximate psychologic disturbances—manifested by hallucinations, delusions, and disordered thought. Also, again unlike other organic brain syndromes, psychosis occurs both in isolation and in association with other, predisposing, psychologic disorders. Several of the latter are themselves readily described in social strategic terms. That disorders described in social strategic terms are associated with a condition readily described only in proximate, mechanistic terms may seem to vitiate the distinction previously drawn between the two types of description. Yet, the dilemma is by no means new, since the interrelation of predisposing psychopathology and psychosis itself has long puzzled psychologic theorists (see, for example, the contrasting views of delusional genesis taken by Freud [1924] and Minkowski [1958]). Furthermore, every behavioral disturbance, whether efficiently described in social strategic terms or not, has proximate causes. And these proximate causes might progress to produce behavioral disturbances no longer confined to the boundaries of particular social strategies. As it turns out, the physiology of psychosis provides some clue as to how that progression occurs.

If psychosis can occur alone or in the course of other illnesses, then it is in some respects the psychopathologic equivalent of fever. Comparison of fever and psychosis, in fact, reveals some important parallels. Just as fever assumes different forms according to the underlying disease process triggering it—the fever of malaria, for example, being characteristically different from that of pneumonia—so psychosis assumes different forms according to the psychopathologic setting in which it occurs. Hallucinations, delusions, and abnormal thought patterns all vary in content and quality according to whether the victim is schizophrenic, manic-depressive, depressed, or paranoid. As is argued later, schizophrenia, manic-depressive disorder, psychotic depression, and paranoid psychosis can each be conceptualized as the result of adding psychosis to a preexisting personality or affective disorder. Thus, delusions of telepathy and magical influence, while not diagnostic of schizophrenia, tend to occur in schizophrenic patients more frequently than the affect-laden delusions typical of depressed or manic-depressive psychotics. Also, just as fever may be chronic or fluctuating, so psychosis may be unremitting, or may wax and wane. As is the case with fever, certain underlying disorders are particularly associated with certain temporal courses. So reliable are the characteristics and temporal course of fever associated with certain organic diseases that reliable diagnoses have been made on that basis alone. The same is true of psychosis. Particular characteristics of hallucinations, delusions, and thought patterns, in combination with temporal information, are enough to reliably distinguish each of the disorders with which psychosis is associated.

Two important predictions follow from this view of psychosis. First, psychoses of many different kinds should share common physiologic and information-processing features. These are features characteristic of psychosis itself. Second, for each major psychotic disorder, an underlying nonpsychotic psychologic disturbance should be evident, unless psychosis has occurred in isolation. In this latter case, clear antecedents capable of explaining its occurrence should exist. In the former cases, those in complete or partial remission from psychotic symptoms per se should nonetheless manifest signs and symptoms of the underlying disorder, and genetic evidence should link this disorder with the psychotic illnesses to which it forms a predisposing factor.

Concerning the first prediction, certain physiologic and information-processing abnormalities do characterize psychotic patients from more than one diagnostic category. Physiologically, patients from different psychotic subgroups all show increased serum CPK (an enzyme), neuromuscular dysfunctions, and diminished skeletal muscle and platelet MAO (another enzyme). These abnormalities either characterize psychosis per se or are associated with certain symptoms of psychosis, such as hallucinations (see Meltzer, 1979, for review and discussion of these physiologic findings). Another abnormality of the same kind involves central nervous system dopamine metabolism. Dopamine, of course, is an interneuronal messenger in vital areas of mammalian brain. Apparently excessive dopamine activity was once thought peculiar to schizophrenia, but recent reviewers have stressed instead its likely role in all psychoses. In particular, dopamine-blocking agents alleviate symptoms of psychosis nonspecifically, without regard to diagnostic category (see Meltzer, 1979). Symptoms limited to specific psychotic disorders, by contrast, frequently require other means for their alleviation. Dopamine hyperactivity in psychosis also provides a clue to the occurrence of psychotic symptoms in otherwise disparate syndromes, since dopamine-dependent systems apparently mediate mammalian responses to a variety of stressful situations and may be modulated by chronic stress levels (Antelman and Caggiula, 1977).

While psychoses of several different kinds share a common physiology, specific psychotic syndromes may possess distinct physiologic features as well. Distinct features associated with schizophrenia and its subtypes, for example, include diminished frontal lobe blood flow, diminished pupillary constrictor responses, various signs of left anterior hemispheric dysfunction, and abnormal ocular pursuit movements (Buchsbaum, 1979). Each of these characterize schizophrenic patients in particular, rather than psychotic patients as a whole, and some may be genuine traits independent of fluctuations in psychotic symptomatology (Iacono, et al., 1981).

What Wernicke (cited in Binswanger, 1958) called "overvalent ideas" are prominently in evidence in psychoses of many different kinds. Both delusions and hallucinatory experiences (cf. Jaynes, 1977) seem to express them. Also, disorganization of thought, language, or both (see Andreason, 1979, 1979a; Dawson, et al., 1980; Rabin, et al., 1979; Schwartz, 1982; Shapiro, 1979) occur in psychoses of many different clinical types (Pope and Lipinski, 1978). Therefore, clinically distinct psychoses may nonetheless manifest a common cognitive disorder. This disorder—various symptoms of which are more or less prominent in any given case—results in dysfunction of virtually every genetically transmitted social strategy, rendering a social strategic view of psychotic disability largely devoid of descriptive value.

Regarding the second prediction, for each of the major psychotic disorders a nonpsychotic counterpart has in fact been clinically described. The correspondence best known is that between schizophrenia and schizotypal personality disorder. Patients with schizotypal personality disorder manifest the chronic social withdrawal and idiosyncratic, autistic thought characteristic of schizophrenia itself but lack frank delusions or hallucinations. Schizophrenic patients in temporary remission from psychotic symptoms remain markedly schizotypal, their social adjustment and idiosyncratic thought patterns being little affected by medications (see, for example, Lipton and Burnett, 1979; Zwerling, 1979). As expected, if schizophrenia results from the superimposition of psychosis on chronic schizotypal personality disorder, there is also strong evidence for genetic association of the two conditions (Baron, et al., 1983; Kety, 1983). For example, when only one member of an identical twin pair suffers from schizophrenia, the unaffected individual is very likely to be schizotypal instead (Inouye, 1963). Even when raised by normal foster parents, children of schizophrenics are likewise characterized by a higher than expected frequency of schizoid traits (Wender, et al., 1974; Heston, 1966).

Whether those who become schizophrenic differ from those who remain schizotypal by virtue of a greater liability to psychosis per se, or whether they have more severe schizotypal personality disorders, resulting in greater probability of psychosis, remains unclear. The "two gene" theory—which treats genetic liability to schizoid personality traits and to psychosis as separate factors—dates back to the time of Kraepelin (Gottesman and Shields, 1982). The bulk of current data, however, suggests that schizotypal illness results from operation of a multifactorial-polygenic system characterized by multiple threshold effects (Gottesman and Shields, 1982). Individuals with lesser genetic predispositions may be schizotypal, while those with greater predispositions are likely to become chronically psychotic. Individuals with intermediate dispositions may fall into either the psychotic or nonpsychotic category, depending on relevant environmental events. One particular version of the multifactorial risk model is that proposed by Meehl (see Gottesman and Shields, 1982), which deserves special attention here. Meehl's hypothesis is that so-called "schizogenes" interact with aversive social events to foster social withdrawal. Social withdrawal, in turn, promotes "cognitive slippage," or autism, which leads to inappropriate social behavior, aversive experiences, and more withdrawal. Although those with fewer schizogenes and favorable environments may remain merely schizotypal, those genetically or environmentally less fortunate will finish the process with chronic schizophrenia. The relevance of Meehl's social-withdrawal model to the present discussion will become more obvious in later chapters, where schizotypy per se is described in social-strategic terms.

The nonpsychotic counterpart of manic-depressive illness is, in all likelihood, cyclothymic personality disorder. Patients with cyclothymic personality suffer periodic cyclic mood swings similar to those experienced by manic-depressives, but fail to develop psychotic symptoms at the extremes of their disorder. Family histories, akin to those for schizotypal personality and schizophrenia, also suggest a genetic association between cyclothymic personality and manic-depressive illness (Kallman, 1954; Wetzel, et al., 1980). For example, patients with manic-depressive illness have excessive numbers of cyclothymic relatives, and patients with cyclothymic personality are likely to have pedigrees remarkable for manic-depressive disease. Identical twins who both suffer nonpsychotic affective lability may have particularly excessive numbers of manic-depressive relatives (Farber, 1981), suggesting that the genetic disposition in these families is a peremptory one. As in the case with schizotypal personality and schizophrenia, whether psychosis and personality disorder are entirely separate genetic factors cannot be satisfactorily answered. Patients with manic-depressive illness may differ from those with cyclothymic personalities by virtue of a superimposed predisposition to psychosis or due to more severe cyclothymia secondarily increasing the probability of psychosis.

The obvious nonpsychotic counterpart of psychotic depression is nonpsychotic depression. Due to diagnostic practices, moreover, the same patient can be said to suffer episodes of both nonpsychotic and psychotic depression, depending on whether delusions and hallucinations are transiently in evidence or not. Schizophrenics, by contrast, are still called schizophrenics even when transiently only schizotypal, and manic-depressives remain manic-depressive even when their mood swings fall within the range of cyclothymic personality disorder. Although psychotic and nonpsychotic depressed patients differ in their response to medictions, demographic and historical features and most symptom constellations nonetheless fail to distinguish them (Frances, et al., 1981; Guze, et al., 1975). Psychotic and nonpsychotic depressions raise the same issue of potentially separate predispositions that occur in relation to schizophrenia and manic-depressive disorder.

Corresponding to paranoid psychosis is paranoid personality disorder. When in remission from their psychotic symptoms, spontaneously psychotic paranoids still manifest markedly paranoid personalities. Although individual cases frequently demonstrate the familial coincidence of paranoid psychosis and paranoid personality, the genetics of these disorders remain poorly characterized. One problem, discussed later, is that at least a subset of paranoid psychotics may have genetic predispositions to schizotypal illness (Gottesman and Shields, 1982), so that paranoid psychotics as a whole may comprise a heterogeneous group.

Finally, consistent with the notion that psychosis manifests an organic brain dysfunction triggered by psychologic trauma, evidence abounds that essentially normal individuals may develop psychosis following either physiologic or psychologic stresses (see Stephens, et al., 1982). The latter must be severe and typically include extreme social losses or isolation. So-called "acute schizophrenia" may represent psychoses of this sort, triggered in nonparanoid victims without either schizotypal or affective illnesses. As for physiologic stresses, these are predictable from the physiology apparently common to all psychoses. Chronic administration of amphetamine-like compounds—which enhance central nervous system dopamine activity—frequently produces psychotic symptoms. These symptoms ordinarily regress after discontinuation of the drug but may continue for some time. Psychologically unremarkable individuals with extreme sensitivity to psychotic side effects of this sort may have a physiologic predisposition to the psychotic process per se (Gold and Bowers, 1978). Without the usual antecedent personality or affective disorders, they might have also previously escaped environmental stresses capable of triggering spontaneous acute psychoses. Chronic alcohol abuse and various brain lesions too may lead to psychoses, even in persons without previous personality disorders. These "symptomatic" psychoses, particularly those attendant on temporal lobe lesions, frequently resemble chronic schizophrenia (Lipowski, 1975), perhaps because much of chronic schizophrenia results from unremitting psychotic disorganization of thought processes. In affective psychoses, by contrast, periods of remission are frequently longlasting.

Infantile Autism

Lastly, mention should be made of infantile autism, another syndrome for which ultimate-causal, social strategic concepts have little or nothing to contribute by way of explanation. In spite of earlier efforts to account for infantile autism in psychologic terms (see, for example, Bettelheim, 1966), it is now increasingly clear that the behavioral disturbances of infantile autism—like those of psychosis—reflect organic brain disease (see Kernberg, 1979, for review). Thus, infantile autism is statistically associated with congenital rubella (German measles) syndrome and possibly with other diffuse viral infections of the brain. Phenylketonuria, a metabolic abnormality, is sometimes associated with an autism-like syndrome, and identical twin studies also suggest a genetic predisposition. Autistic children are characterized by abnormal, immature EEG patterns, abnormal rapid eye movement sleep patterns, focal and diffuse cerebral seizure-like activity, and abnormal cortical responses to sensory stimulation. They may suffer convulsions, cognitive deficits of a type suggesting organic brain disease, or both. In recent years, interneuronal messengers have also been studied intensively and are likely abnormal in at least some autistic children.

As in psychosis and other organic brain syndromes, the cerebral dysfunction responsible for infantile autism results in failure of specific information-processing mechanisms. The mechanisms most affected in infantile autism seem to subserve communication in its most general form. Thus, autistic infants fail to babble, to respond to rhythmic language patterns, or to modulate their voices as do normal infants. Early language deficits are followed either by complete failure to acquire language or by specific impairments rendering communication tenuous. Rutter and Bartak (1971) argue that cognitive deficits responsible for failure of language development play a primary etiologic role in the autistic syndrome. Yet, autistic infants also show poor eye contact, regularly avert their gaze from others, and fail to develop social smiles. Facial expression in general is absent, and other nonverbal gestures are also infrequent.

Tinbergen and Tinbergen (1972) shed some important light on how the autistic child's communicative failure might result in the full clinical syndrome. According to these authors, for many higher primates contact with others of their species is always potentially fearprovoking. Fear produced by such contact is largely relieved through use of *phylogenetically ritualized* gestures (Appendix E), which serve to inhibit aggression. Without these gestures, unmodulated anxiety might inhibit social relations. According to Tinbergen and Tinbergen, the autistic child is unable to use communication devices to attenuate contact-fear and therefore is unable to participate in normal social activities. Those activities that contain threatening or aggressive elements, such as looking at a face, are particularly difficult for the autistic child. Progressive withdrawal from human contact, and severe social inadequacy, eventually result from this deficiency.

At least some of the diverse abnormal behaviors shown by autistic children are plausibly attributed to severe social withdrawal. Head-banging, hand-flapping, self-mutilation, self-stimulation, and ritualistic behaviors in particular may belong in this class, since nonhuman primates raised in isolation develop similar stereotypies (Salzen, 1979). Mason and Green (1962) even suggest that some stereotypies in isolate-reared, nonhuman primates are self-directed fragments of attachment behaviors normally sensible in relation to the mother, a theory that accounts not only for their form, but also for their elicitation by fear-provoking stimuli. Other abnormal behaviors, however, may be direct manifestations of the poorly characterized cerebral lesions responsible for autism in the first place. Gaze deviations, awkwardness, toe-walking, and abnormal truncal movements in particular are plausibly included in this category.

As in other organic brain syndromes, social failures in autism are so diffuse as to defy attempts to usefully classify them. Virtually every genetically transmitted social response rule outlined in previous chapters fails to develop normally in the autistic child. In fact, it was presumably that diffuseness that first led Kanner (1943) to describe autism as a "disturbance of affective contact" rather than as a failure of one social ability or another. Even Mahler and Furer (1972)—who believe that a constitutionally predisposed failure of the maternal-child relationship causes infantile autism—stress the diffuse, rather than focal, nature of the resulting "ego impairment." Their position is consistent with that outlined here, as long as the failed attachment relationship is seen as one among other disrupted relationships, and if the social implications of impaired "ego functions" are translated into concrete terms. In particular, failure of the maternal-infant relationship may account for at least some of the more dramatic secondary symptoms of autism, as already noted. In a similar vein, Ornitz (1971) attributed infantile autism to perceptual disturbances, at least some of which result in widespread social disability.

In summary, certain psychopathologic syndromes are best delineated in terms of the information-processing capacities affected by them. These include the organic brain syndromes, psychosis in general, and infantile autism. In each of these syndromes, central nervous system lesions probably result in dysfunction of specific mental capacities, which, in turn, leads to widespread failure of genetically transmitted social strategies. This latter failure, because of its diffuseness, is difficult to easily characterize. By contrast, later chapters discuss syndromes efficiently described in terms of one social strategy or another. Included in this category are those nonpsychotic disorders in which psychosis frequently supervenes, as well as others in which a psychotic overlay is less common.

13

Dysfunction of Specific Social Strategies I

Attachment

Abnormal behavior patterns may result from excessively salient proximity-maintenance strategies. These patterns include agoraphobia, pathologic mourning, depression, and borderline syndrome. Each of these can be described as a dysfunction of attachment strategies consequent to genetic and environmental factors.

Excessively Salient Proximity Maintenance

Attachment, or proximity-maintaining, social strategies are the foremost organizers of juvenile behavior, but they play lesser roles in normal adult life. This follows, of course, from the narrow definition previously given to proximity-seeking strategies and differs from the position held by Bowlby and others (Hartog, 1980; Reynolds, 1981; Weiss, 1982). Although attachment-related tactics certainly characterize adult relationships (see Weiss, 1982), the ensembles in which they function are best conceptualized in terms of other social strategies. Given that proximity-maintaining strategies are interpreted in the narrowest, childhood sense, if follows that their vicissitudes result in adult psychopathology only when they are abnormally salient. But what is abnormal salience, given that fragments of the attachment ensemble persist even in normal persons? Childhood attachment strategies wane with age, not because they disappear as deep behavioral structures, but because the conditions eliciting them become progressively more stringent. As children become less dependent upon the caretaker's constant presence, exigencies eliciting manifest proximity seeking become more and more unusual ones. By the time normal individuals become adults, situations causing them to manifest childlike proximity maintenance become very restricted indeed and generally consist of traumatic events outside the range of daily experience. Bowlby (1969) describes the recrudescence of childlike proximity-maintaining behaviors among adults following major catastrophes. Clinging, cuddling, and urgent touching of trusted potential altruists are common means used by severely traumatized adults to modulate their fear.

If normal adults manifest narrowly defined proximity-maintaining strategies only in response to trauma, then abnormal persistence of these strategies must consist in their manifestation following lesser degrees of stress. Thus, individuals with normal and abnormal attachment histories should be indistinguishable in the absence of stress, and should become noticeably different only when stress increases to moderate levels. This prediction, which has been made as well by Bowlby (1973), has been verified for rhesus monkeys raised with various degrees of maternal deprivation (Hinde and Spencer-Booth, 1971). It has also been verified with human adults, who demonstrate adverse effects of childhood loss largely when current psychosocial stresses are present (Brown, 1982). Adults with the least stringent criteria for eliciting attachment strategies may also suffer certain psychopathologic consequences. It is the thesis of this chapter that certain forms of adult psychopathology, including agoraphobia, pathologic grief, depression, and borderline personality disorders, are caused in this way. Etiologic factors responsible for the persistence of proximity-maintaining strategies will be shown to include both genetic and environmental factors, and the latter will be related to developmental history.

Agoraphobia

In the agoraphobic, perhaps, attachment strategies are most clearly evident (see Bowlby, 1973). "Agoraphobia," of course, literally means "fear of open spaces," but the term as it is currently used refers to a syndrome phenomenologically, epidemiologically, and prognostically distinct from other phobias, either simple or social (Gray, 1978; Mathews, et al., 1981). Characteristically, agoraphobic victims suffer severe anxiety whenever they leave their homes, unless they are closely accompanied by a well-known friend or relative. Simple phobias (of snakes or heights, for example) will not be discussed here except to note, as did Bowlby (1973), that feared objects or situations tend to be ones associated with grave dangers in the prehistoric environment, so that fear of them may be innately easy to learn. Social phobias (of public speaking, for example) are mentioned in Appendix E. As the result of their anxiety, agoraphobics come to depend on one or more trusted caretakers. Without a caretaker, they are housebound; with one they may be able to leave the house and may even pursue other activities. Gradually, caretakers—usually including the spouse—are forced to become full-time attendants. Withdrawal or anger on a caretaker's part is met with more symptoms, despair, and occasionally suicide attempts. To the agoraphobic, access to the caretaker is vital, and physical proximity is the only means for anxiety reduction.

The nature of the anxiety experienced by the agoraphobic and the means for its relief are both of considerable theoretical interest (see Klein, 1980). Bowlby (1973) suggests that pathologic anxiety in adults is homologous with infantile separation anxiety, an hypothesis that is possibly overly simple. Agoraphobic anxiety, which is likely related to proximity maintenance, is characterized by panic attacks, feelings of unreality, and fears of imminent catastrophe. It is quite distinct, however, from anxiety suffered in certain other disorders. Disorders resulting from sexual competitive conflicts (Chapter 15), for example, are clinically characterized by fears of bodily injury, humiliation, or punishment. Disorders resulting from dysfunction of group-related strategies (Chapter 14) are characterized by paranoid anxieties and by fear of ostracism and scapegoating. As expected, though, agoraphobic anxiety does resemble anxiety associated with depression and borderline personality disorder, both of which may also be related to attachment strategies. Feelings of unreality—especially concerning personal identity—are also frequent in certain types of mourning (Bowlby, 1980). Significantly, too, pharmacologic interventions successful against neurotic anxiety associated, for example, with sexual competitive conflicts, are generally ineffective against panic attacks of the sort experienced by agoraphobics. Instead, these may respond to medications usually used for depression (Grunhaus, et al., 1981).

Agoraphobic patients, according to Bowlby (1980), have early life histories compatible with the later salience of attachment strategies. Parental loss, disinterest, threats of abandonment, or illness are common in the childhood lives of those who later become agoraphobic. A particularly important pattern, which Bowlby also cites for cases of school refusal, involves a reversal of the normal attachment relationship. The child must stay at home in order to care for the mentally or physically ill attachment figure. Compulsive care giving occasionally coincides with the most intense dependency needs, and both may be consequent to patterns of this sort.

Pathologic Mourning

However, unfamiliar situations are not the only ones able to elicit attachment behaviors. Loss of proximity itself may be sufficient. In children, loss of proximity is predictably followed by behaviors that have proximity as their manifest goal. In adults, loss of proximity to a trusted potential altruist triggers mourning responses, which, as Bowlby (1980) points out, are compounded of attachment-related behaviors and have proximity maintenance as their raison d'etre.

In particular, initial angry denial and subsequent depression characterizing normal mourning closely resemble the Protest and subsequent Despair stages of infantile separation responses. In chronic pathologic mourning, alternating anger, yearning, and despair continue indefinitely, precluding new relationships and distorting the pattern of daily life. The predisposition to chronic mourning, Bowlby (1980) and others (see, for example, Volkan, 1970) argue, consists of an early sensitization to attachment losses. Parental loss, withdrawal, disinterest, or threats of abandonment are thought to be common for those who become chronic mourners, just as for agoraphobics. Although little statistical evidence exists concerning parental loss in human mourning, maternally deprived nonhuman primates do show an apparent sensitization effect to losses experienced later in life (Young, et al., 1973). Particular cognitions predisposing to chronic mourning may include the belief that attachment figure's are above criticism, that they must be cared for, and that one is to blame should they be lost (Bowlby, 1980). That chronic mourners are ill prepared to accept losses is suggested, too, by their prolonged absence of emotional response—or "numbing"—following news of a loved one's death (Parkes, 1970).

Like the agoraphobic and all others whose important relationships largely subserve attachment strategies, the person prone to chronic mourning forms ambivalent relationships with loved ones (Bowlby, 1980; Parkes and Weiss, 1983). Freud (1916), of course, considered psychologic introjection of ambivalently loved lost persons to be etiologically important to pathologic grief. Psychologically incorporated into the mourner's ego, the lost ambivalent love object, according to Freud, continues as the target of hostile feelings, which are now manifested as self-hatred. In a previous chapter, though, conflicts were shown to occur between dependent and caretaker individuals when the former require a higher rate of investment than the latter are willing to provide. Hostility between excessively dependent adults and their loved ones may result from discrepancies of this kind. If so, the significance of ambivalent relationships lies less in their etiologic importance than in revealing excessive dependency (see Parkes and Weiss, 1983). Dependency itself is highly predictive of chronic mourning (Parkes and Weiss, 1983). As for introjection and identification with the lost loved one (see Lindemann, 1944), this may be more defensive than anything else. Bowlby's (1980) discussion of mislocation, identification, and other efforts to retain the lost love object is highly relevant here.

One particular form of exaggerated identification with the lost person, development of symptoms from his or her terminal illness, may occur for reasons other than retentive ones. In particular, feelings of guilt toward the deceased may be prominent among survivors, and symptom formation may be secondary to the simultaneous fear and desire of talion, or "eye-for-an-eye," punishment. Intense guilt may result from hostile feelings typical of pathologically dependent relationships or may be secondary to other factors. Symptom formation, too, may serve to obtain care taking and attention previously given to the deceased. Families that ignore the bereaved's emotional needs may particularly encourage symptom mimicry or development of unrelated psychogenic illness. These issues are also thoroughly covered by Bowlby (1980).

Not only normal and chronic mourning, but other grief syndromes, too, can be accounted for within the framework provided by attachment strategies. The first of these is failure to mourn, which is usually accompanied by a rigidly independent and aloof personality style. Bowlby (1980) argues that pseudoindependence and failure to mourn follow repetitive childhood rebuffs at the hands of attachment figures or the loss of attachment figures altogether. The rebuffed, deserted, or bereaved child denies attachment needs altogether. Being frustrated, though, these needs continue stronger than ever, requiring more and more rigid defenses.

Second, there is the severe mourning frequent in bereaved parents (see Raphael, 1983). From the parental viewpoint, the function of proximity maintenance is not to receive but to provide altruistic aid when it is most required. Parents temporarily separated from their child may suffer severe anxiety, which can only be alleviated by certain knowledge of the child's well-being. Knowledge, that is, that the child requires no altruistic aid. Therefore, insofar as parental grief results from activity of parental attachment strategies, it should differ from that attendant upon loss of potential caretakers. Tormenting anxiety about the lost child, together with guilty recriminations for having allowed the loss, should be most prominent, while panic for one's own well-being, protest, and anger might be less apparent. Clinically, this appears to be true. Bereaved parents, particularly mothers whose children have died in preventable accidents, frequently suffer extremes of guilt and severe anxiety over the child's well-being. Fantasies that the child is lost in an afterworld, and reunion fantasies in particular, often lead to suicidal acts, in the desperate hope of resuming parental care. Elements of this kind are sometimes seen when the dependent party in any care-taking relationship has died and are not limited just to parents.

Depression

"Unipolar" depression, or depression without manic episodes, also resembles the chronic type of pathologic mourning, from which it can be distinguished only by knowledge of antecedent grief. Unfortunately, clinical evidence relating depression to childhood loss of the attachment figure has received little support from large-scale studies (Crook and Eliot, 1980; Tennant, et al., 1980, 1981). Certainly, the majority of depressed adults have no history of outright parental loss (Pfohl, et al., 1983). Some of the complex factors potentially responsible for the discrepancy between clinical experience and large-scale study results are illustrated by Brown and his co-workers (Brown, 1982), who have published the best-known studies with positive findings. According to Brown, early parental loss, insofar as it leads to later depression, does so only through interaction with current psychosocial stressors. Because psychosocial stress levels are dependent on socioeconomic class, a statistical relation between childhood loss and current depression may be readily demonstrated only among lower-class subjects or among other subjects exposed to unusual life exigencies. For example, among female subjects the relation between childhood loss of the mother and later depression may be mediated in part by premarital pregnancies (Brown, 1982). Possibly, some of Brown's female subjects were prone to premarital pregnancies due to displaced attachment yearnings of their own, or even to obtain more secure relationships with the fathers. Childhood losses, moreover, result from more than one cause, and their effects may differ accordingly. Brown and Harris (1978), for example, found that depressions following remediable and irremediable childhood losses tend to be agitated and retarded, respectively. Remediable losses include those from desertion or divorce; irremediable losses are those from parental death. Agitated depressions—during which psychomotor activity is increased—possibly signify protest and yearning. Retarded depressions—during which psychomotor activity is slowed—possibly signify despair and hopelessness. Suicidal preoccupations may also result from childhood losses and in many cases will not be accompanied by overt depression (Adam, 1982).

As for current losses, Brown and Harris (1978) have shown that objective loss, usually that of a close relative, preceded a majority of cases of both psychotic and neurotic depression in at least one London sample. However, many of the events precipitating depressions are not losses of loved ones. Instead, blows to self-esteem, pride, financial security, or other important values seem capable of precipitating depression in predisposed persons, so that their interpretation within the framework of attachment strategy is seemingly problematic. Arieti and Bemporad (1978), for example, note that depression follows the subjective loss of either a "dominant other" or "dominant goal." The "dominant other" described by Arieti and Bemporad closely resembles the attachment figure described by Bowlby and presents no conceptual difficulty. The "dominant goal," though, is usually on the order of making money or achieving fame and has no obvious connection to attachment needs at all. The answer to this puzzle, which explains how attachment-related behaviors may be triggered by blows of widely varying kinds, is twofold. First, as Arieti and Bemporad note, the dominant goal is frequently an agenda for pleasing real or fantasized dominant others or for calling oneself to their attention. Its frustration, therefore, is tantamount to permanent separation from the attachment figure. Miller (1981) also describes cases of this type in which grandiose schemes intended to please an earlier attachment figure alternate with depressive episodes. Second, dominant goals are frequently competitive projects, whose success or failure is used as a measure of resource holding power. In Chapter 7, estimated resource holding power and clinically manifested self-esteem were shown to coincide, so that the former may be at least one component of the latter. In fact, diminished self-esteem may be the most regular feature of depression (Prosen, et al., 1983). By reducing estimated resource holding power, and therefore self-esteem, failure of a dominant goal may increase the sense of vulnerability. In children, vulnerability regularly triggers increased attachment behaviors (Chapter 6), and the same may be true for adults with strong underlying dependency needs. Thus, failure of a dominant goal subserving other than simply attachment ends may have as its primary consequence increased attachment yearning, from which depressive symptoms will follow directly.

In recent years, attention has also been directed toward potentially pathogenic cognitions typical of depressed patients. The importance of cognitive, as opposed to purely environmental, factors in depressive illness is illustrated by certain epidemiologic evidence. Henderson (1982a), for example, found that perceived inadequacy of social supports, rather than objective measures of them, correlate best with onset of "care-eliciting" neuroses (see also Flaherty, et al., 1983). The construed social world, rather than the social world per se, is the better predictor of at least some psychologic morbidity. Among the specific cognitions frequently held responsible for depressive tendencies are "learned helplessness" (Seligman, 1975), which is actually based on an animal model, and Beck's (1976) "depressive triad." The latter consists of negative expectations about the future, oneself, and one's capacity to make a difference. At least in nonhuman animals, cognitions resembling learned helplessness and the depressive triad are apparently manifested following frustration of early attachment needs. Thus, rhesus monkeys separated from their mothers for short periods grow up to be deficient in tasks requiring initiative. Previously separated animals were slower to try new tasks, made desultory attempts, and gave up quickly if not immediately successful (Spencer-Booth and Hinde, 1971).

One aspect of the maternal-infant relationship potentially significant for the development of cognitions resembling learned helplessness and the depressive triad is parental provision of "response-contingent" stimulation. Stimulation contingent upon the infant's own behavior is essential to normal development (Lewis and Goldberg, 1969; Watson, 1971) and may play a special role in maturation of problem-solving behaviors dependent on a sense of effectiveness. Maternally deprived rhesus monkeys raised with inanimate surrogates fail to explore novel stimuli and fail to actively seek solutions to new problems. If raised with mechanical surrogates, though, these behaviors are preserved, apparently due to the response-contingent stimulation a moving surrogate provides (Mason, 1979). Human mothers, in particular, attempt to maximize response-contingent stimulation for their infants. Adult speech and gestural changes, and imitation of infantile facial expressions and vocalizations, are well suited to reinforce the human infant's own behavior (Papousek and Papousek, 1979). Imitative exaggeration of infantile expressions and vocalizations by normal adults may be largely unconscious (Trevarthen, 1979).

The stereotypic and unconscious manner in which parents provide feedback to their infants suggests that parental behavior may be governed by innate tactics serving to optimize response-contingent reinforcement. Certainly, parental inclusive fitness might be served by biasing the infant's cognitive models in favor of later initiative, as well as by specific developmental gains, such as gestural development, that are promoted by high levels of contingent feedback. In psychoanalytic terms, what is at issue here is the development of infantile omnipotence, which Freud thought resulted from parental responses to infantile vocalizations (see Brenner, 1973). Although omnipotent feelings are part and parcel of certain psychologic disorders, potent if not omnipotent feelings dating from infancy may be requisite to normal functioning as well.

No human infant is likely to suffer the complete absence of response-contingent stimulation achieved with nonhuman primates in the laboratory. Minimal care required for the human infant's survival necessitates a modicum of interaction with adult human beings. Yet, insofar as human infants can be deprived of response-contingent stimulation, those reared by inadequate, unreliable, emotionally disinterested, or emotionally unavailable mothers will be those who suffer. Mothers who feel emotionally disinterested in their offspring, for example, can hardly be expected to provide as much response-contingent stimulation as mothers who are normally involved. The exquisite sensitivity of infants to even transient loss of response-contingent stimulation from the mother is demonstrated by Trevarthen (1979), who has shown that human infants become agitated if their mothers momentarily confront them with flat, unmirroring facial expressions. Similar results have been obtained by Brazelton and his coworkers (1975). When tested with the "strange situation" technique (described at the end of this chapter), children of emotionally unresponsive mothers are frequently classified as "avoidant" (Main and Weston, 1982), suggesting that they expect little good to come from direct efforts to meet their needs. Interactions with rejecting mothers might bias cognitive models against initiatory behaviors and at the same time lead to abnormally persistent attachment strategies. As part of their later depressive illness, children raised in this way will also manifest learned helplessness or the so-called depressive triad.

In this fashion, the relative emotional unresponsiveness of chronically depressed parents may account for the development of psychopathology in their children (see Pound, 1982; Beardslee, et al., 1983; Parker, 1983). Not surprisingly, the developmental impact of maternal depression may be even more severe than that of maternal psychosis (Sameroff, et al., 1982). Diminution of response-contingent stimulation and enhanced early attachment anxiety resulting from maternal unresponsiveness may plausibly mediate extragenetic familial transmission of at least some depressive disorders.

Like typical cognitions, somatic features accompanying depression may also be explicable in terms of attachment exigencies (see Henderson, 1982a; Coryell and Norten, 1981). Hypochrondriacal complaints in particular may be seen as cues to elicit care-taking behavior. As noted in a previous chapter, the cost-benefit curve determining the level of parental investment shifts in favor of higher rates during periods of childhood illness. Feigned illness and its detection are mechanisms by which child and caretaker seek to maintain rates of parental investment at their own preferred level. Clinically, depressive hypochondriasis is frequently connected with dependency fantasies of a frankly infantile form and is largely social in its unconscious meaning.

Somatic symptoms of an entirely different kind also accompany depressive disorders. These include sleeplessness, weight loss, anorexia, decreased sexual appetite, gastrointestinal and autonomic disturbances, and extreme hypoactivity, among other symptoms. Significantly, nonhuman primates deprived of maternal care also become hypoactive (Kaufman and Rosenblum, 1967), forging yet another link between depression and attachment exigencies. Gray (1978) argues that physiologic disturbances accompanying severe depression are analogous to those that occur in hibernating mammals. Hypoactivity and diminution of appetitive behaviors may serve a function analogous to that of hibernation. Both by reducing metabolic demands and by inhibiting demanding or angry behaviors that might release aggressive responses from noncaretaking adults, hypoactivity and other vegetative changes could promote a marginal form of survival for immature primates transiently deprived of maternal care. At least in depressed adults, manifest hostility is seldom expressed when vegetative symptoms are present (Pilowsky and Spence, 1975). Sleeplessness, too, might protect juveniles normally shielded by maternal watchfulness. This, of course, is highly speculative and more a matter for physiologic than psychologic research.

Insofar as unipolar depression reflects the individual's attachment history, genetic factors predisposing toward it may be such as to effect attachment strategies. These may alter maternal-infant relationships either indirectly (Appendix E) or directly. Genetically based alterations in appraisal processes might belong in this latter category. Pathologic anxiety of the sort associated with attachment-related disorders is, in fact, likely to be heritable (Woodruff, et al., 1974; Surman, et al., 1983). It can also accompany certain physiologic abnormalities, such as enhanced exercise-induced lactate accumulation (Pitts and McClure, 1967; Grosz and Farmer, 1972) and mitral valve prolapse (Crowe, et al., 1979), which might themselves have a genetic component. Individuals genetically predisposed to overwhelming anxiety of this sort could, like brain-injured patients suffering from so-called catastrophic reactions (Slater and Roth, 1969), respond to even small stressors with unmodulated anxiety attacks. Since distress of this kind is a potent trigger for proximity maintenance, patients with genetic predispositions to anxiety would probably experience more unsatisfactory attachment relationships than those lacking them. Familial associations between anxiety disorder and depression (Leckman, et al., 1983), the frequency of depression in the course of chronic anxiety neurosis (Dealy, et al., 1981), and personality resemblances between anxiety neurotics and recovered unipolar depressives (Murray and Blackburn, 1974) suggest the importance of anxiety as a proximate mechanism through which a depressive tendency might be inherited.

Genetic factors, too, might directly imbalance the social valuation experienced as depression. Affected individuals might have had relatively normal childhood attachment experiences but nonetheless, during their periodic depressions, act as if recrudescent attachment strategies were organizing their mental life. In theory, primary instabilities of the appraisal process responsible for depressive affect should be distinguishable from secondary dysfunction related to unresolved attachment needs on the basis of mental and behavioral life between depressions. Those whose thought and behavior continue to be dominated by attachment strategies even during remissions (see, for example, Akiskal, et al., 1983; Hirschfeld, et al., 1983; Matussek and Feil, 1983) are perhaps more likely to have had etiologically significant early childhood experiences. Those whose thoughts and behavior during remission are normal or follow a different pattern of deviance (Akiskal, et al., 1983; Matussek and Feil, 1983) are perhaps more likely to have primary instabilities of neuroendocrine appraisal processes. Whether distinctions of this kind can actually be made is a matter for future research.

A neuroendocrine instability resulting in some cases of unipolar depression might also be related to the biologic disturbance presumably responsible for cyclothymic personality disorder. If so, bipolar affective illness—affective illness characterized by both "ups" and "downs"—would be genetically related to at least one type of unipolar depression, consistent with Gershon and co-workers' (1975) "liability" model (see also Winokur, 1980; Baron, et al., 1981). Yet, other patients with unipolar depression may have genetic predispositions unrelated to bipolar illness, consistent with the model proposed by Cadoret and Winokur (see Sperber and Jarvik, 1976).

That genes predisposing to bipolar and some cases of unipolar affective illness act by producing instabilities of neuroendocrine appraisal processes, while most cases of unipolar depression result from a variety of attachment-related developmental events, would also explain some current familial data. Some cases of bipolar illness, for instance, appear to be transmitted via a single dominant gene, while unipolar illness, consistent with multiple routes of causation, appears to be transmitted polygenically (see Stone, 1980). Twin studies show higher intertwin concordance rates for bipolar illness, which hypothetically depends on unstable appraisal processes, than for unipolar illness, most cases of which hypothetically result from interpersonal, albeit genetically influenced, mediating events (Allen, 1976; Bertelsen, et al., 1977). From her sample of identical twins raised apart, Farber (1981) concluded that affective lability per se, even in the absence of clear bipolar illness, is nearly always a concordant trait and frequently occurs when other family members suffer from manic-depressive illness. Affective lability and depressive traits, moreover, were clearly segregated in Farber's twin sets. The potential force of genetically unstable appraisal processes is also illustrated by reexamining the famous Rosanoff twins, who, by contemporary standards, would likely be diagnosed as manic-depressives (Farber, 1981). Although raised and living apart, and in spite of significant differences in premorbid personality, these twin males suffered the onset of an affective psychosis within three months of each other. Although treated at separate locations, they pursued dramatically synchronized waxing and waning courses until one died at the age of thirty-three.

Little more can be said in the present context concerning affective genetics. Future behavioral-genetic studies, particularly those employing gene linkage techniques (Weitkamp, et al., 1981), promise to reveal the true relationship of unipolar and bipolar disease. Readers interested in reviews of this complex field are referred to Stone (1980) and Henderson (1982).

Borderline Personality

Without a doubt, the most severe disturbance likely resulting from persistent attachment strategies is so-called borderline illness. The term "borderline" was first applied to a group of nonschizophrenic patients who, unlike neurotics, could not be successfully psychoanalyzed. Not surprisingly, distinction of borderline patients from schizophrenics on the one hand and from neurotics on the other has attracted considerable interest. Kernberg (1967), for instance, treated the borderline state as a form of ego organization intermediate between those typical of neurotic and psychotic patients. Poor ego integration in the borderline patient is said to be manifested by simultaneous maintenance of sharply contradictory attitudes, poor anxiety tolerance, poor impulse control, and an inadequate capacity for sublimation. On the other hand, borderline reality testing is largely intact and sets the borderline apart from those who are frankly schizophrenic. Grinker, Werble, and Drye (1968), however, treated borderline illness as a syndrome distinct from other conditions, and they distinguished four subtypes. All subtypes are characterized by abnormal anger, defects in interpersonal relationships, lack of stable self-identity, and depression, but one subtype (III) also has features resembling schizotypal personality disorder. Gunderson and Kolb (1978) argued that borderline patients differ from schizophrenics in that their affect is not flat, they are dependent rather than isolative, and they more commonly abuse substances. They are said to differ from neurotics in that they experience brief psychoses, are sexually deviant, are antisocial, and have poor achievement records.

To study how the borderline diagnosis is actually employed, Spitzer, Endicott, and Gibbon (1979) constructed a questionnaire for the characterization of patients said to be borderline. Items included in the questionnaire fell into two sets: One, culled from Wender, Rosenthal, and Kety's (1968) study of schizophrenic inheritance, was intended to identify schizotypal traits. The other, culled from work by Gunderson and Kernberg, was intended to identify abnormal affective traits. Statistical analysis of patient descriptions by thousands of psychiatrists treating ostensibly borderline patients revealed distinctly separate assortments of the two sets of items. Borderline patients, in effect, fell into two separate groups, one with largely schizotypal and the other with largely affective abnormalities. Traits characterizing the latter group are now embodied in the DSM-III diagnosis, Borderline Personality Disorder (American Psychiatric Association, 1980).

But Spitzer, Endicott, and Gibbon's (1979) clear distinction of affectively unstable and schizotypal patients goes only part way toward clearing up the diagnostic confusion. Close examination of the DSM-III criteria for borderline personality disorder reveals that considerable diagnostic overlap exists with cyclothymic disorder. Both conditions, for example, are characterized by fluctuating moods, alternation of inflated self-esteem with feelings of inadequacy, impulsivity, social and occupational impairment, and irritability. Cyclothymic, or "cycloid," personality (Kretschmer, cited in Stone, 1980) has long been considered a less severe variant of florid manic-depressive illness and is frequent in relatives of manic-depressive patients (Kallman, 1954; Wetzel, et al., 1980). The relation between cyclothymic personality and manic-depressive illness was discussed briefly in a previous chapter. Other diagnoses potentially related to cyclothymic disorder include so-called "hysteroid dysphoria" (Klein, 1975), which Stone

(1980) claims can be characterized by bipolar mood swings, and "emotionally unstable character disorder" (Klein, 1967), which is characterized by prominent mood swings and hysterical character traits. If borderlines are to be usefully distinguished from those with cyclothymia and related disorders, special care must be taken to exclude those individuals whose illnesses are largely comprised of mood swings. Only those patients whose mood swings are accompanied by self-mutilation, impulsivity, sexual deviation, anger, pathologic anxiety, and primitive defenses typical of borderline illness should be considered in this category, and individuals with pedigrees suggesting manic-depressive disease should be given other diagnoses.

When the schizotypal personalities and those likely to be cyclothymic are removed, the remaining borderlines have some remarkable traits. Their thoughts and feelings are distorted by processes usually described under the rubrics "splitting" and "lack of object constancy." They experience pathologic anxiety, depression, anger, and fearfulness. They mutilate themselves, are sexually perverse, and have prominent gender confusion. Frank psychotics aside, they are the most difficult patients clinicians encounter and benefit least from most forms of therapy. How, then, can the signs and the symptoms of this extraordinary disorder be explicated in terms of attachment strategies?

To begin with "splitting," terminologic confusion and theoretical biases alike have largely obfuscated its operational meaning. While the problem cannot be fully addressed here, at least some of the time splitting refers to highly intensified affects (Akhtar and Byrne, 1983), particularly rapid alternations between dependent idealization and furious devaluation. The degree to which idealization and contempt are carried, the intensity of feelings with which they are associated, the rapidity with which alternation occurs, and the patient's apparent inability to maintain a middle ground differentiate the phenomena in question from cyclical transferences of the kind seen with narcissistic patients (Chapter 15). Typically, the borderline patient first idealizes some individual, often the therapist, to whom he or she relates more or less as beneficiary. The idealized person is thought to be incapable of evil and maximally possessed of every positive attribute. Others are simultaneously devalued, feared, and hated, to exactly the same degree as the idealized person is admired and loved. At the first disappointment, though, perceived roles suddenly reverse themselves. The formerly perfect person will now be the object of furious anger. Contempt will replace admiration, fear will replace security, and loathing will replace love. Once thought incapable of evil, the object of this switch is now thought incapable of good. Others, by contrast, may be suddenly rehabilitated and placed on the same pedestal. New disappointments, however, will inevitably result in new promotions and devaluations, so that no judgment is ever final.

Significantly, only those both willing and able to meet borderlines' emotional and physical needs are usually idealized by them. Failure to meet those needs is generally what triggers devaluation. This failure may be literal, as when the therapist refuses to get the patient a drink of water, insists on seeing the patient at a regular hour, or requests that the bill be paid. It may also be figurative, as when the therapist fails to understand what the patient is trying to communicate. It is the fragility of positive feelings, and their tendency to be swept away in the fury following minor disappointments, that results in the disruption of apparent therapeutic alliances with borderline patients (see Adler, 1979).

In fact, the rapid sequence of dependent idealization and furious anger by which splitting is sometimes recognized can be conceptualized as a cyclical form of proximity seeking. Those who seem reliably altruistic and attentive to the borderline patient are accorded only the most positive feelings. The patient wishes to be near them, feels devoted to them, and experiences security in their presence. They have become "good mothers" to the patient, although in an ethologic, not psychoanalytic, sense, and the patient becomes like a happily ensconced child. However, at the first sign of inattention or neglect the patient experiences intense anger. This anger, in light of which all positive memories are transformed into their opposites, resembles the anger of children threatened with abandonment. Bowlby (1973) comments on the "furious," "violent," and "dysfunctional" anger of children threatened with parental desertion, but intense anger also occurs in the relationship between emotionally cold mothers and their avoidant babies (see Main and Weston, 1982). At times of disappointment, the formerly "good mothers" become "bad mothers" to the borderline patient and are treated accordingly.

What splitting often signifies, then, are certain rapid fluctuations of interpersonal states. They occur when patients desperately seek dependent relationships but interpret even minor disappointments as total abandonment. Not just borderlines, but depressed, agoraphobic, and pathologically mourning patients too usually seek dependent relationships and perceive withdrawal as abandonment. This is consistent with their common strategic dysfunction. Lindemann (1960) demonstrated a relationship between childhood separations and later behavior patterns that were alternately clinging and rejecting. Nonborderlines, however, have higher thresholds for both proximity seeking and feelings of abandonment, and their behavior is in either case better modulated. In referring to this phenomenon, either "accelerated attachment cycling" or "intensified attachment cycling" would be preferable to "splitting," which is now tainted by theoretical connotations.

If splitting is confusing, "lack of object constancy" is even more so. Psychoanalytic use of "object constancy" was initiated by Hartmann (1952), who used it to designate the stage—postulated by psychoanalytic theory—when the infant first valued the mother continuously and for her own sake. Prior to the stage of object constancy—according to this theory—the infant valued the mother only instrumentally, as the source of somatic satisfactions. Modern objections to this theory were discussed in a previous chapter. Piagetians, of course, already used "object constancy" in reference to the apparent stability of infantile object representations as manifested by continued pursuit of temporarily hidden objects. Prior to development of object constancy, infants fail to seek hidden objects, as if "out of sight" really means "out of mind" for them. Although object constancy was first thought to develop at around nine months, more recent research (Bower, 1974) has progressively lowered this age, which is also relevant to the present topic. Shortly after his initial paper, Hartmann (1953) linked the Piagetian concept to his own, and the theoretical confusion has consequently blossomed. In the absence of object constancy, internal representations of other persons are said by psychoanalysts to be unstable, irregularly cathected, or capable of merger, fusion, fission, or even outright destruction (see Blanck and Blanck, 1974). With object constancy, representations of others survive their absence, remain cathected, and are said to be capable of several beneficent acts, especially the provision of reassurance when actual persons are separated from each other.

As in the case of splitting, terminologic confusion regarding object constancy may be partially resolved by its operational use. In practice, lack of object constancy is diagnosed when borderline patients manifest a highly characteristic separation response. When an idealized person, usually the therapist, is temporarily absent, the borderline patient will predictably deteriorate. Anxiety, depression, self-mutilation, and suicide attempts will occur and frequently necessitate hospitalization until the therapist returns. So regular are these decompensations for some patients that hospitalization is done preemptively, before the separation even occurs. Subjectively, patients with this sort of response report feeling abandoned and doubt profoundly that the relationship can ever be resumed. Even if they believe in the therapist's eventual return, they doubt that he or she will want to resume treating them, will still care about them, or will even remember their histories.

The relation between borderline separation intolerance and object constancy in its original psychoanalytic, Piagetian, or hybridized sense is far from obvious. Concerning the first, previously discussed research has discredited the developmental theory on which it rests. A few remarks are in order concerning Piagetian object constancy. Although borderline separation intolerance is said by psychoanalytic theorists to result from instability of object representations in the absence of actual contact, little evidence exists linking separation intolerance to phenomena of the sort discussed by Piaget. According to Piaget (1954), infants lacking object constancy fail to appreciate the existence of objects temporarily hidden from view. Yet, borderline patients do not doubt the absent therapist's existence, only that the relationship can eventually be resumed. Those few patients claiming to doubt the very existence of temporarily absent persons—at least in this author's experience—have invariably been coached in such fears by previous psychoanalytic interpretations. If, in fact, these feelings were spontaneous, then they should be associated with other problems with Piagetian object constancy. But, these same patients are able to find keys, wallets, automobiles, and other personal effects temporarily out of sight and express no doubt as to their continued existence. Nor do persons other than the therapist—or other attachment figures—disappear from the patient's mind during brief absences. According to recent research (Bower, 1974), moreover, individuals lacking appreciation of object constancy would operate on a cognitive level closely approaching the neonatal, an astonishing regression even for these very disturbed patients. The relation of object constancy in its hybridized, modern sense to borderline separation intolerance is equally opaque. This hybrid concept, the result of a peculiar marriage of Freudian and Piagetian ideas, is itself so unclear, and its behavioral correlates so ill-defined, that either everything or nothing can be explicated with it, depending upon one's prejudice and scientific bent.

But how might borderline separation intolerance actually be accounted for if the various uses of object constancy are of no help? As in the case of other behaviors typical of borderline patients, proximity seeking strategies of the kind discussed by Bowlby provide the Rosetta stone. In particular, it is highly likely that as children mature symbolic and cognitive means are found to alleviate the anxiety previously associated with short separations. Proximity maintenance as a whole may come to be symbolically mediated as children mature (Cohen, 1974), but self-reassurances are also likely to be important. Thus, although one-year-olds separated from mother in unfamiliar circumstances show overt anxiety, as evidenced by crying, protests, and manifest fear, two- and particularly three-year-olds left in equally unfamiliar circumstances attempt to reassure themselves against the anxiety they would otherwise feel. Such reassurances typically take the form of self-reminders, particularly of where mother is, and when she will return, but also of her devotion to them. Anxious three-year-olds, for instance, might ritualistically recite "Mommy loves me" or "I'm a good boy/girl" in order to calm themselves, since both propositions imply the mother's reliable return. If very specific plans for the separation have been shared with the child, these too may alleviate fear (Ainsworth, 1982). Other children may clutch reminders of mother, such as her photograph, or other mementos of her affection for them. These methods of self-reassurance, which are made possible by cognitive developments following the first year of life, may break down for two- or three-year-old children under unfavorable circumstances, or following unexpected disappointments, and crying, protests, and overt fear typical of the younger child will then emerge. But when anxiety is not excessive, and when the situation is otherwise favorable to the child, self-reassurance will largely prevent the more severe forms of separation response.

Comparison of one-year-old to three-year-old children, and of borderline to normal adults, reveals parallel differences in the forms taken by their separation responses. The borderline's diminished capacity to allay his or her anxiety during brief separations from important attachment figures is much like the one-year-old child's incapacity for self-reassurance.

In neither case can anxiety—once it becomes severe—be reduced by recourse to symbolic, linguistic, or cognitive processes. But, since borderline patients are not cognitively impaired, their resemblance to one-year-old childen in this respect is unlikely to result primarily from cognitive maldevelopment. Certainly, in every other respect than separation responses they show themselves more advanced than one-year-olds. A more probable hypothesis is that the separation anxiety experienced by borderline individuals is too severe to be easily relieved by cognitive processes of the sort normally effective. If so, the borderline patient temporarily separated from an attachment figure is much like the unusually stressed two- or three-year-old, whose self-reassurances break down in the face of illness, fear, or other disappointments coincident with separation. Just as "splitting" would be better called "accelerated" or "intensified attachment cycling," so borderline phenomena attributed to "lack of object constancy" would be better attributed to "undampened separation anxiety," which lacks the muting effect that symbolic and cognitive processes have on normally experienced separation fear.

Abnormal affects prominent in borderline patients also point toward disordered attachment strategies. The relation of depression to proximity maintenance has been discussed. Borderline anxiety closely resembles that experienced by agoraphobics. Panic attacks occur, accompanied by fears of catastrophe and feelings of unreality. Fear of humiliation or personal injury is very much in the background, which is to be expected given the secondary role played by same-sex competitive strategies in borderline pathology. Abnormal anger typical of borderline patients requires more comment. Mention has already been made of the intense anger elicited by perceived desertion and of the anger seen in children with abnormal attachment relationships. Although specific exacerbations of borderline anger do often occur following perceived abandonments, other connections between agonistic behaviors and attachment experiences may also contribute to their occurrence. Reynolds (1981), for instance, concluded from his review of the literature that hyperaggressive and hyperfearful social responses typified isolation-reared nonhuman primates. These animals, Reynolds argued, "are abnormal in modulating their level of fear and aggression to social stimuli . . . and are incapable of maintaining fine gradations in their agonistic interactions" (Reynolds, 1981, p. 107). Proximate causal mechanisms responsible for disinhibition of anger and fear following attachment deprivation remain unknown, but failure of deprived animals to accurately interpret social gestures may play a significant role (Miller, 1971). Excessive fearfulness and aberrant responses to social and gestural stimuli are among the features of what Mason (see Pugh, 1977) calls the "primate deprivation syndrome," which occurs in rhesus monkeys raised without adequate maternal care.

Borderline self-mutilation, too, points toward a connection with early attachment strategies. Dramatic as it sometimes is, self-mutilation resembling the borderline's can occur in isolation-reared primates, for whom it may represent a self-directed manifestation of their generalized hyperaggressiveness (Salzen, 1979). Brandt and co-workers (1971) demonstrated that isolation-reared monkeys behave in a self-threatening manner, biting and hitting themselves when brought into visual contact with unfamiliar animals. Their limbs in particular are a favorite target of self-mutilating primates (Mason, Davenport, and Menzel, 1968), just as they are for human borderlines. Pugh (1977) notes that many manifestations of the primate deprivation syndrome may result from otherwise functional behaviors occurring outside the environment of adaptation. Self-mutilation in particular may be an aberrant offshoot of hostile tactics normally subserving attachment demands that become redirected internally in the absence of a maternal "target."

Sexual deviations can also be laid at the foot of early attachment difficulties. Failure of gender appropriate behavior patterns is part of the primate deprivation syndrome, which is followed by adult sexual dysfunction. The importance of premarital pregnancy in women with early attachment losses has already been mentioned, although it is not clear that these pregnancies result from dysfunctional sexual patterns.

In summary, the signs and symptoms of borderline personality disorder, including accelerated attachment cycling, separation intolerance, anxiety, depression, anger, self-mutilation, and sexual deviations, may all be attributable to developmentally anomalous proximity maintenance strategies. It differs from unipolar depression by what are most likely quantitative factors, perhaps related to the age at which attachment experiences became atypical or to the extent of their deviation from the adaptive norm. Consistent with this model, borderline personality and persistent mood disorder frequently overlap, and those borderlines with a prominent affective component to their illness may have a better prognosis than those in whom other symptoms are most salient (Pope, et al., 1983). As expected from the close relation between the two syndromes, Stone (1980) found that hospitalized borderline patients without schizotypal features had pedigrees remarkable for affective illness. This has been corroborated by Soloff and Millward (1983). Loranger and co-workers (1982) found that borderline pedigrees were distinct from those of bipolar or schizophrenic patients, and were remarkable for the frequent occurrence of borderline and unipolar illness. The environmental factors associated with borderline personality disorder include very early maternal separation (Bradley, 1979), abnormal parenting behavior (Johansen, 1983), and a characteristic pattern of child neglect (Gunderson, et al., 1980).

Clinical efforts to help borderline patients have centered largely on their common preoccupations. As clearly as the signs and symptoms of their illness, these point to dysfunction of early attachment experiences, particularly of the so-called separation-individuation phase (Mahler, 1971). As described in a previous chapter, the separation-individuation phase corresponds to that of the weaning conflict, when maternal parental investments suddenly decline in spite of infantile resistance. Evidence from the primate deprivation syndrome, however, suggests that more than insight is required for borderlines. What the deprived nonhuman primate seems to require are "corrective emotional experiences" (Alexander and French, 1946), to use the term in a different setting from that in which it is usually applied. Thus, prolonged exposure to normally reared animals may be helpful, particularly if these are nonthreatening juveniles (Suomi and Harlow, 1972; Rogers, 1973), and benefits may also occur from contact with nonprimate pets (Mason and Kenney, 1974). Possibly, the art of treating borderlines consists more in avoiding hyperfearful, hyperaggressive social responses than in promoting insight alone.

Finally, note should be made of the salience of attachment strategies in those patients who are neither agoraphobic, mourning, depressed, or borderline, but who may have predispositions to one or more of these disorders. Dependent personalities and child abusers (see DeLozier, 1982) likely belong in this category. Frequently, too, patients complaining only of chronic dissatisfaction present either behavioral or ideational evidence of unusually salient attachment concerns. Bowlby (1980) cites various behavioral signs of strong adult attachment needs, including sleeping with children, care-taking efforts directed toward the therapist, and strong reactions to loss of pets, among others. Ideationally, attachment needs manifest themselves in fantasies, affective responses to tragedy or fiction, and in responses to temporary absences. Lubin (1980), in his study of Van Gogh's painting, provides numerous excellent examples of how unsatisfied attachment needs may subtly betray themselves in creative efforts as well. Kuhn's (1958) fascinating case, "Rudolph," shows how murderous wishes toward women may also result from childhood attachment losses.

The interrelation of chronic pain and depression (Kramlinger, et al., 1983), and the effects of opiates on separation responses (Panksepp, et al., 1978; Fabre-Nys, et al., 1982), suggest that attachment strategies may play a role in at least some cases of narcotics addiction.

The full role of childhood attachment history in adult psychopathology is likely to be clarified, eventually, by long-term studies using psychologic measuring instruments designed on the basis of Bowlby's work. The "strange situation" technique, for example, is a method for rating attachment behaviors of infants and young children (Ainsworth, 1982). Categorizations from the strange situation technique are stable over time, are concurrently and prospectively valid, and predict important behavioral characteristics up to at least five years posttesting. It has been widely employed in child-development research and will doubtless shed considerable light on psychopathology in coming decades. Instruments are also available now to measure attachment needs in adolescents and adults (see DeLozier, 1982), and these too will be used in coming studies of psychopathology.

14

Dysfunction of Specific Social Strategies II

Group-Related Behaviors

Schizotypal and paranoid personality disorders can be efficiently described in terms of group-related social strategies. Genetic and environmental factors leading to schizotypy can be understood in this framework, as can potentially therapeutic environmental changes. The interrelation of paranoid and schizotypal symptoms is also partially explicable from this point of view.

Schizotypal Signs and Symptoms

In previous chapters, social strategies were described that result in formation of cognitively cohesive "ingroups." Because these strategies are both ubiquitous and evolutionarily stable, it is probable that they depend on genetically transmitted propensities for their development and maintenance. Perceptions of authority and the social distribution of knowledge were treated as proximate mechanisms subserving cognitive conformity, while ethnicity and xenophobia define group boundaries within which consensus is expected to operate. Linguistic communication makes human consensus practicable and widens its scope beyond that achieved by other social animals. Having outlined social strategies responsible for group formation and consensus, it is now appropriate to inquire into the psychopathologic results of their developmental failure. It is the thesis of this chapter that failure of orientation to the ingroup and to its consensual reality results in schizotypy, with an attendant risk of schizophrenia. In addition, abnormalities in the perception of ingroup members, who are felt to be outgroup participants, result in paranoid personality disorders or paranoid psychoses in psychotically predisposed individuals.

Addressing the first theory, the most salient features of schizotypal disorder are social withdrawal and autism, of which the former may be primary (Gunderson, et al., 1983). Schizotypal withdrawal is global, often progressive, and frequently associated with feelings of being different from all other persons. The schizotype dreads attention, since others might notice what he perceives as his own oddity. For the same reason, self-revelation is avoided. He fears others, whom he may believe are hostile. Yet, towards them, he himself may harbor violent thoughts (Spotnitz, 1976). Inability to relax except when alone leads to social avoidance. But, when alone, the schizotype may be lonely, depending on the degree to which human company has been forsaken.

In terms of genetically transmitted social strategies, schizotypal attitudes toward social relationships can parsimoniously be ascribed to failure of ingroup, outgroup orientation. The schizotypal personality, in other words, fails to perceive himself as a member of the ingroups that social situations would ordinarily place him in and to which he would ordinarily feel some sense of belonging. He fears detection and consequent hostility and gains no relief from the camaraderie that ordinarily buffers agonistic feelings within social groups. One is appropriately reminded of Tinbergen and Tinbergen's (1972) hypothesis about infantile autism, described in a previous chapter. Self-revelation and complex social environments are both anathemas to the schizotype, who would prefer to live as an unseen ghost.

Nor is the ghost metaphor entirely arbitrary when applied to the schizotype. Social isolation is frequently the primary personal meaning of death, so to be socially isolated is to be effectively dead regardless of vital functions. So-called "hex deaths," in particular, illustrate this principle (Cannon, 1942). Lifton (1979) argues that to be unrelated to others is to pursue "psychic death," but that pursuit of relationships may be equally terrifying to schizotypal patients.

Just as global withdrawal signifies the patient's failure to feel part of an ingroup, so schizotypal autism manifests failure to adopt that group's consensual world view. If, as Berger and Luckman (1966) argue, consensual reality is defended from idiosyncratic thought patterns only through continuous and significant exchanges with other group members, then schizotypal autism may even reflect schizotypal withdrawal. The close relation of "logical" and "demonstrable" thought was noted in a previous chapter. Cohen and Camhi (1967) argue that even frankly schizophrenic individuals produce bizarre associations less due to a failure in the associative process, than due to a failure to self-edit associations in line with those consensually appropriate. Individuals with or without schizotypal traits alike are prone to certain conceptual errors, but only the schizotype is likely to adhere to these in the face of consensual disapproval.

Prominent among schizotypal conceptual errors are confusions of interpersonal boundaries and certain beliefs in magical influence. The former are most salient in schizophrenic delusions and comprise several of the "first rank" symptoms said by Schneider (1959) to be diagnostic of schizophrenia. Although Piaget believed that interpersonal boundary confusion typified the young child, boundary confusion in chronic schizophrenic patients may less reflect regression than the prolonged experience of auditory hallucinations. These, after all, are voices, and as such may be mistaken for direct links with other persons. In nonpsychotic patients, preoccupations with telepathy and magical influence may partly reflect disordered relationships with consensual authority figures. "Seeing through" and controlling lesser individuals are among the prerogatives most commonly associated with authority status in most societies (Sennett, 1981). In an Ibo tribe, for example, healers are believed capable of visualizing the body's interior (Sennett, 1981). Powers of thought control, telepathy, and bodily influence, all typically schizotypal preoccupations, are quite regularly ascribed to authority figures in various societies.

Finally, apparent confusion of interpersonal boundaries might result from certain linguistic mistakes. Consistently correct language use may require a carefully cultivated consensual viewpoint inaccessible to the schizotype. Modern theories of linguistic communication imply that truly consensual information must always be provided alongside information that is new (see, for example, Haviland and Clark, 1974). With inadequate attention to consensual information, sentences may seem to presume information or to imply that the listener is privy to whatever is in the speaker's mind. Clinically, schizotypal patients whose speech seems abnormal in this respect are not infrequently encountered but the general importance of the phenomenon cannot really be spoken to here.

Schizotypal nonconformity in thought and world view is least evident in situations for which overlearned socially acceptable responses exist and becomes more evident in unstructured situations where etiquette provides less guidance. Hence, projective tests are particularly valuable in detection of subtle schizotypal traits (see Rapaport, et al., 1968). Another situation in which schizotypal nonconformity stands revealed is in response to verbal suggestions. Suggestibility, of course, is at least partially a tendency to accept information given by authority figures. Schizotypal resistance to suggestion, manifested variously as either suspicion, guardedness, or simple incredulousness, is well known. Hypnosis, for example, is rarely achieved with significantly schizotypal subjects, and tests of hypnotizability provide valuable clues to otherwise hidden schizotypy (Spiegel and Spiegel, 1978).

Numerous other anomalies marking the schizotype's life history—occupational, intellectual, and marital—all can be viewed as secondary to his or her pervasive social withdrawal and autistic thought patterns, which together form the core of the schizotypal syndrome. Most of these are obvious and require little in the way of explanation. Feeling himself an outsider, and thinking like an outsider, the schizotype cannot shoulder the insider's daily life.

Schizotypal Disorder and Primary Process Thought

The present view of schizotypy is actually far from new and differs from certain classic accounts only by its placement in a social strategic framework. Jaspers (1963), for instance, considered social withdrawal etiologically significant to schizotypal autism, and Freud originally considered decathexis of the external world and reemergence of primary process thought jointly responsible for schizotypal symptoms (see Fenichel, 1945). "Decathexis," of course, is the libido-theory concomitant of manifest social withdrawal. Although "primary process thought," was said to differ from secondary process thought in that it follows no logical rules, employs symbols and plastic representations in place of language, and uses none of what may now be called linguistic operators, a case can be made that it is really just nonconsensual, at least as it is actually used.

Consider, for instance, two hypothetical portraits: One realistic and the other depicting a horse's head atop the subject's neck. The former would likely be counted a manifestation of secondary, the latter, perhaps, of primary thought processes. The hypothesis suggested here is that a chimerical, as opposed to realistic, portrait is considered a manifestation of primary process thought simply because no one but the artist sees a horse's head on the subject's neck. In placing it there, the artist has departed from what is consensually agreed upon. Not all is lost, however, since a consensually intelligible reason for the departure will still save the day. The artist, for instance, may prefer to comment on the patron's intellect than to collect a fee. In providing such a reason, the artist certifies that his or her excursion was only transient, so to speak, and that he or she still lives in the consensual realm. Primary process, as analysts like to say, is "in the ego's service." Without consensually intelligible reasons, though, the departure from consensual reality could no longer be explained away, and the artist's mental health might well be impugned. Such is the connection between perceptual and cognitive conformity on the one hand and perceived sanity on the other.

Numerous other pairs likely considered primary and secondary thought manifestations—including verbal ones—can easily be imagined, all of which plausibly differ in the degree to which they express consensual or nonconsensual reality.

That primary process thoughts are private, rather than consensually accepted, would also explain their relative tendency to take plastic, rather than linguistic, form. Although not essential to primary process thought, plastic representation is the most likely means for its expression. The tendency of nonconsensual thoughts to take nonverbal form follows, in fact, from the relatively private uses to which nonverbal thoughts may be put. Language, by contrast, is the very instrument with which consensual thoughts are imposed on individual group members (Chapter 10). Consequently, departure from the consensual world of the human group may be best accomplished by loosening the linguistic chains that bind each member's thought patterns to those that are normative or by thinking in nonverbal terms. This in turn suggests that the thoughts of preverbal children, since they only occur in nonverbal forms, should be largely nonconsensual. In fact, this must be so, given the child's unfamiliarity with group reality. This is the basis for one well-known theory of childhood amnesia (Schachtel, 1947). Analysts, of course, consider primary process thought characteristic of young children, which is their justification for calling it primary in the first place.

If primary process thought is operationally just nonconsensual, then Freud's early description of schizotypal illness actually coincides with that developed from a social strategic viewpoint. Schizotypy, according to Freud, is manifested by object decathexis—social withdrawal in behavioral terms—and by primary process—or nonconsensual—thought patterns. The emphasis Freud and other psychoanalysts later placed on primitive defenses in schizotypal illness (see Gunderson, 1979) cannot be accounted for in this framework, though it too is basically consistent with schizotypal disregard for what others consider rational. The schizotype, in effect, may be less constrained in his or her self-deceptions by what is consensually plausible and so might invent defensive fictions that are transparent to normal observers. By contrast, defensive fictions invented by nonschizotypal patients are carefully crafted to appear consensually valid.

An interesting corollary to all this is that the distinction between creativity and autism is really just pragmatic. Those who think nonconsensual thoughts for consensually validated reasons are deemed creative; those who think nonconsensual thoughts for wholly private or uncommunicable purposes are less likely to be thought creative than autistic. But if autistic and creative thoughts differ only in their immediate uses, then schizotypes might be prone to having both types, not just autistic ones. On occasion, schizotypal cognitive freedom might result in new ideas, combinations, and world views, not only mere autism. Park's (1928) "marginal man" is relevant here. Freed from bondage to the consensual reality of any one group, the marginal man, according to Park, is uniquely situated to achieve intellectual progress. Also, quite aside from purely cognitive factors, psychologic disengagement in itself may provide greater freedom for artistic observation. Writing of Joseph Conrad, whose life and work are remarkable for distinctly schizoid preoccupations, Karl (1979) described this latter factor as "narrative distance." Numerous authors have also observed a positive relation between disengagement and loneliness, on the one hand, and creative endeavors on the other (Hartog, 1980; Calhoun, 1980; Cohen, 1980; Parkinson, 1980).

Although little data is available concerning schizotypy per se, frankly schizophrenic individuals are not remarkable for their creative powers. Perhaps because their lives are socially and intellectually impoverished, chronic schizophrenics—like other severely disturbed patients (Rothenberg, 1983)—actually score lower than normal on several measures of creative thought (see Rabin, et al., 1979). Nonpsychotic relatives of schizophrenics, many of whom might be schizotypal, do show enhanced creative powers, however. Karlsson (1966) described individuals he considered "genetic carriers" of thought disorder who were highly creative and possessed enhanced associative capacities. Heston and Denny (1969) described highly creative, nonpsychotic adoptees whose biologic parents were schizophrenic. Anthony (1968) coined the term "superphrenic" to describe creative and original youngsters at high genetic risk for schizophrenia. Kauffman and co-workers (1979) found that offspring of schizophrenic parents were more creative and original than offspring of either normal or depressed mothers.

Taken together, these observations suggest a simple hypothesis: Those less severely affected by schizotypal predispositions are, due to their relative freedom from the bonds of consensual cognitions, unusually creative persons. More severely schizotypal individuals, however, become progressively impoverished, autistic, and unproductive and consequently show no hint of creative potential. If this is so, schizotypal genes might be compared to those causing sickle-cell anemia. These enhance the well-being of carriers while impairing those with greater genetic loadings. Akin to sickle genes, "schizogenes" might survive in human populations by virtue of the social benefits accruing to creative individuals.

Proximate Causation of Schizotypal Disorders

Genetic predispositions to schizotypal illness were mentioned in a previous chapter. That genetic predispositions to characteristically schizotypal social deficits might occur should occasion little surprise. Since evolutionarily stable, ubiquitous social strategies likely depend for their occurrence upon at least some proximate mental mechanisms built into brain structure and function, genetic propensities of many different kinds might affect the group-related social strategies most relevant to schizotypal traits. For example, innate gestural tactics subserving affective communication may be particularly important for creation and maintenance of nonfamilial social interactions. The characteristically "flattened" affect of some schizotypes suggests that abnormal interpretation and production of innate gestures may play an etiologic role in schizotypal social perceptions (see Pilowsky and Bassett, 1980). Schizotypal gaze aversion may have much the same significance (Grumet, 1983). Nongenetic physiologic factors resulting in chronic social withdrawal may also be clues to the cerebral abnormalities associated with genetically predisposed schizotypy. Animal models of schizotypy, for example, may be provided by certain lesion studies. Nonhuman primates with amygdalar brain lesions typically withdraw from socially complex situations and may even become total isolates (Reynolds, 1981). Lesions of the frontal and temporal poles in both nonhuman primates and human beings may result in flattened affect and social disinterest. Much further research is needed in this important area.

More can be said concerning environmental factors associated with schizotypal illness, both on a cultural and a familial level. On a cultural level, some intriguing hints are contained in those societies that have recently suffered sharp increases in the incidence of schizotypal illness. Although ascertainment difficulties largely preclude study of schizotypy per se, much is now known concerning the culture-specific incidence of schizophrenia, its psychotic counterpart. Insofar as schizophrenia is a form of schizotypy in which, due to increased severity or coinciding factors, chronic psychosis has supervened, then factors increasing the incidence of schizophrenia may also be those predisposing to schizotypy. In this regard, the increased incidence of schizophrenia in recently Westernized areas of the third world (see, for example, Dunham, 1976; Torrey, 1979) is particularly interesting. Since schizotypy is comprised of simultaneous social withdrawal and nonconsensual cognitive tendencies, rapid cultural change, accompanied by the breakdown of community bonds and previously dominant consensual world views alike, would plausibly increase its incidence. Living in consensually fragmented societies individuals marginally predisposed for genetic or other reasons to social withdrawal and autism might develop more florid schizotypal traits than they would have developed in other circumstances.

That traditional, cognitively coherent, and highly centripetal societies may push schizotypally predisposed individuals toward normalcy may also explain the better prognosis of schizophrenics living in nonindustrialized areas of the world (Sartorius, et al., 1978; Waxler, 1979; Warner, 1983), as well as the increased incidence of schizophrenia in those who have left their countries of origin (Eitinger, 1960). At least some of the latter cases, like the excess numbers of schizophrenics in rural areas (Dohrenwend and Dohrenwend, 1974) and urban slums (Farris and Dunham, 1939; Dohrenwend and Dohrenwend, 1974; Goodman, et al., 1983), may result from excessive migration of those with schizotypal traits (see Dunham, 1976). In general, individuals with little emotional involvement in their community of origin might be expected to more readily emigrate and, in the more severe cases, to seek out either isolated rural or anonymous urban settings.

Family-related environmental factors also suggest the correctness of a social strategic approach. Data gathered by family therapists is particularly interesting in this regard and has been summarized by several recent reviews (see, for example, Wynne, et al., 1979). Basically, schizophrenic families of origin are characterized by disturbed and paradoxical communication patterns that critically impair transmission of information between family members. Just as in a consensually fragmented society, individuals predisposed to autism might not find in such families salient viewpoints in which to anchor their own thoughts. Acting over many years, disturbed family commmunication patterns might prevent formation of consensual cognitive substrata, particularly since parents normally act as group-designated authority figures with respect to their children. That absence of a clearly communicated familial world view is insufficient by itself to cause florid schizophrenia is suggested by adoption studies (see Gottesman and Shields, 1982), but poor family communication may act synergistically with genetic factors in those at risk for schizotypy.

Although family factors may contribute to the development of schizotypal illness, it is striking that schizotypal traits of every kind first come to medical attention around the time individuals disengage themselves from their families of origin. Manifestation of schizotypal traits on threatened or real separation from the family of origin, however, is only to be expected given the group-related dysfunction these traits represent. Following disengagement from the family of origin, group-related social strategies must become especially salient factors in the organization of social behavior. Prior to that time, their developmental failure might remain hidden behind a facade of relatively normal parent-child interactions. That a critical transition from dependence on familial and kin-related social strategies to dependence on group-related social strategies occurs during adolescence is evidenced also by the increased severity of loneliness in early as compared to late adolescence (Ostrov and Offer, 1980) and by typical adolescent preoccupations with ingroup membership, social acceptance, and fear of exclusion. Previously, loneliness was described as an affectively experienced social appraisal process subserving ingroup strategies in particular. Its amelioration in late adolescence suggests the resolution of adaptive problems related to early ingroup experiences. The symbiotic closeness of schizotypal patients with their families of origin, and their great sensitivity to family bereavement, may result from the attrition of extrafamilial social life rather than from pathology intrinsic to the family itself.

In discussing socialization, Luckman (1979) makes several points relevant to societal and family influences on schizotypy. In particular, he argues that primary socialization, occurring in the home, and secondary socialization, occurring when the child leaves home, are nearly identical in traditional societies. Socialization, of course, consists in large part of indoctrination into consensually defined reality. In modern societies, he argues, there is no unitary world view of the kind encountered in preliterate groups, so that primary and secondary socialization more often than not place the individual in disjoint social realities. In any event, the connection between primary and secondary socialization is highly tenuous, and the continuity of social indoctrination is no longer ensured. The fact that schizotypal traits first manifest themselves as a failure of secondary socialization following an apparently successful primary socialization, and that the demise of traditional society may in at least some instances have been followed by increased schizotypal illness, together suggest that disjoint socialization processes may worsen the outlook for schizotypally predisposed individuals. In effect, those living in traditional cultures may be partially innoculated against a failure of secondary socialization by their primary socialization experience, which inducts them into one and the same consensual reality. Also, the convergence of primary and secondary socialization may be partially responsible for the improved outlook for schizotypal illness in traditional societies. Further studies in this very important field may either confirm or disprove these speculations, but would certainly be relevant to understanding the life histories of schizotypal patients.

Treatment of Schizotypal Disorders

If schizotypal traits result from dysfunction of group-related social strategies, a dysfunction exacerbated by socially isolative, fragmented societies or by families with distorted communication patterns, then therapeutic interventions aimed at combating social withdrawal and at increasing saliency of consensual world views might ameliorate them somewhat. In particular, interventions of this type might interrupt the progressive social deterioration typical of both severely schizotypal and frankly schizophrenic individuals. Unfortunately, though, enthusiasm for psychotherapy in severe schizotypal disorders has waned considerably, largely as the result of a few widely misinterpreted studies, so that a fair hearing is now hard to obtain. Gunderson (1979) reviews the most influential of these studies, however, and concludes that long-term therapy may well improve even chronic schizophrenics. At least some misinterpreted studies naively compare psychotherapy with psychotic patients to drug therapy. Insofar as psychosis supervenes in schizotypal illness, its effective amelioration with drugs should be a prerequisite for, not an alternative to, psychotherapeutic interventions.

But even if psychotherapy in general may be effective in schizotypy, do data support the importance of overcoming autism and social isolation? In fact, based on his review of the literature, Gunderson (1979) concluded that psychotherapeutic interventions most likely to aid the schizophrenic patient are those that confront him with consensual reality. The therapist, in effect, serves as a "reality anchor" for the otherwise autistic patient. Gunderson refers to therapy of this kind as the "real life approach" and contrasts it with methods eliciting fantasies and unconscious material. The latter may actually be harmful to schizotypal patients, whose hold on consensual reality is already tenuous.

Clear consensual messages are also crucial in determining the outcome of schizophrenic milieu therapy, according to Mosher and Gunderson (1979). Even family therapy, according to these authors, must have as its major goal the definition and validation of a "consensual family reality" (Mosher and Gunderson, 1979, p. 430). Disturbed communication patterns render a consensual reality otherwise unattainable for many "schizophrenic" families.

Clinically, the value of nonthreatening social situations—as an antidote to schizotypal isolation—is well known. Residential treatment centers seem particularly valuable in this regard and are frequently associated with gradual improvement. An ultimate goal for residential treatment settings might be to match the long-term outcomes now spontaneously achieved in rural, nonindustrial societies, where social conditions are apparently more hospitable to schizotypally predisposed individuals (Sartorius, et al., 1978). Unfortunately, lack of financial support has largely vitiated the long-term usefulness of residential treatment. All too often, therapists must stand by while schizophrenic patients who improved in residential treatment settings are discharged and returned to the same communities in which they once again deteriorate.

Schizophrenic Subtypes

Before leaving the topic of schizotypy, a few words might be added on schizophrenic subtypes. Ever since Kraepelin proposed unifying symptomatically disparate presentations of what is now called schizophrenia, controversy has existed concerning their proper designation. Certainly, this issue cannot be resolved on purely theoretical grounds. Yet, some observations are emphasized by the social strategic model. First, simple schizophrenia, a subtype actually added by Bleuler, appears to be the schizophrenic syndrome most closely related to schizotypal personality (see also Andreasen and Olsen, 1982). Psychotic symptoms are minimal in simple schizophrenics, while social withdrawal and autism are profound (Carpenter and Strauss, 1979). In hebephrenia and paranoid schizophrenia, by contrast, psychosis is prominent and the schizotypal picture emerges clearly only during remissions from psychotic symptoms. Catatonia is perhaps best considered a manifestation of severe psychosis. Motoric symptoms appear in nonschizophrenic psychoses as well as in the course of schizophrenia (Abrams and Taylor, 1976) and in animal studies have been associated with central nervous system dopamine excess (see McKinney and Moran, 1981). The ostensibly better prognosis of catatonic patients

(Astrup, et al., 1962) may result from the nonschizotypal nature of underlying pathology in at least some of those suffering sudden florid psychoses with motor manifestations.

Similar remarks apply to so-called acute or reactive schizophrenia (see Stephens, et al., 1982). Patients with acute schizophrenia have little or no genetic loading for schizotypy and accomplish relatively normal social adjustments when in remission from psychosis. Their similarity in this regard to those with periodic affective psychoses, and their tendency to psychotic decompensations following traumatic life events (hence the designation reactive), lead some to categorize acute schizophrenics with affectively disordered patients. This is in spite of the fact that they may lack prominent affective distress. More stringent definition of schizophrenia is thereby accomplished at the expense of more ill-defined affective disorders (Carpenter and Strauss, 1979). An alternative solution, suggested in a previous chapter, would consider so-called acute schizophrenia a form of stress-induced psychosis, occurring in the absence of either schizotypal or affective disorders. Those prone to acute schizophrenic reactions would likely be those biologically predisposed to psychosis per se, certainly in response to stress and perhaps in response to dopamine-releasing agents as well (Chapter 12). Their reliably better long-term prognosis than that of chronic or process schizophrenics (Strauss and Carpenter, 1979), would result from their not actually being schizophrenic at all. If so, "low threshold psychosis" might be a preferable name for what is now called acute schizophrenia. Only detailed biochemical, clinical, genetic, and prognostic data can resolve this issue, however, and the present remarks must be taken in a speculative vein.

Paranoia

Finally, mention should be made of paranoia. That paranoia can complicate schizotypal illness is demonstrated by the frequent occurrence of paranoid ideation or even delusions in patients with schizotypal personality or schizophrenia. Paranoia, however, can also occur in the absence of overt schizotypal traits. In particular, paranoid personalities typically lack the bizarre and autistic thought patterns frequent in schizotypes. The fact that paranoid delusions can occur without other schizophrenic stigmata was noted by Kraepelin and is reflected in diagnostic systems that distinguish paranoid psychoses of a certain type from schizophrenia (see Kendler, 1980). In an earlier chapter, paranoid psychosis was treated as the psychotic counterpart of paranoid personality disorder, a position supported by clinical experience if not by systematic studies.

What is most remarkable about paranoid delusions is that the unfortunate patient sees those around him as potentially hostile. Those individuals are thought to possibly be members of an ill-intentioned group, either of private plotters or public enemies, who have banded together against their hapless victim. In effect, the delusional paranoid believes himself in the midst of hostile outgroup members who have infiltrated his own ingroup. If an American, he frequently believes that friends and passersby may belong to the KGB; if a Russian, that they may belong to the CIA. If a liberal, he imagines they may be FBI agents; if a conservative, that they may be Communists. In every case, the delusional paranoid experiences feelings appropriate only if he or she were potentially exposed to outgroup enemies. The paranoid delusion, in effect, would be psychologically appropriate only if the patient were a foreign spy.

The paranoid delusion, however, differs from nondelusional paranoid thought only by virtue of its systematization and fixity. Paranoid personalities typically imagine that others may be out to get them. Plots are seen at the root of every difficulty, and outgroup influences are perceived behind every setback. Between individuals, the camaraderie and trust that normally distinguish ingroup relations are notably tenuous, and ingroup bonds of reciprocal altruism are never taken for granted.

The paranoid individual, whether delusional or not, therefore suffers a dysfunction of group-related social strategies closely akin to that responsible for schizotypal illness. This explains why paranoia, like schizophrenia, is frequent among those who have emigrated to a new country (Eitinger, 1960), or among those in a culturally or linguistically strange environment (Allodi, 1982). Paranoia is also common among those who have recently left an unusually cohesive ingroup (see Galanter, 1983). The relation between the social strategic dysfunctions of paranoia and schizotypy also accounts for the occurrence of paranoid ideas in schizotypal illness as well as their occurrence without the full picture of schizotypy. While the paranoid imagines that others may be outgroup members, the schizotype fails to feel part of any ingroup. The schizotype, therefore, may or may not be paranoid, but the paranoid will not be schizotypal. Paranoia and paranoid delusions may complicate schizotypy, but extremes of autistic thought will not complicate paranoia.

That paranoid ideation depends on dysfunction of group-related social strategies is evidenced as well by studies of so-called authoritarian personalities (Adorno, et al., 1950). Extremes of ethnicity and paranoid features coexist in these cases, just as extreme social withdrawal and paranoid features coexist in some cases of schizotypy.

The frequent coincidence of male paranoia and homophobia is discussed in the next chapter, where homophobia is shown to be potentially secondary to the same group-related social perceptions responsible for paranoia in the first place.

15

Dysfunction of Specific Social Strategies III

Sexual Competition and Disorders

Oedipal disorders, and their association with impaired self-esteem, are easily explicated from a social strategic viewpoint. Sexual disorders, on the other hand, are likely heterogeneous. Homosexual behavior in particular has a ritualized significance that makes it psychologically important.

Oedipal Disorders

Fortunately, the very conflict to which classical psychoanalytic theory ascribes the most importance is most easily explicated in social strategic terms. Consideration of sexually related social strategies explains why boys might compete with their fathers, why girls might compete with their mothers, and even some of the circumstances in which these competitions might be exacerbated. Consideration of attachment-related strategies explains, too, why these competitions would be conflict laden and why they are eventually suppressed in favor of more important childhood needs. In some respects, of course, a social strategic view turns psychoanalytic theory upside down. Rather than causing adult sexual competition, childhood competition with the same-sex parent is merely its first manifestation. Adult sexual competition is not childish; instead, childhood sexual competition is precocious. In the main, however, the implications of the two viewpoints are largely the same. In childhood sexual competition, potent emotional conflicts may be mobilized, which continue to influence behavior even into maturity. In childhood, too, models are formed and tactics learned that are never entirely modified. Their influence can be discerned in responses to adult sexual competition and, particularly, in transference feelings directed toward the therapist.

Behavioral syndromes classically attributed to the Oedipal conflict include neurotic inhibitions and anxiety states, hysterical and obsessive-compulsive disorders, and masochistic behaviors of every kind. Therefore, a social strategic treatment of the Oedipal complex, and of adult sexual competition, provides the foundation for an ultimate causal account of many abnormal behavior patterns not dealt with in previous chapters. Attention here will be restricted to two specific, theoretically interesting, features of Oedipal psychopathology. Readers are referred to comprehensive reference works for descriptions of behavioral syndromes (Slater and Roth, 1969, or Gray, 1978, for example). Specifically, Oedipal treatments of these disorders are to be found in Fenichel (1945).

The first noteworthy feature of the Oedipal conflict, and of same-sex competitive strategies in general, is that their pathogenic effects seem to depend on disavowal of hostile intentions. Pathogenic repression, of course, is central to the Freudian view of Oedipal psychopathology, and the importance of disavowal is still emphasized even by those theorists who have abandoned Freud's hypothetical constructs (see, for example, Schafer, 1976, 1978). Typically, competitive, hostility-ridden patients seeking treatment initially deny all but the friendliest feelings. Time and skill are usually required to dispel this self-deception, which seems to be an essential prerequisite to real improvement.

Insofar as disavowal is frequently associated with potentially hostile behaviors, it might be susceptible to a social strategic analysis. However, virtually the only work along this line is that of Alexander and colleagues (Alexander, 1975, 1979; Alexander and Noonan, 1979), who suggest that the capacity for self-deception could enhance inclusive fitness if it improved the ability to dissemble suppressed motives. Humans, of course, are exquisitely sensitive to hidden hostile intentions. Therefore, suppression of intentional states together with the behaviors they lead to might protect competitively disadvantaged individuals from otherwise dangerous exposure.

However, although self-deception is at the heart of clinically evident defense mechanisms (Schafer, 1976), little evidence exists that it actually aids in the suppression of manifest behavioral clues. Bowlby (1980), for one, seems to support that view when he argues that "systematic exclusion" of normally activating information could serve to deactivate behavioral subsystems. Yet clinical experience occasionally suggests just the opposite. Insofar as the meaning of otherwise clear-cut acts are denied, disavowal often seems to relax behavioral control. Loss of behavioral control leads to social ostracism, which more often than not is the immediate cause for seeking psychotherapy. Only when disavowal is reversed does the patient regain control over the hostile behaviors at the root of his social problems.

Sloman and co-workers (1979) argue that the neurotic process increases selective pressures against competitively unfit genes. In this way, it may speed the selection of higher cognitive processes. Since self-deception is the most salient aspect of the neurotic process, their observations cast further doubt on Alexander's hypothesis.

Therefore, an important proximate mediator of Oedipal psychopathology—the extraordinary human capacity for disavowal and self-deception—is only tenuously accounted for from an inclusive fitness viewpoint. This is in spite of the fact that the Oedipal conflict itself, and same-sex competition in general, is easily treated within the same framework. Possibly, the capacity for disavowal and self-deception is an incidental effect of cognitive capacities that are themselves immediately advantageous, or it may be an effect of language skills, as one theorist argues (Jaynes, 1977). But in either of these cases, it should currently be treated as a purely proximate problem.

Oedipal Disorders and Self-esteem

The second feature of Oedipal disorders of interest from a social strategic viewpoint is their tendency to coincide with disordered self-esteem. Disordered self-esteem has long been considered etiologically significant in many mental disorders (see Freud, 1933; Fenichel, 1945; Bursten, 1982) and is also undoubtedly consequent to psychopathology of any type. However, in an earlier chapter we took the view that at least part of clinically manifested self-esteem is homologous with resource holding power, as defined by the theory of interpersonal conflict. Therefore, it is worthwhile to examine the implications of such an homology for the possibly specific relationship between Oedipal disorders and abnormal self-regard. Resource holding power, to refresh the reader's memory, refers to a hypothetical dimension on which individuals might compare themselves with others as a means of predicting the likely outcome of potential conflict (Parker, 1978).

Older theories of self-esteem will not be reviewed here, except to note that each depends on libido theory, Freudian structural theory, or other reified constructs. By contrast, the rationale for considering self-esteem at least partly homologous with resource holding power is based on the fact that both rest on the same determining factors. Human contests, and consequently resource holding power, depend not only on physical ability but also on complex social factors coincident with those frequently seen to affect self-esteem. Prestige, verbal and political skills, wealth, birthright, and social connections are critical elements determining both judgments. Other factors that superficially only affect self-esteem turn out, on closer inspection, to also affect resource holding power. Moral virtue and religious faith, for example, are often thought of as sources of individual power, and consensual belief systems lend prestige to the notion that those who have them are ultimately undefeatable.

Both clinically evident self-esteem and resource holding power are compound judgments, so that weaknesses in one area can be compensated for by strengths in another. One school of psychology, in fact, rests on the need individuals have to regulate their self-esteem by compensating for real or imagined weaknesses (Ansbacher and Ansbacher, 1956). This is accomplished by overdeveloping talents in other areas and is easily explicable if resource holding power is one component of clinical self-esteem.

Since resource holding power is an estimation of the capacity for successful conflict, the behavior of individuals with disordered self-esteem might reveal, perhaps subtly, disordered responses to potentially inimical social encounters. Those with excessive self-esteem, for example, might be excessively ready to engage in conflicts (that are not, in human societies, ordinarily violent ones) and might be excessively ready to escalate them once they have started. Consensual belief systems, of course, may produce certain exceptions to this rule. The very religious, for instance, feel both invulnerable and worthy of self-esteem only insofar as they obey their faith, which may require them to renounce conflict entirely. Taking similar exceptions into account, those with diminished self-esteem might show the opposite tendencies. Fearful of potential opponents, they might avoid conflict whenever possible. Social strategies requiring conflict may be erratically pursued, or neglected entirely, depending on the degree to which self-esteem is diminished.

Both these predictions seem to be true. In mania, overly inflated self-esteem occurs together with excessive interpersonal aggression. In depression, impaired self-esteem occurs together with diminished interpersonal aggression, so that anger is frequently said to be "turned inward."

However, impaired self-esteem is frequently more complex and shows itself in more elaborate ways. Kohut (1971, 1977) and his followers (Goldberg, 1978), for example, have described patients whose diminished self-esteem is manifested in alternately idealizing and disparaging attitudes toward the psychotherapist. When idealizing, patients of this sort attempt to please the therapist, with whom they hope to curry special favors and whom they hope to emulate. Kohut argues that these idealizing attitudes resemble the feelings of normal children toward their parents that are gradually surrendered with growing awareness of parental limitations. In patients, though, disparaging attitudes suddenly supervene, usually following minor disappointments. The therapist might have been late for an appointment, misunderstood an important communication, or in some other fashion failed to live up to his or her idealized image. When disparaging, the patient adopts a derogatory and arrogant manner. The therapist may be treated with disdain or may be considered an alter ego, significant only as a reflection of the patient's own importance.

The idealizing attitude presents no conceptual problem. This is merely the placatory, alliance-seeking behavior expected from one with no confidence in his capacity to stand on his own. By obtaining an idealized ally, the patient allays his anxiety. However, through acts of commission or omission the therapist inevitably reminds the idealizing patient of their true relationship, which is not that of allies at all. When this occurs, the attitude toward the therapist becomes disparaging, though it nonetheless remains sufficiently defensive that the patient's true feelings still show through. With disparagement, according to Kohut (1971, p. 106), the patient attempts to garner the "perfection and power" previously monopolized by the therapist. Taking for himself what had been the other's pedestal, he denies shrilly that he needs an ally, or that the therapist would be a good one in any event. Eventually, though, setbacks deflate the patient's grandiose defense and return him, humble once again, to his fantasied protector.

As noted, insofar as self-esteem and resource holding power coincide, those with impaired self-esteem should suffer secondary impairments in the pursuit of conflict-ridden social strategies. Consistent with this prediction, some of the patients described by Kohut and his followers—before their problems with self-esteem were appreciated—had been treated for years on the presumption they suffered from typical Oedipal neuroses. Apparently, a prominent aspect of the syndrome these patients displayed was inhibition and anxiety in competition with others of their own sex. From this, Kohut (1977) deduced the importance of self-esteem to confident relations with the same-sex parent and, by implication, to the adult world too. Kohut speculated that the classical Oedipal conflict may be symptomatic of defects in self-esteem, rather than developmentally obligatory, and that with adequate self-esteem, the Oedipal phase may be considerably less traumatic than assumed by classical analysts. Only the child with impaired self-esteem, according to this view, is likely to become mired in "unassimilated lust and hostility" (Kohut, 1977, p. 247). Emergence of sexually competitive attitudes in patients with impaired self-esteem often signifies recovery, according to Kohut.

Some may assert that no child could compete successfully with his or her parent, no matter how positive his or her self-esteem. Sheer differences in physical strength seem to preclude it. The error here, of course, lies in assuming that competition between parent and child is violent, so that physical strength is the determining factor. If Kohut is correct, then fantasies of hostile competition with the parent indicate poor self-esteem and are not normal to the Oedipal period at all. Like the hapless citizen of a dictatorship, the Oedipal child with impaired self-esteem will nurture fantasies of violent revolution. If he perceived himself as potent in the first place, he would have no need for these fantasies. Competition, furthermore, is commonplace between parent and child, and has been discussed under the rubric of parent-child conflict. There is certainly no reason to assume that parent-child sexual conflicts should be fundamentally different from those over other resources, all of which occur in a social arena. That these are considered irresolvable, in fact, may be more a reflection of Victorian morality than of human biology.

Sexual Disorders

Both in psychologic theory and in clinical practice sexual competition and sexual disorders are closely related topics. In theory, at least, the relation is likely chimerical, since it is largely based on Freudian libido theory. As the result of Oedipal conflict, libidinal energy is said to regress from genital to pregenital sexual appetites, satisfaction of which entails perversion. Freud (1917), of course, illustrated this model with one of his most elegant metaphors, which likened libido to an advancing army, but its simplicity is actually deceptive. In fact, it embodies several complex assumptions, all of which are likely to be false. Libido theory itself, the putative functional equivalence of various somatic appetites, their ostensible developmental ordering, and the relation between component somatic appetites and perverse sexual behavior are all highly problematic. Whether perversion and sexual competition are linked in clinical practice is also questionable, since few objective criteria exist by which the relative importance of sexual competition can be judged for individual patients.

The social strategic viewpoint adopted here does suggest that certain sexual deviants may also be troubled by sexual competitive issues, but the relation is neither uniform nor simple. Instead, sexual deviations are likely to be highly heterogeneous; even individuals with the same sexual pattern may have come by their deviations in different ways. Nor does a social strategic approach answer many of the questions raised by sexual deviation. Some deviations, for example, are best addressed in proximate causal terms. Others are easily interpreted with neither proximate nor ultimate causal concepts. While on the subject, an attempt will be made here to summarize the few points that follow from the social strategic model.

Regardless of whether or not it is properly considered a psychologic disorder, homosexuality deserves to be discussed first due to its frequency and cultural importance. Attention will be directed here mainly toward male homosexuality, which, in our society, is considerably more common than its female counterpart (Mellen, 1981). Not only are male homosexual impulses accorded prominent roles in certain psychologic theories, but phobic preoccupation with male homosexuality characterizes certain psychiatric illnesses. From an inclusive fitness point of view, both male and female homosexuality are particularly puzzling, especially in light of their frequency in the absence of cultural restraints.

Several lines of evidence suggest that homosexual "object choice"—or preference for those of the same sex—results from dysfunction of proximate sexual mechanisms built into the central nervous system. Whether or not organic factors account for all cases of homosexuality, environmental events likely play less of an etiologic role than that attributed to them by most psychologic theories. Significantly, nineteenth century medical investigators already believed that homosexual object choice resulted from organic, and not environmental, factors, so that current research has moved the clock back to pre-Freudian times. Among the modern findings supporting the role of organic factors has been documentation that at least some homosexuals manifest gender-inappropriate behaviors long before inappropriate object choice. By self-report, as many as two thirds of male homosexuals may have been effeminate in childhood, compared to only a small fraction of heterosexual men (Saghir and Robins, 1973). Bell, Weinberg, and Hammersmith (1981) studied demographically matched samples of homosexual and heterosexual men and women. They concluded that of maternal and paternal traits, parental relationship, birth order, sibling constellation, and early experiences of many kinds, childhood gender nonconformity was virtually the only significant predictor of later homosexual preference. This was true for both effeminate and noneffeminate males and for females and appeared independent of other environmental variables.

At the same time, investigators have demonstrated that the mammalian central nervous system, initially bipotential, becomes committed to male or female gender-typical response patterns early in the course of development. What nineteenth century developmental biologists discovered to be true of the urogenital system has, in the twentieth century, also been shown to be true of the brain. Remarkably, moreover, central nervous system commitment may be anomalous with chromosomal sex, predisposing the individual to produce gender-inappropriate behaviors throughout his or her life span. Only a small deductive leap need be made to conclude that early-appearing gender-inappropriate behaviors of at least some homosexuals may result from anomalous brain commitment. Since gender-related infantile play practices are more than culturally determined (see Goodall [1971] and Kummer [1968] for descriptions of homologous differences in nonhuman primates), this hypothesis is particularly plausible and has become the basis of much modern research into the biology of homosexuality.

Evidence for central nervous system sexual bipotentiality and developmental commitment, and for the link between anomalous early commitment and later behavior in humans, is too complex to be fully summarized here. At least part of central nervous system commitment, however, seems to depend on prenatal androgen, or male hormone, levels. Testosterone administered early in life to experimental animals can affect gender-related aspects of later behavior, including persistence in conflicts, perseverance in pursuit of environmental resources, and distractibility from behavioral goals (see, for example, Andrew, 1976). Similar effects have been demonstrated in human children (Breuer, 1982). Adult animals previously exposed to testosterone also show changes in sexual behavior, but these can be compared with human sexual patterns only with difficulty. Human females with infantile adrenogenital syndrome—who are exposed to high androgen levels prenatally and postnatally—manifest as adults a pattern of sexual behavior resembling the male in all respects except object choice (see Symons, 1979). These women, for example, are aroused by visual stimuli, have an increased number of erotic dreams, and experience an appetitive, driven sexuality less common among other women. Their object choice, however, remains heterosexual. Another natural experiment, testicular feminization syndrome, casts more light on prenatal androgen effects. Genetic males with testicular feminization syndrome lack cellular receptor sites necessary for androgenic hormone effects. Accordingly, although they have normal or high levels of prenatal and postnatal androgens, they develop female external genitalia. Occasionally, chromosomal sex is not discovered until late in childhood or even in adolescence. Significantly, these genetic males also typically manifest what would be normal female object choice (Mellen, 1981; Bell, Weinberg, and Hammersmith, 1981), suggesting that however male genes commit the central nervous system to male object choice, androgen effects play a necessary role. Not surprisingly, the pattern of sexual behavior shown by males with testicular feminization syndrome is also typically female. Finally, 5-alpha-reductase deficiency (Imperato-McGinley, et al., 1979) must be mentioned. Like patients with testicular feminization syndrome, genetically male subjects with 5-alpha-reductase deficiency are raised as the females they superficially appear to be. However, because effective intrauterine and postnatal testosterone levels are normal in subjects with 5-alpha-reductase deficiency, testosterone surges during puberty result in the sudden emergence of previously latent male sexual patterns, including male object choice.

Whether differences in either androgen levels (Kolodny, et al., 1971) or in the metabolic fate of androgens (Margolese and Janiger, 1973) could account for anomalous early commitment in at least some homosexual males has been clouded in controversy. For the most part, this is far beyond the present scope. Obstacles to the demonstration of abnormal androgen-brain interactions in male homosexuals include the technical difficulties of measuring hormone products, the impossibility of ascertaining their effects on the neural sites most relevant to sexual object choice, and the possibly transient nature of the abnormality later reflected in permanent behavioral change.

Homoerotic behaviors, though, may have psychologic significance not predictable from etiologic knowledge alone. Among higher primates, for instance, male homoerotic activities in particular are laden with ritualized meaning, most certainly of a phylogenetic type (Appendix E). In humans, the same ritualized significance might explain the importance of male homoerotic preoccupations in more than one psychiatric syndrome. Among higher primates, "sociosexual presenting" (Hinde and Stevenson-Hinde, 1976) between members of the same sex may reinstate dominance relationships. Submissive males present themselves, much like females, and are mounted by dominant males. Presentation and subsequent mounting defuse encounters that might otherwise become violent (Kummer, 1979a). Sexual competitive strategies in particular may be served in this way. In some primate species, males even develop specialized anatomic structures mimicking the perineal swellings of estrous females. These are employed to appease more dominant animals (Clutton-Brock and Harvey, 1976).

Although homosexual behaviors of the human male involve sexual penetration, and therefore differ from the dominance gestures of nonhuman primates, they nonetheless convey much the same ritualized significance. This is demonstrated in numerous vulgar figures of speech, which are used by heterosexual men to express anger, and by the behavior of men in certain environments, such as prisons, which deprive them of sexual companionship and create intense rivalries at the same time. Homosexual assault is a perquisite of prison dominance (Roth, 1971), and less powerful men refusing to provide normally female sexual favors may find themselves victims of superior violence.

Among the most striking of Freud's accomplishments was his recognizing, without benefit of ethologic evidence, the dominance-submission aspect of male homoerotic activity. The "negative Oedipal complex" (Freud, 1923) consists of passive homosexual fantasies or impulses unconsciously intended to placate a more powerful male whom the patient actually hates. Whether the negative Oedipal complex—the signaling value, in other words, of passive homoerotic behavior—actually motivates some cases of sustained homosexuality is highly problematic. Evidence of likely organic dysfunction militates against its etiologic importance. Also, contrary to the Freudian prediction, homosexual men switch passive and active sex-roles rather freely (Trimmer, 1978). Yet, transient homosexual fantasies encountered in psychotherapy of heterosexual, competitive men may be explained in this way. For such patients, transient passive homoerotic fantasies may have the same significance as other impulses toward submission and point to suppressed competitive strivings directed at other men. Interpretation of their ritualized significance, rather than of their apparent sexual content, will be requisite to clinical progress.

Noting the remarkable tendency of the male paranoid to fear homosexual assault, to detect homosexual taunts in innocent remarks, and to suspect plots against his masculinity, Freud (1911) also hypothesized that projection of passive homosexual impulses plays an etiologic role in paranoia. This, of course, is consistent with the general analytic principle—so often correct—to suspect that which people most vehemently deny. However, since dysfunctions of group-related social strategies account quite well for other aspects of paranoid ideation (Chapter 14), some group-related explanation should be sought for this particular aspect of paranoid illness as well. Clues to an association of group-related and homoerotic behaviors may be found in the study of nonhuman primates. In several species of nonhuman primates those at the bottom of the male dominance hierarchy are forcibly extruded from the social group. Group extrusion occurs, of course, so that more dominant males can monopolize available females (see Fox, 1980). Typically, subordinate or juvenile males forcibly extruded by their more dominant fellows continue to live near the social group and continue to strive for readmission and concomitant access to females. In some species, these peripheralized males may even aid in group defense. Relations between peripheralized males and those remaining in the social group remain tense, however, and submissive gestures by the extruded males are frequently required in order to ward off attacks. Among these gestures, of course, are frequent presentations, to which group males respond by mounting the inferior animal. In effect then, peripheralized males are tolerated only insofar as they occasionally act like females.

The relevance of primate male peripheralization to human social life is demonstrated, in fact, by certain cultural institutions. These correspond to the male paranoid's worst nightmare. The so-called berdache, for example, occurred in certain American Indian tribes (Fox, 1980). Young men in these tribes were forced to accomplish painful and dangerous feats as part of their male initiation rites. Not incidentally, these feats served to kill some young men before they were of marriageable age, increasing the number of potential wives for those already initiated. Young men failing to accomplish their prescribed feats—if they were still alive—were offered a simple choice: They could leave the tribe, which usually meant certain death at the hands of neighboring tribal groups, or they could continue to live in the tribe as women. Males remaining in the group under these circumstances, the berdaches, dressed as women, performed female chores, socialized with women, and entertained men in typically feminine ways. Male sexual behavior by a berdache was met with Draconian punishment. The berdache, in effect, was extruded from the group as a man, but tolerated as a woman, not unlike a peripheralized nonhuman primate.

The male paranoid, who imagines himself in his enemy's camp—that is, to be living among inimical outgroup members—seems to fear becoming a berdache or, in any event, its latter-day equivalent. His preoccupation with homosexual assault, with imagined insults to his masculinity, and with imputations of femininity are all consistent with this fear, which may be part and parcel of his self-perceived estrangement from the male social group. If this is so, paranoid homosexual preoccupation and the negative Oedipal complex both result from the ritualized meaning of male homoerotic behaviors. Male neurotics, anxious to disavow their hatred of other men, claim instead to be submissive. They illustrate this with passive homoerotic fantasies. Male paranoids fear the sexual implication of their group estrangement or of their failure to participate in what Young (1962) referred to as the group's "male solidarity." Believing that others will label them, they become sensitive to the slightest hints.

Significantly, paranoid-like rejection and fear of feminine traits is also prominent among males with authoritarian personalities (Adorno, et al., 1950), who also manifest group-related pathology, and among males with strongly racist attitudes (Cottle, Edwards, and Pleck, 1970).

Finally, organic events responsible for development of homosexual object choice may be genetically predisposed. This is demonstrated by the higher concordance rates for homosexuality in identical, as opposed to fraternal, twins (Heston and Shields, 1968) and by other familial evidence. The complete reproductive failure of obligative homosexuals would seem to ensure that extraordinarily steep selective pressures exist in favor of physiologic events reliably resulting in normal object choice. Yet, at least male homosexual object choice is common, whenever cultural penalties are removed. Therefore, factors countervailing diminished reproductive success must be operative in determining the inclusive fitness of genes predisposing individuals to its development.

Genes predisposing to homosexual object choice, for example, may confer inclusive fitness advantages on heterosexual individuals carrying a lower genetic load, much the way sickle-cell anemia genes protect the heterozygote from malaria. This is the individual, of course, who carries only one abnormal gene. Because his or her other gene for hemoglobin is of the normal kind, the heterozygote is also spared from sickle-cell disease. Likewise, advantages conferred on more numerous heterosexual individuals may cancel the steep selective pressures exerted by reproductive failure of relatively fewer homosexuals. Mellen (1981) suggests a model of this type when he argues that feminizing genes serve to moderate extreme masculine traits previously adaptive but now maladaptive to human males. Homosexual males, he argues, become homosexual because they carry a heavier than ordinary load of these attenuating genes. Actually, even if the behavioral effects of genes predisposing to homosexual object choice were independent of genetic load, if obligative homosexuality were a sufficiently improbable result, then beneficial effects of the sort hypothesized by Mellen could still outweigh the disadvantages imposed on those who do become homosexual.

Inclusive fitness consequences of homosexuality might even be positive. This might be the case, for example, if homosexuality were a specialized altruistic role, as Wilson (1978a) has suggested, or if its development depended on environmental parameters signifying poor reproductive prospects. This is not as unlikely as it may seem. In rodents, at least, physiologic changes of the sort that might result from environmental overcrowding also inhibit reproductive maturation (Christian, 1964). If nothing else, theories of this type remind us how little is actually known concerning homosexually relevant selective pressures and how difficult their quantification might actually be, even within the modern environment.

Frank dysfunction is only one way in which proximate mental mechanisms might enter the study of sexual deviations. In some circumstances even their normal functioning might be such as to make deviations more likely, particularly if these are mild and have relatively less impact on reproductive success. Sexual fetishism may be caused in this way. Some features of severe fetishism suggest that it results from functioning of the same mental processes responsible for normal sexual behavior. Due to their excessive sensitivity, their activity in an abnormal environment, or plain bad luck, these have resulted instead in formation of crippling fetishes. First, severe fetishism is an exclusively male disorder. Yalom (1980), in fact, reports that he was unable to discover a single case of female sexual fetishism in the psychiatric literature. Although severe cases of fetishism might result in attrition of normal sexual interests (Stekel, 1930), mild fetishism also characterizes nearly all normal males, for whom fetishes appear as conditions of sexual excitement subordinate to the goal of sexual intercourse. Thus, essentially normal men who require for their maximal sexual excitement that their mates wear particular underwear, comb their hair in a particular fashion, or accent particular bodily parts are frequently encountered. While not exclusive to the male sex, conditions of this type are likely to be much less prominent in female sexual excitement, for which emotional rather than material circumstances are more important (Symons, 1979). Second, fetish choices are remarkably restricted, and the same objects tend to be chosen both by severe fetishists and by normal males as well. Of the millions of objects, manufactured and natural, that enter the fetishist's environment, he will predictably settle his sexual interest on just a few. These include bodily parts, such as breasts, buttocks, feet, hands, and hair, and articles of feminine clothing, particularly intimate apparel.

Fetishism's restriction to the male sex, its prominence even in normal male sexuality, and the fact that its objects are usually in close proximity to, or even parts of, the female body, all suggest that the mechanisms subserving normal male arousal have somehow gone awry. The importance of male sexual responsiveness to purely sensory cues has been discussed in a previous chapter and suggests that finely tuned mechanisms must exist to mediate it. These would result in male arousal not only to invariant anatomic stimuli, but also to culturally determined signs of sexual availability. Thus, plasticity is required, which, under certain circumstances, could result in fetishistic displacement of intercourse itself as the prime object of masculine desire. Females, being less dependent for their sexual arousal on purely sensory cues, would be correspondingly protected against fetishistic fixations both in their normal variety and in their extreme forms.

Voyeurism, insofar as it manifests disengagement of a proximate mechanism from the strategic ensemble in which it normally functions, may result from processes akin to those that produce fetishism. Thus, the voyeur—who, like the fetishist, is also usually male (Trimmer, 1978)—takes as his sexual end-point visual stimulation normally only antecedent to intercourse. As in the case of fetishism, a normally adaptive part-function appears to have replaced the strategic whole.

Processes resulting in other sexual deviations may best be conçeived in ultimate causal, or social strategic, terms. Male sadism and exhibitionism in particular may result from processes of this kind. As for male sadism, differences in male and female sexual patterns may account for some of its manifestations. The similarity of sexual behavior patterns between heterosexual and homosexual females, and the promiscuity typical of male homosexuals, both indicate that heterosexual males make greater compromises in their sexual lives than do females. That is, in order to obtain sexual partners, heterosexual males must largely adopt the nonpromiscuous sexual pattern preferred by females (Chapter 8). It is within this context that male sadistic fantasies, which concern a compromise more in the male's favor, or even a triumph of the male sexual will entirely, can best be understood. These fantasies depict the female as either sexually submissive, claiming nothing in return for sexual access, or as helpless, so that the male has sexual access without the necessity of having to bargain for it. Wishes for submissive or helpless females are the nidus, too, of more elaborate fantasies, in which rape, bondage, and corporal punishment play various roles. In each of these, the core wish can still be recognized: The male should not have to court the female nor compromise with her in order to have his way.

If the origin of male sadism lies in the necessity to compromise with women, then males who imagine themselves to have compromised more should be the most sadistic. These are males who—either in reality or in fantasy—are less able to compete with other men for female sexual favors. Therefore, males with Oedipal psychopathology may be especially prone to sexual sadism, which might correlate also with fluctuations in their subjectively perceived resource holding power, or self-esteem. This may account for the connection between sexual sadism and castration anxiety noted by classical analysts (see Fenichel, 1945). Since fluctuations in self-esteem frequently result from defeats or successes in competition with other men, exacerbations of sexual sadism may appear in these patients as manifestations of displaced aggression. In fact, however, the relation between transient defeats and sadistic sexual fantasies is likely to be more complicated than the term displacement implies. Similar confusion may exist between sexual sadism and punitive aggression used to deter female infidelity. Although both are likely to be heightened in neurotically inferior males, their psychologic significances remain distinct. Only the characteristic fantasy element, reduction or elimination of the female's power of sexual refusal, reliably distinguishes male sexual sadism from other forms of interpersonal violence.

As described in a previous chapter, women will most often respond to the nudity of strange males as a threat, rather than as an invitation. Therefore, from a social strategic viewpoint, male exhibitionism is to rape very much what assault is to outright battery. It is the threat without the consequent act. Like sadism, it implies denial of female sexual choice. How exhibitionists differ from rapists on the one hand and sadists on the other, and how they are alike, is highly relevant to a social strategic treatment of perversions, but is beyond the scope of this chapter.

16
Public Mental Health

Both technologic innovations and socioeconomic factors affect the likelihood of particular social dysfunctions. Technologic innovations of particular importance may include new methods of contraception and obstetric care, new methods for feeding infants, and new means of communication. Important socioeconomic factors may include alienation, anomie, and the incidence and meaning of poverty in any given society.

Technologic Innovations

Implications of abnormal psychology are never limited to the clinic; they extend as well to the social environment in which mental disorders actually form. In previous chapters, attention has been given to the patient's personal environment, consisting of his or her friends and relatives, which affects for better or worse the patient's strategic functioning. Attention here will be directed toward the larger social environment and toward some of its features likely to militate for or against mental health. Social strategic analyses of what constitutes a mentally healthy society, or at least a society promoting mental health, could occupy an entire separate volume. Accordingly, the remarks here are sketchy and incomplete and are intended only to illustrate future possibilities.

First, a social strategic viewpoint suggests that certain technologic innovations—which otherwise appear perfectly innocuous—might have far-ranging impact on the mental health of those who use them. Perhaps the clearest examples of such innovations come from modern obstetric care. Employment of increasingly sophisticated obstetric technologies has frequently interfered with the maternal-infant interaction—and with its emotional setting—in such a way as to attenuate the development of maternal attachment strategies. Some of these adverse effects have been mentioned in previous chapters, but readers interested in a more comprehensive treatment of the subject are referred to Trowell's (1982) excellent article. As the result of psychologic research, both obstetricians and nurses are currently more concerned with preserving early maternal-infant interactions.

Similar remarks apply to newer methods of feeding small infants. In this case, though, the psychologic results, both salutary and detrimental, are largely unknown. The potential effects of the infant's nutritional state and the importance of nonnutritive sucking were briefly mentioned elsewhere (see Appendix E, Chapter 6). Major changes in infant-feeding practices, affecting both the nutritional value of what infants receive and the opportunities they have for physical contact with the mother, have swept the Western world. In the United States alone, for instance, the percentage of infants breastfed by the time of hospital discharge dropped from sixty-five percent in 1946 to only twenty-seven percent in 1966 (Knoedel, 1977). Even those women who do breastfeed may wean their children earlier than was once customary. In underdeveloped countries, aggressive marketing of milk substitutes has created major public health problems in the last two decades. Although no one has demonstrated that new feeding practices have any effect on later psychologic health, inadequate information exists to reach an informed judgment. Possibly, an effect might be found only on extraordinary attachment relationships, such as those formed by mothers who were once abused children. Prospective studies are badly needed here, in spite of the numerous methodologic difficulties inherent in them.

But before their birth and feeding, infants must be conceived, and here as well technology has had its say. The social strategic results of effective universal contraception are likely to be both short- and long-term. With regard to the latter, contraception helps the female in her effort to find a reliable father for her children (Tiger, 1979a). Its universal use, insofar as it prevented the conception of children outside of long-term relationships, would also reduce the inclusive fitness value of male sexual promiscuity. Given thousands of years, males might evolve who are less promiscuous and make better fathers, a change in masculine psychology that would certainly be for the better. The short-term effects depend on the individual results of having fewer or no children. For example, at least some of those who will choose to remain childless could be happier if they made the opposite decision. On the other hand, many of them may lead better lives as the result of forgoing children. For a variety of reasons, some of which were touched on in previous chapters, many of them would only be made unhappy by children, who, in turn, would likely be harmed by them. Unfortunately, whether a decision to remain childless is advantageous or not in any given case may only become evident as the person ages. The finality of such a decision emerges more clearly with age, along with its long-term consequences. Similar considerations apply to the number of children parents choose to bear, should they wish to be parents in the first place. Once again, empirical studies, particularly with subjects at risk for psychologic disorder, are badly needed.

New methods of communication may also affect genetically transmitted social strategies. Televisions shows, for instance, introduce isolated viewers to a vividly portrayed social group. Fictive members of this group appear weekly in the viewer's home. In the case of soap operas, their appearances are even more frequent. In some American cities, characters in well-known shows are more familiar than the next door neighbor. Viewers overinvolved with fictive television groups may come to lack real relationships and may assimilate apparently consensual world views that have actually been distorted for dramatic or commercial reasons. On the other hand, those who are isolated for any reason—including schizotypes—may conceivably gain through their television sets vicarious access to an otherwise inaccessible group. To what extent loneliness and, in the case of schizotypes, cognitive autism may be ameliorated in this fashion is really not known.

Future uses of computer terminals—so that work may take place in the home—may have similar complex effects. A real source of both group identification and normative cognitions, the workplace, may give way to solitary interactions with a video screen, with unpredictable effects on the mental health of those who could tolerate going to work. On the other hand, those who for physical or psychologic reasons cannot go to work would then be able to keep their employment. Employment itself signifies group involvement, and income affects the pursuit of nearly every social strategy, at least in our society, so common sense informs us that at least these few people might be enormously benefited by the opportunity to work in their homes.

Other technologic innovations with probable impact on genetically transmitted social strategies are easily enumerated and may be of great importance in determining future trends in psychopathology.

Socioeconomic Factors

Not only technologic innovations but social and economic factors as well are of great significance from a social strategic viewpoint. Alienation and anomie, for example, may worsen the functioning of those predisposed to schizotypy. Extreme pluralism may have much the same effect, though a somewhat increased incidence of schizotypal disorder is a very small price for an intellectually diverse society.

By far the most destructive socioeconomic factor in most patients' lives, and the only one discussed in any detail here, is poverty. In our society, at least, poverty means a chronic and severe lack of money, at least in comparison with most other people. Therefore, to understand the social strategic effects of poverty, the same framework must first be applied to money. This, of course, is a practical framework, very different from the purely symbolic framework of psychoanalytic theory. Much has been made, for instance, of money's symbolic connections: with feces, with babies, with male genitalia. Yet, just as automobiles may stand for penises even as they are used for transportation, so money may stand for things unrelated to its actual use. In fact, none of money's symbolic connections really clarifies its normal use or tells us why essentially normal individuals so desperately fear to be without it.

From a social strategic viewpoint, the most salient aspect of money is its tactical flexibility. In our society, the uses of money point toward nearly every social strategy and, thus, toward nearly every psychologic meaning of which men and women are capable. Money confers control over resources of all kinds, including nutritional, housing, and medicinal ones on which life itself depends. Associated as it is with resource control, pursuit of money has become an arena, too, for sexual competition, and money is the coin in which many parental investments are made. Not only parental investments, but altruistic investments of every kind can be made more easily with money, so its acquisition also subserves kin and reciprocal altruism. Ingroup memberships, too, frequently depend on money, and acceptance in exclusive country clubs, social circles, or elite societies, as well as the desire to live in exclusive neighborhoods, are among the most powerful stimuli to its accumulation. Many of the groups formed by money are purely symbolic (for example, "The type of man/woman who drives a Porsche"), their desirability being the products of advertising agencies, but their lure is no less potent for their unreality.

That money subserves these social strategies is less a biologic fact, however, than a social one. The confusion of biologic and social facts of precisely this sort was the error made by social Darwinists, when they assumed that because the poor starved, competition to be rich was a fact of nature. Instead, that money can serve most of these purposes reflects societal organization, which so defines money, and property ownership of all kinds (see Godelier, 1979), that its social strategic uses follow inevitably. In a society, for instance, that provided children and others with genuinely equal food, housing, medical care, and education, acquiring large amounts of money would no longer subserve either parental or kin-related altruistic strategies. Sexual competition, too, would less likely be served by money and would more likely occur in other arenas. Ingroups formed along other than money lines would further weaken the motivation for pursuing it.

Perhaps the only function of money that is more than simply conventional is its use in reciprocal altruism. This follows from the nature of money itself, which dictates an inevitable relation to the social strategy in question. Reynolds (1981), for instance, argues that human object exchanges in general—for which currency provides a mediating utility function—are evolutionary extrapolations of so-called *prestational behaviors* as they appear in nonhuman primates. As described by Reynolds, prestational behaviors are those subserving reciprocal altruism. Thus, barter, which is one step removed from the use of money, can be seen as the mutually advantageous coincidence of two altruistic and reciprocal acts, in which objects are donated to other persons (see the discussion of mutualism in Chapter 10). By removing the need for simultaneity, and by embedding barter in an extended system of object exchanges, invention of currency enhances the scope of reciprocal altruism and extends its role in societies composed largely of strangers.

It is a curious measure of how money is used in our society that its one inherent function will seem to many readers to be the least salient.

In any society, being deprived of money will be a psychologic hardship only in proportion to the uses that society makes of money. In our society, therefore, being deprived of money is psychologically a very serious matter. In our society, to chronically and severely lack money is to be unable to adequately care for one's children, to be powerless, to be considered a failure, to be an eternal outsider in relation to the very groups society at large so much admires, and to have little scope for participation in altruistic interchanges with either family or friends. Therefore, poverty in our society is a psychologic death sentence, an obstacle to all the activities from which distinctively human lives are made. Though the poor among us may continue to enjoy the sun, the moon, and all the beauties of nature (if they can get to it)—human life, at least from a sociobiologic viewpoint, is largely a social affair. Which particular disorders most characterize those forced into this living death is a matter only the epidemiologists can settle. To some extent, these disorders may reflect the social strategies most vulnerable to disruption, or may emerge as desperate if dysfunctional efforts—such as through drug abuse—to retain what is left of life. But the general principle is clear: In failing to take poverty and its potential social strategic meanings seriously enough, students of abnormal psychology will inevitably confine themselves to excessively personal psychologic stressors. Here, even more than in sexual education, psychologic theory might have something useful to say about public mental health.

Appendices

Appendix A
The Epigenetic Landscape

The well-known *epigenetic landscape* (Waddington, 1956) likens behavioral development to the pathway taken by a ball rolling downhill. The hillside over which the ball rolls is eroded by ramifying furrows, so that the particular course taken depends on initial position and impetus at each of the branch points the ball encounters. No possible position or impetus, which are likened to environmental influences, can cause the ball to diverge from the existing furrows, which are likened to genetically determined potential developmental pathways. Thus, the epigenetic landscape implies that genes provide potential behavioral pathways, of which certain ones are selected by environmental factors.

The epigenetic landscape embodies several assumptions not contained in the notion of instinct-training interlocking (Chapter 2). One assumption is that genes play a restrictive role in behavioral development. They reduce the otherwise infinite number of alternative pathways for behavioral development at any one moment to those represented by the relatively few furrows the rolling ball might actually encounter. This assumption is unfortunate. Although genes may play a largely restrictive role in generating culture (Chapter 3), there is less reason to view their role in individual development in the same terms. Another assumption of the epigenetic landscape is that developmental pathways taken early in life are more important that those taken later. Because the pathways ramify, those at the top of the epigenetic landscape critically restrict those at the bottom. This assumption, like the first, may be misleading. Recent psychiatric research has demonstrated the capacity of adult experience to reverse unfavorable early beginnings, which, in any event, is what psychotherapy is all about. Overstating the persistence of early developmental commitments militates against psychotherapy in exactly the same fashion that complete genetic determinism would. Lastly, the epigenetic landscape assumes that developmental pathways, and therefore behavioral outcomes, are discrete. Balls must follow available channels; pathways intermediate between these are not considered possible. There is little evidence for discrete behavioral options in men and women, and the usual experience of gradual rather than sudden change in clinical situations militates against their existence.

Bateson (1976) suggested that Waddington's epigenetic landscape be supplemented with the notion of *equifinality.* Equifinality is the tendency of self-correcting systems to converge over time on the same stable outcome. Equifinality, however, fails to ameliorate the other assumptions of the epigenetic landscape and is itself of doubtful validity when applied to human behavior. In fact, as applied to behavioral development, equifinality does little more than state the robustness of normal behavioral outcomes to abnormal environmental exigencies, a matter that should be separately studied for each behavior and environment of interest. Because assumptions required for the epigenetic landscape model, with or without equifinality, are unproven for behaviors of psychiatric interest, an interactionist approach based on the notion of instinct-training interlocking is preferable. For purposes of this study, instinct-training interlocking is used as the model for intercalation of genetic and environmentally transmitted information.

Appendix B
The Genetic Viewpoint in Psychologic Theory

In Chapter 2, Freudian sexual theory was shown to reflect a basically Darwinian agenda. Here, two other manifestations of Freud's genetic viewpoint are cited along with other well-known theories essentially genetic in character. First, there is the Freudian notion of psychosexual stage (Sulloway, 1979). Freud saw the childhood progression of sexual interest as a genetically determined developmental sequence. This was akin to developmental sequences marking fetal development, which, at the time, were widely thought to recapitulate the evolutionary history of the species. Thus, Freud thought, the primordial history of the mind itself could be seen in childhood sexual interests.

As with sexual motives, though, the Freudian treatment of psychosexual stage ignores the wider context that we now know to be selectively crucial (Chapter 2). Just as purely sexual motives are biologically intelligible only alongside other innate predispositions serving to obtain sexual opportunities, so the childhood progression of bodily appetites can only be understood by reference to the social developments of which they are key elements. By way of example, the social strategy of the newborn and infant is to develop a close attachment to, and influence over, a female adult caretaker from whom he or she can obtain nourishment and protection. Rosenblatt (1976) has demonstrated that infantile attachment strategies of many mammalian species are served initially by thermotactile, later by olfactory, and still later by visual approach behaviors. Thus, thermotactile, olfactory, and visual stimulus preferences actually subserve social, not simply somatic, ends. In humans, so-called oral needs, far from being the engines of behavior during infancy, are likewise subordinate to the same attachment strategies. Innate dispositions to suck, for example, function not only to obtain nourishment, but also, at least in most primate species, serve to keep the infant safely at the breast (Bowlby, 1969). No intelligible picture of the selective pressures on thermotactile, olfactory, or visual stimulus preferences, or on so-called oral needs, can result if these preferences and needs are torn from their natural setting as tactics in an overall plan to obtain nourishment and protection from an adult female. Similar remarks apply as well to psychosexual developments following the oral stage.

Freud's genetic viewpoint is evident on reading *Totem and Taboo* (1913). His conjecture on the origin of exogamy laws is an evolutionary one, if once again in an outmoded, in this case Lamarckian, framework. Fox (1980), for example, places *Totem and Taboo* in a Darwinian framework and finds its fundamental hypothesis to be biologically sensible. In the Darwinian framework, of course, dispositions do not develop following single events, even one as momentous as Freud's parricide, but from the countless repetitions of similar events over many generations. Had Freud attempted to carry out the Darwinian behavioral program with consistently Darwinian concepts, he might have made of *Totem and Taboo* the earliest work of sociobiology.

Other psychiatric theorists as well have attempted to place mental life in an implicitly genetic context, in each case failing for lack of the conceptual tools now available from ethology and sociobiology. Most of the resulting models rest on the same outmoded somatic impulse theory first contrived by Freud, but others, most notably Jung's (1953) concept of the archetype, are real innovations. The Jungian archetype, although still of considerable interest, is flawed in its original conception by its Lamarckian roots and by the absence of ethologic context. More is said about it in Appendix E. Other theories based on a genetic viewpoint see in organic processes innate urges, considered psychologically prior to the actual behaviors that manifest them. Still others are frankly vitalistic and represent extreme generalizations of the libido theory. Examples of the former category are Freud's (1920) own theory of Eros and Thanatos and theories, like Klein's (1948), that are derivative from it. In the latter category belongs Reich's (1949) biophysical theory. These and other psychologic theories are essentially based on the genetic viewpoint, and each miscarried due to some conceptual flaw.

Appendix C
The Hierarchic Position of Genetic Influence

That the highest levels of behavioral structure must be genetically transmitted contradicts Freudian theory. At the same time, it is highly consistent with more modern psychologic thinking. Freud, of course, considered somatic appetites the vehicles of genetic influence. These appetites, he thought, must first be disciplined by culture if truly adaptive behavior is to occur. From the present viewpoint, though, somatic appetites are response rules of the lowest order. Sucking, for instance, manifests a terminal response rule superior only to that which governs swallowing. Higher order response rules are needed to bring "suckable" objects within reach in the first place. Sexual responses, too, depend on other response rules to make their realization possible. By resting his system on somatic appetites, Freud attempted to build human behavior from the bottom up. To apply the genetic viewpoint, though, it must be built from the top down (Chapter 3).

Freud, however, subscribed to the notion that genetically determined responses should be stereotyped. Since they culminate in stereotyped ways, somatic appetites fulfilled the nineteenth century image of what something biologically determined should be. Yet, the assumption made here suggests that their repetitive, automatic quality is less the indication of their genetic origin than of their extraordinarily low position in response rule hierarchies The lowest levels of such hierarchies govern behaviors for which unusual contingencies are few and far between. Nursing and sexual intercourse, for example, are limited in their variety by mechanical constraints, if they are actually to occur. Only at higher levels of response rule hierarchies is tactical flexibility, and therefore variability of manifested behavior, requisite to achieving adaptive goals. For example, the response strategy that dictates male seductive efforts toward sexually accessible females must result in a wide variety of unstereotyped behaviors highly dependent on social feedback and cultural mores. No single repetitive behavior, only a class of behaviors recognizable by their common predictable outcome, result from the operation of this response strategy.

That behavior is organized from the top down and that the highest level response rules are genetically transmitted are consistent with several major trends in modern behavioral theory. Exemplified by the influential work of Miller, Galanter, and Pribram (1960) and reinforced by both neurophysiologic studies and cybernetic analyses, pyramidal models of behavioral organization serve a critical role in modern psychology. These models view behavior as the result of downward ramifications of feedback loops, subroutines, goal-orientations, or, as in the present discussion, response rules. In ethology, too, Dawkins (1976) has argued for the necessity of hierarchically ordered genetic behavioral programs. Evolutionary simplicity, cybernetic economy, and advantages of "local" executive control are cited in favor of hierarchic ordering. Eibl-Eibesfeldt (1979) discusses the displacement, in ethologic theory, of "universal movement patterns" by "universal strategies of interaction."

In spite of the Freudian preoccupation with lower order stereotyped response rules, psychiatry has also moved toward a strategic view of biologic influence. To mention only one modern theorist, Bowlby (1969) used the term "plan hierarchy" to refer to nested subroutines serving innate attachment purposes. Along with linear chaining and causally hierarchic integration, plan hierarchies were considered responsible for the overall organization of behavior.

Appendix D
The Primacy of Social Life in Modern Psychologic Theory

The Social Arena

As mentioned in Chapter 4, modern behavioral scientists now emphasize the importance of social life, and of social context, to the interpretation of human behavior. It is least surprising, perhaps, that sociologists and anthropologists would take this position. Berger and Luckman, for instance, argue that specifically human phenomena are "inextricably intertwined" with human sociality, and that Homo sapiens is actually "Homo socius" (Berger and Luckman, 1966, p. 51). Montagu goes so far as to define "person" as "an interdependent system of social relationships" (Montagu, 1966, p. 70), which would seem to deny the very possibility of asocial man. More surprising, perhaps, is that students of affective and cognitive processes have recently joined the same camp. Pugh (1977), whose theory of mental functioning is described in Chapter 5, argued that human motivational structures are specifically oriented toward social exigencies rather than toward those imposed by the nonhuman environment. This fact, he thought, explains the human capacity for adaptation to widely varying physical environments. Into each of these men and women import the social systems in which their motivational lives are actually lived.

As for cognition, Humphrey (1976) and Chance (1962) argue that human cognitive capacities evolved largely due to the advantages they confer in dealing with the social, rather than the nonhuman, environment. A similar point has been made with respect to nonhuman primates (Breuer, 1982). As a result, according to Humphrey, human intellect is more akin to a "dedicated " game player—like an electronic chess machine—than to a general purpose computer. The games played by human intellect, of course, are the genetically transmitted social strategies outlined in Chapters 6 through 11. The resulting tendency to read social meaning into asocial natural events, according to Humphrey, also accounts for common superstitions, such as those ubiquitous among gamblers, and perhaps for some aspects of religious belief as well. Chance argues that a positive feedback loop exists between cognitive ability and social complexity, which was responsible for the rapid emergence of human thought as we know it today. According to Chance, greater cognitive abilities lead to more and more complex social environments, which, in turn, create greater selective pressures in favor of cognitive ability. Developmental studies (Trevarthen, 1974; Charlesworth, 1979) confirm that cognitive capacities are largely social in their origin, and that their first uses in life are mainly interpersonal. Cognitive functions reflect the activity of cerebral tissue, and cerebral tissue, to paraphrase Mark and Ervin (1970), embodies yesterday's sociology.

In psychiatry, a social emphasis has been variably overt and implicit. An overt social emphasis characterizes the psychologic tradition founded by Adolph Meyer. Workers in that tradition include Sullivan, whose psychiatric system is called "interpersonal," Fromm-Reichmann, Rosen, Will, and Arieti. Generally, those in the Meyerian tradition plumb psychopathology for its socially adaptive content, or at least for the social purposes the patient might hope to accomplish with it. A closely related approach is taken by other modern theorists, who see psychopathology less as aberrant social adaptation than as social failure. Wolman, for example, argues that all nonorganic mental disorders are "sociogenic" and should be classified according to the "patterns of maladjustment" occurring in the patient's social life (Wolman, 1979, p. 388). The preeminent psychologic tradition with an implicit social emphasis is the Freudian. As noted previously, Freudian psychoanalytic theory treats mental life as the derivative product of transformed somatic impulses. Yet, it was the social, not the physical, world in which somatic impulses met their match, according to Freud, and the uses of somatic impulses, once in harness, were also largely social. Modern revisions of psychoanalytic theory have moved social life even closer to center stage (see Greenberg and Mitchell, 1983).

Suicide

The fact that social adaptation dominates current psychiatric thought is illustrated by recent studies of suicide and anorexia nervosa. Because their interpersonal significance is hidden behind apparent social disinterest, suicide and anorexia nervosa are all too easily interpreted in other than social terms. Suicide, for example, removes mentally disturbed individuals from the social arena entirely. It thus prevents interpersonally adaptive behaviors. The same is all too often true of anorexia nervosa. The anorexic's struggle appears to be one with nature and appetite. When it ends in starvation all social goals have apparently been sacrificed. Yet, in spite of appearances to the contrary, both suicide and anorexia nervosa are now widely understood as serving social purposes. They differ from other social behaviors only in the extent to which their intended effects are fanciful and indirect and not in the degree to which they are directed at the human world.

It is well known, for example, that suicidal fantasies frequently follow bereavement. Fantasies of self-destruction can follow early losses, as of a parent, by many years (Adam, 1982). In these instances, so called liebestod fantasies may play an important etiologic role. Rather than seeking his or her own annihilation, the would-be suicide sees in self-destruction the opportunity for reunion with the lost person (Lifton, 1979). Suicidal fantasies, however, are also frequent among adults who suffered childhood loss of a parent for reasons other than death (Adam, 1982). Here liebestod fantasies can play no causal role. Bowlby (1980), however, cites other social motives contributing to death wishes in such cases. These include the desire for revenge, the desire to coerce the return of an absent attachment figure (Chapter 6), the need to assuage guilt over anger at the absent person, and the wish to elicit help from third parties, among others. The so-called "psychosemantic fallacy," through which the would-be suicide imagines that the self he destroys will be present to witness the social effects of his own destruction (Farborow and Schneidman, 1959), plays an important role in suicidal behaviors motivated by dependency or revenge wishes.

Tiger (1979a) makes the interesting point that relatively few suicide attempts are such as to do what laymen would consider violent injury. Thus, in spite of the availability of methods for violent and instantaneous self-destruction, suicidal methods are generally chosen to kill with the least external damage. The preponderance of cosmetically inoffensive suicide attempts is consistent with the social purposes suicide usually serves and with the notion that most suicidal individuals have, at least in fantasy, not actually renounced self-preservation. Only in schizophrenia is suicide frequently violent (Lindelius and Kay, 1973), most likely as the result of delusional thinking. Of the nonpsychotic exceptions to Tiger's rule, many are intended as expressions of hostility toward those who will discover the suicide's body.

Significantly, too, even the inclusive fitness effects of suicide may depend on largely social factors. In some circumstances, beneficial effects on kin—whose reproductive fitness might be correspondingly enhanced—could balance the suicide's loss of his or her own reproductive opportunities. In fact, the clinical circumstances in which suicide frequently occurs suggest that genetic tolerance for it is highly restrictive. Perceived uselessness to loved ones and the feeling of being a burden are grave prognostic signs in the patient with suicidal ideation (Gray, 1978). These perceptions compound the increased suicidal risks resulting from age and illness, both of which signify decreased reproductive prospects. Conversely, the fear that one's self-destruction might harm loved ones seems to provide a bulwark against suicidal impulses and generally reassures the anxious clinician. In certain impoverished societies, culturally sanctioned self-destruction likewise serves to aid kin, in this case through preservation of resources for those with better reproductive prospects.

Anorexia Nervosa

As for anorexia nervosa, the problem for a social psychology lies in demonstrating that the apparent denial of physiologic needs has other than physiologic significance. Drive-defense, or Freudian, psychology actually faced a similar problem, in that it was necessary to show how denial of one physiologic need could be determined by exigencies of another. The classical psychoanalytic resolution of this problem, that anorexia symbolized a renunciation of oral impregnation fantasies (Waller, et al., 1940), dominated psychologic treatment of anorexia until recent years. Bruch (1973), who has pioneered the social investigation of anorexia nervosa, claims never to have encountered this dynamic except among those to whom it had been suggested by previous therapists. To establish that denial of physiologic needs serves social ends, however, requires that anorexic manipulation of eating behavior have tactical significance in the "interpersonal field" (Bruch, 1973, p. 5). This clinical fact, if the term is not oxymoronic, has now been firmly established by Bruch and others. Thus, even in the presence of normal physiologic responses to either satiation or deprivation (Silverstone and Russell, 1967; Stunkard, 1959), anorexics and, for that matter, the pathologically obese can be shown to employ abnormal eating behaviors for social purposes.

Both universal and idiosyncratic factors may conspire to distort eating behavior in socially significant ways. So-called oral behaviors are innate social tactics from the very beginning of life. The significance of feeding, weaning, and nonnutritive sucking to maternal-infant attachment strategies is discussed in Chapter 6. Genetic and cultural *ritualization* processes by which gluttony or food refusal assume communicative value are discussed in Appendix E. That food refusal in particular has ritualized social significance for normal persons is evidenced by the universal power of self-induced starvation. To "fast against others"—sometimes to quite literally starve on their doorstep—is understood as a powerful and coercive social tactic that cannot be readily ignored (Bruch, 1973). On a more personal level, those prone to distort eating behaviors for social ends lack age-appropriate social skills, or tactics in the terminology employed here, with which they could pursue social ends more directly. In particular, social incompetence manifested in lack of self-direction, autonomy, and sense of personal effectiveness is notable in all the case histories reported by Bruch (1973). In objective studies, those with eating disorders are frequently found to have poor family, occupational, and community adjustments (see, for example, Johnson and Berndt, 1983). Social ineffectiveness, dependency, isolativeness, and lack of self-identity create a picture superficially resembling schizotypy (Chapter 14), although attachment concerns more typical of depressed and borderline patients (Chapter 13) are more often than not the critical factors. Certain specific cognitions are also prerequisite to the social use of eating behaviors. Bruch (1973), for example, cites disidentification with and contempt for the body—which may even be viewed as someone else's property—as a common precondition to development of eating disorders, and other social cognitions may play critical roles in particular cases.

One essential distinction, which Bruch (1973) considers the dividing line between atypical and primary anorexia, is whether food refusal per se or only emaciation is necessary to the patient's social purposes. When food refusal is the important factor, weight loss is an accidental by-product and is usually not severe. Specific social purposes served by food refusal, which often occurs in the course of other psychiatric disorders, are to express criticism of or hostility toward attachment figures, to demonstrate moral superiority over those not strong enough to resist "pleasures of the flesh," or to proclaim independence and autonomy from suffocating parental caretakers.

Specific social purposes served by emaciation tend to be somewhat different. Bruch (1973) describes primary anorexics as excessively sensitive to both criticism and praise. Typically, a cruel remark causes an initially overweight young woman to diet. As she loses weight, the future anorexic reaps praise, together with a sense of social competence that had previously eluded her. Sexual uncertainties brought on by puberty can be put off by achieving an asexual page boy appearance—even menstruation can be halted through emaciation—and the prepubertal state of childhood can be symbolically lengthened. These latter motives are particularly clear for "Nadia" and "Ellen West," well-known patients described by Janet and Binswanger, respectively (see Binswanger, 1958). For the anorexic patient, emaciation and illness will further galvanize attention that may never have been voluntarily given, even as further food refusal demonstrates pseudoindependence and moral superiority.

Because anorexia is a form of social dysfunction, recovery cannot be equated either with resumption of eating or with weight gain. Eating and weight gain may occur without improvement in social functioning (Bruch, 1973) or may be followed by suicide (Blinder, et al., 1970), another social tactic for those lacking alternative skills. Bruch (1973) described long-term follow-up data on forty-five primary anorexic patients. Of the twenty-four with normal follow-up weights, only thirteen led anything resembling a normal social life. The remainder led severely restricted lives dogged with continuing obsessional preoccupations. Similar remarks apply to the psychologic meaning of gluttony and obesity and to their psychotherapeutic treatment.

Thus, even superficially private phenomena are treated by modern psychotherapists as fundamentally social.

Appendix E Specific Proximate Mechanisms

Perceptual Mechanisms

A proximate causal model was presented in Chapter 5. Acting in concert, perceptual mechanisms, cognitive models, appraisal processes, and behavioral subroutines produce adherence to genetically transmitted response strategies. Here, attention is directed to each separate mental mechanism and to their psychologic implications.

Innate perceptual mechanisms attuned to reproductively meaningful aspects of human social interactions are well documented. Mechanisms of this kind are responsible for the attentional salience of the human face and for categorical perception of speech sounds, which occurs even before language is learned. Other examples might be given, but two will suffice to illustrate operation of these mechanisms as a whole. First, however, the information-processing function of a perceptual mechanism is greatly clarified by consideration of the philosophic position that Robinson (1979) calls "constructive realism."

Constructive realism, which treats sensory reports as "natural signs" of real objects and events, is distinct from "common sense realism," which argues that sensory reports reproduce natural objects or events on a point-by-point basis. Both are consistent with evolutionary theory, since either signal validity or reproductive veracity may be enforced by natural selection. Modern neurophysiologic evidence, however, suggests that no perceptual mechanisms are merely reproductive, as common sense realism argues, but that filtering of irrelevant information occurs at all levels of the sensory pathways. Reproductive information is retained only when knowledge of "things as they are" (Robinson, 1979, p. 39) is essential to behavioral performance. Perception approaches the model of constructive realism when what is required is not a response to a specific physical configuration, but a rejoinder to a situation the physical details of which are unimportant. This is the case, for instance, in using certain common objects, the actual details of which are only poorly represented in memory (Nickerson and Adams, 1982). This is also the case for most if not all social perceptions, which more often than not are less important for their physical details than for what they signify. Smiles, laughter, and crying, for example, need not be perceived in physical detail, but only as signs of social situations that are likely to demand adaptive responses. As a result, social functioning in particular should be highly dependent on perceptual mechanisms that are essentially semiotic. From physical configurations these mechanisms extract natural signs, the signal validity of which is insured by natural selection. Social perceptions, in other words, should approach the model of constructive realism.

Of all the physical configurations from which natural signs relevant to social functioning can be extracted, none is more important than the human face. Consequently, the human facial gestalt commands special attention from the first hours of life (Spitz, 1965), long before conditioning experiences could produce an interest in it. Apparently, the human face is a preferred visual stimulus from the very beginning. Later in life, faces must be identified as familiar or unfamiliar, and if the former, then according to their owner. So important are facial recognition mechanisms to biologic survival that they are subserved by neuroanatomic regions distinct from those involved in pattern recognition as a whole. Thus, damage to inferior temporal and occipital cortex can result in inability to recognize familiar faces without concomitant impairments in other pattern recognition tasks (Geshwind, 1979). Also, special aspects of facial appearance, such as foreshortened features, are apparently used as innate clues to immaturity and trigger affective responses important to maternal-infant interactions in many mammalian species (Chapter 6).

Studies of speech sound categorization provide a more detailed view of an innate perceptual mechanism attuned to socially important signals. Although human speech sounds actually vary continuously along whatever dimensions are measured, certain boundary processes effectively "quantize" speech sounds into categorically perceived phonemes. These are then used as linguistic building blocks (for a review of categorical speech perception see Marler, 1979). Like facial recognition mechanisms, phonemic categorization processes depend on specialized cortical loci distinct from those subserving other linguistic and intellectual functions (Luria, 1981). Conditioning experiments have demonstrated that categorical perception of speech sounds occurs in infants as early as one month of age (Eimas, et al., 1971). Not only can appearance of these categorical processes not be accounted for by differential reinforcement schedules resulting from adult language use, but some of the categorical distinctions made by infants may not even be employed in the particular language they will later learn. Thus, infants can make sound distinctions they will later lose through disuse.

Presumably, innate sound categorization mechanisms provide for economy in the acquisition and maintenance of later linguistic skills. One theory of this economy is presented by Liberman (1979), who argues that the innate categorization of speech sounds proceeds as if governed by knowledge of the distinct movements available to the human vocal tract. Ploog (1979) made the same point as Liberman. The "key to the phonetic code," according to Ploog (1979, p. 709), "is the manner of its production." In other words, innate categorization mechanisms recover from a degraded, continuous auditory signal information concerning discrete sequential movements made by the vocal tract from which it originated. If Liberman and Ploog are correct, the function of speech is to inform the listener of the movements of the speaker's vocal tract. The relation of phonemic classification mechanisms to potential movements of the human vocal tract may also explain why infants, whose vocal tracts are equipotential with respect to all human languages, are able to make phonemic distinctions irrelevant to the language they will later acquire.

Actually, the "motor theory" of phonemic classification is only one aspect of so-called "synthetic theory," which argues that all aspects of speech perception, from phonemic to propositional, proceed by formation of educated guesses concerning the speaker's behavior or intent (Clark and Clark, 1977). Speech interpretation at the highest levels may depend on the same principle. Luria (1981), for instance, argues that comprehension of the "inner sense" of linguistic communications—meaning beyond even propositional content—depends on reconstruction of the motivational state that led the speaker to communicate in the first place. Clear examples in which inner sense and propositional content diverge are provided by proverbs and certain indirect requests. When a speaker, for example, tells a self-pitying listener that "every cloud has a silver lining," the motive for the vocal act is understood to be encouragement or criticism, depending on the particular relationship and situation. It is utterly divorced from the communication of factual information concerning clouds. Similarly, "Do you mind closing the window?" is understood not to be motivated by curiosity concerning the listener's tolerance for effort, but to signify a desire that he or she close the window. Because motivational reconstruction is inevitably self-referential—it proceeds, that is, on the basis of what the listener would be intending were he or she to emit the same vocalizations—the synthetic theory in general is of considerable psychologic interest. Insofar as other social perceptions proceed on the same principle, synthetic theory may be a model for projective defenses. Knowing, for example, that one's own behavior is motivated by hatred, greed, or lust, one might be likely to infer that motive in others' behavior. When one's own actions are disavowed (see Schafer, 1978), the clinical picture of projection might then emerge.

Finally, that human infants possess innate phonemic categorization processes, like species-specific sensitivities to avian songs (Ploog, 1979), violates the so-called "principle of equipotentiality," an assumption of many behaviorists. Discriminant cues that fall into different innate sound categories can more readily be learned than those within a category. If humans stand more ready to learn some distinctions than others, then that readiness, and not merely reinforcement schedules, determines behavioral outcomes. Insofar as social categorizations in general follow the model of speech perception, then simple behavioral theories of social life will be found to be vitiated.

Cognitive Models

That animals form internal representations or maps of the physical environment has been known since Tolman (1932) first demonstrated unreinforced maze learning. Primates in particular have a propensity to organize discrete learned associations into coherent spatial models (Menzel, 1973). That at least higher animals also form self-representations is indicated by certain experiments and by the predictive importance of *resource holding power*. Gallup (1970, 1977), for example, demonstrated that apes can recognize their mirror images, and that they associate points on the image with correct locations on their own bodies. Resource holding power, which is discussed in Chapter 7, is the individual's capacity to hold resources against hostile members of the same species. Estimates of one's own resource holding power, in comparison to estimates of an opponent's resource holding power, determine inimical tactics. Humans, of course, form representations not only of the environment and of themselves, but also of other persons and of their motivational structure (Heider, 1958). Proximate mechanisms causing the accretion of these models are briefly discussed in Chapter 5. Specific cognitive models are discussed in Chapters 13 through 15, in relation to the psychopathologic syndromes in which they are prominent. Here, only the question of stereotypic models need be discussed.

Although it is difficult to understand how linguistically encoded memory stores could be genetically acquired, similar constraints do not apply to memory stores encoded in nonlinguistic form. Readers interested in alternative forms of memory and thought encoding and their psychologic significance are referred to the large amount of literature accumulated in this area (see, for example, Anderson and Bower, 1973; Chomsky, 1957; Kintsch, 1972; Kosslyn, 1975; Norman, 1976; Paivio, 1971; Piaget, 1955; Rumelhart, et al., 1972; Searle, 1969; Shapiro, 1979; Shepard, et al., 1975; Tulving, 1972; Vygotsky, 1962). Since linguistic encoding requires both a lexicon and syntax, genetic transmission of linguistically encoded information would seem to require a wholly private language code existing from the moment of birth. Means would have to exist, moreover, for the integration of innate linguistic information with later-acquired information encoded in the same form, a requirement that further strains credulity. By contrast, innately acquired nonlinguistic memories presuppose only iconic templates to which later experience could be gradually assimilated. Not only is this presupposition plausible, but something like it is known to occur, at least on the elementary levels required for visual and auditory stimulus recognition. The innate responsiveness of the newborn infant to the human face, for example, betrays an innate iconic representation of facial features. This is true regardless of whether that representation is discretely stored or is somehow a distributed feature of infantile perceptual processing as a whole. In the present model, cognitive models are functionally continuous with perceptual feature detectors. Both serve to refine sensory input to central decision mechanisms.

On the output side, the motor theory of phoneme classification has implications for innate memory. Since young children can distinguish phonemes they themselves cannot distinctively pronounce (Clark and Clark, 1977), the motor theory implies that innate knowledge of motor sequences necessary to produce a behavioral result antedates the capacity for actually performing those sequences.

The more interesting question, and one that poses a greater imaginative challenge, is whether higher order nonlinguistic models—templates not on the order of visual patterns or even motor sequences, but pertaining instead to social or moral patterns—can be acquired through genetic transmission. These models, unlike those relevant to visual perception or motor acts, would show their activity through stereotypically experienced nonlinguistic ideas. These might be predictably elicited by specific social situations but would not be entirely explicable in terms of the individual's learning history. Nor could they be accounted for by universal features of the human environment. They would be conceptually similar to Jung's (1953) archetypal images, which are also nonlinguistic ideas elicited in response to specific environmental exigencies. Lumsden and Wilson (1981), too, speculate that innate prototypic "knowledge structures" may account for archetypal phenomena.

Unfortunately, Jung's notion of the archetype has been received with even more incredulity than it deserves. In part, disbelief in archetypal phenomena resulted from a failure to place them in an information-processing context that might make them scientifically more palatable. In part, disbelief resulted from Jung's Lamarckian framework. If contemporary men and women were predisposed to ideas merely because their ancestors had experienced them, humanity would be burdened by even more foolishness than is presently the case. In a Darwinian framework, however, the archetype appears more sensible. If individuals whose brain structure predisposed them to produce certain socially complex nonlinguistic ideas were more fit than those with different brain structure, then the predisposition to produce those ideas would become fixed by natural selection. This would occur regardless of whether enhanced fitness was directly related to either the particular brain structure, the consequent ideas, or both. Here, "socially complex" means that the ideas in question refer to social exigencies rather than to audiovisual stimulus features.

Yet another source of disdain for Jungian archetypes lies in the bitter intramural rivalries between Freudian and Jungian analysts. The former have painted their opponents as "soft-headed," a characterization furthered by Jung's overly mystical approach to what should be an evolutionary issue (see Rieff, 1968). Although Jungians may well be "soft-headed," and Freudians the virtuous opposite, the archetypal notion has never belonged to the critically deficient. In fact, under the rubric "primal fantasy," Freud (1917) himself proposed a closely related concept, which became essential to the Freudian view of religion (Freud, 1927, 1939; Rizzuto, 1979). Encompassing many of the sexual and punishment fantasies of childhood, primal fantasies, according to Freud, comprise part of the human phylogenetic endowment. "In them," Freud wrote, "the individual reaches beyond his own experience into primeval experience at points where his own experience has been too rudimentary." Freud, too, founded his concept on Lamarckian principles, which resulted in particularly unfortunate consequences for his theory of incest fantasies.

Although familial obsessional and phobic ideas (Epstein, 1980) and dream content (Epstein and Collie, 1976) have been documented, it is extremely difficult to prove that more common ideas are innate. To establish that particular common ideas result from innate memory contents, methods must be found for objectively judging homologies between products from different cultures. Evidence must exist that homologies detected in this way are neither coincidental nor result from common cultural or environmental features. Evidence must be gathered that they occur in homologous social situations, in order to demonstrate equivalence of meaning. Experimental alternatives to cumbersome naturalistic studies of this kind are prohibited by ethical considerations. And even if methodologically sophisticated studies were addressed to these issues, they would nonetheless fail to carry much weight among most social scientists, who argue endlessly over the merits of far more straightforward studies. Still, it is worth noting that the existence of genetically transmitted nonlinguistic world models relevant to complex social decisions is neither neurologically nor sociobiologically nonsensical and requires no Lamarckian assumptions. Inherited nonlinguistic models present no particular problem of integration with acquired models of the same kind and would be consistent with data on inherited audiovisual stimulus templates. Like templates, models relevant to complex social functioning may be either discretely stored or be a distributed property of neural structures. The purported practical advantages of their emergence and recognition, as in Jungian dream analysis, is beyond the scope of this study.

Finally, genetic factors unrelated to brain structure or function may nonetheless predispose individuals toward certain idiosyncratic world models. These may be of particular importance to abnormal psychology. Dunn (1979), for example, noted that among mammals a strong inverse relationship exists between milk protein content and frequency of infant feedings. Even within a species, milk protein content and frequency of feedings are inversely related. Bottle-fed human infants for instance, receive higher protein milk than breast-fed infants and sleep correspondingly longer between feedings. It is easy to imagine that a maternal genetic tendency to produce higher protein breast milk might lead to longer infant sleep periods, to less stress on the mother, to a more placid infant-mother relationship, and eventually to formation of an infantile world model in which others are thought to be willing helpers. Because the infant would also inherit the maternal genes governing milk protein content, genetic endowment and cognitive models would coincide, although without any mediating neural changes. Numerous examples of distal genetic predispositions to particular cognitive models, all equally hypothetical, are easily imagined.

Appraisal Processes

A fundamental discovery of modern psychiatric research is that affects are subjective correlates of definable neurophysiologic states. This view of affect, with its extraordinary implications for abnormal psychology, is based on several types of experimental and clinical evidence. Studies of antidepressants and lithium, for example, demonstrate that alleviation of strong affects requires specific neurochemical changes, depending upon the affect involved, and that neurochemical properties of pharmacologic agents can be used to predict their clinical usefulness in mood disorders. Conversely, drugs or diseases inducing mood disorders exert consistent neurochemical influences in the opposite direction. Physical manipulation of the brain, such as electroconvulsive treatment, or stimulation or lesioning of specific brain structures, is also regularly associated with prominent affective changes, which may occur in the absence of apparent cognitive impairments. These and many other facts overwhelmingly support the theory that specific affects accompany specific neurophysiologic states in the same way that a variety of physical sensations accompany physiologic states (for example, hunger with low blood sugar).

Whether the correlation of subjectively experienced affect and neurophysiologic state is best conceived in materialistic or idealistic terms, or even in terms of psychophysical parallelism, is not at issue here. Nor is the chain of mediating events particularly relevant. Various models of the interrelationship of subjective experience and physiologic states are well reviewed elsewhere (Gray, 1978). What is significant in the present context is why correlations should exist between subjective experience and physiologic states in the first place. In particular, why are a few central nervous system parameters sufficiently linked with central attentional and information-processing mechanisms as to be correlated with affective experience? What distinguishes these parameters from countless others having no specific representation in subjective life? What function do such associations perform?

Subjective perceptions of bodily processes are of some relevance here. These suggest that subjective attention is allocated to bodily parameters only when central decision processes must take part in their regulation. Bodily parameters never represented in subjective experience are those that never require centrally generated behaviors for their regulation. Blood pressure is such a parameter, as are the vast majority of physiologic measures only distally related to overt behavior. Bodily parameters that do enter subjective experience also go unrepresented most of the time but come to subjective attention when centrally generated behaviors are required to supplement their lower order control. Blood sugar, for example, becomes associated with subjective sensations only when endocrine-metabolic processes fail to maintain it, so that eating behavior is required. Before Banting and Best discovered insulin no overt behavior could acutely lower blood sugar. Hence, humans have few or no sensations associated with excessively high blood sugar levels. Body temperature and arterial oxygen levels follow the same pattern. Body temperature is subjectively experienced only when overt behavior, such as seeking shelter, is requisite to its maintenance. Oxygen supply manifests itself in subjective life only after lower order respiratory mechanisms have failed to prevent its depletion. In each of these instances, the correlation of bodily parameter and subjective experience signifies the need for central decision processes to generate behaviors supplementary to lower order regulatory mechanisms.

If the correlation between affective experience and neurophysiologic state follows the pattern of other subjectively experienced bodily parameters, then the affective experience must also signify the need for overt behavior. But what are the biologically vital parameters for which behaviors are required? What critical exigencies are reflected in the neurophysiologic states associated with subjective affects? Hunger clearly reflects prior appraisals of blood sugar (among other parameters). What appraisals have occurred prior to experiences of depression, euphoria, love, or anger?

In terms of a social strategic model, the answers are obvious. Correlations between affective experience and neurophysiologic states signify, for the most part, social appraisals. They signal the social engagement of central decision processes, from which socially adaptive behaviors emerge. At times of emotional experience, the biologically critical exigencies stimulating centrally generated responses are largely social in nature and only secondarily related to the nonhuman environment. Subjective experience verifies the social nature of most emotions: Typically, we get angry when fighting with others, lonely when lacking in company, anxious when others threaten us, and happy when they satisfy our needs. Affects experienced following nonsocial appraisals, such as when threatened by falling rocks, are of circumscribed psychologic importance if nonetheless vital to physical survival. They constitute a minority of emotional experiences and may be subjectively distinct from their more frequent social counterparts. The neurophysiologic mechanisms associated with affectively experienced neurophysiologic states are therefore social appraisal processes, committed to noting selectively critical complex social configurations. In terms of the model of strategic responding outlined in Chapter 5, they superimpose valuations on social configurations detected by antecedent perceptual mechanisms and data reduction (or cognitive) processes and comprise the final mental mechanisms prior to the central decision process itself.

That affects signify active appraisals, and are not the passive consequences of situational factors, was appreciated by Aristotle and is a key tenet of modern philosophies of mind (see Sennett, 1981). Extension of personal responsibility into the emotional sphere, a point important to several modern psychotherapeutic methods, stems from this viewpoint. The specifically social nature of affectively experienced appraisals has been noted as well by students of animal behavior. Reynolds (1981, p. 171), for example, considered the social nature of emotional experience "fundamental" to the ethologic viewpoint and described affectivity as a "system specialized for the assessment and programming of social action."

It should be obvious that the neurophysiologic states associated with subjective affect will act as reinforcers. That is, behaviors leading to the environmental configurations that elicit those states will be strengthened or attenuated, depending on whether the configuration is positively or negatively valued. Therefore, the social strategic model being developed here is essentially a learning theory model of social interaction. It differs from behaviorist learning theories only in that the reinforcing valence of selectively critical social configurations is held to be genetically determined and embedded in the neurophysiologic processes that lead to affectively experienced states.

Disinterest in the selective origin of reinforcement has comprised the most extraordinary intellectual blind spot of modern behavioral science (see Robinson, 1979, for the following references). Pavlov, for example, studied associations between relatively restricted stimuli and responses. He evinced little interest in the unconditioned stimuli or responses to which associations actually formed. Similarly, Thorndike's "Law of Effect" stated that discomfort or satisfaction to the "animal will" would respectively weaken or enhance stimulus-response bonds. Yet, the "animal will" itself lay outside the boundary of Thorndike's psychologic system. Hull and Spence attempted to remedy this situation by tying primary reinforcers to the defense of physiologic homeostasis, a solution that accounts for learning by starved, thirsty, or pained animals but fails even to account for reinforcement by sexual satisfaction. In any event, modern behavioral scientists see the defense of homeostasis occurring more peripherally and, in large part, at the social level. By maintaining his or her place in a social group, for example, the individual ensures access to physiologically required resources. Had Hull and Spence really appreciated the complexity of homeostatic defense, they would have arrived at an entirely different psychology: a psychology in which a detailed biologic structuralism forms the body on which wags an associationist tail, rather than vice versa.

Unfortunately, Hull and Spence are the high point of this sorry behaviorist history. So-called "contiguity" theorists, who argued that mere contiguity between stimulus and response results in learned associations, wrote of "visceral clues" and stimulus-created "problems" to account for the adaptive course of learning. Yet, they never regarded these as proper objects of psychologic study. Skinner and his followers went so far as to define reinforcers by their effects: Reinforcers, according to Skinner, are those procedures or stimuli the presence or removal of which alters response probability. Biologic, or any other, accounts of reinforcers were specifically eschewed. Not surprisingly, Skinnerian psychology has been most closely identified with the training of unnatural behaviors in a species living only in laboratories. Even the modern cognitive behaviorists, who reintroduced mediating cognitive processes between stimulus and response, have actually done nothing to remedy the bankrupt behaviorist treatment of reinforcement, from which their own accounts still suffer.

The marked hostility of many behaviorists toward biologic accounts of reinforcement stands in sharp contrast to the curious affection for behaviorist notions found among many physiologic psychologists (Robinson, 1979). Robinson attributes this unrequited love of behaviorism, which has had conferred on it a bogus respectability, to a shared ontologic viewpoint. Both behaviorists and physiologic psychologists aim for a purely proximate, mechanistic account of animal behavior. Uncritical acceptance of behaviorist ideas by biologic psychologists is an intellectual oddity potentially corrected by an ultimate causal account of subjectively teleologic mental events.

That a model featuring innate social strategies may devolve into a form of social learning theory should only surprise those who draw sharp and outdated boundaries between the innate and acquired. Alexander (1979) also emphasized the importance of social learning in the development of evolutionarily significant behavior patterns, and Symons (1979) noted that learning abilities are essential for expression of species-typical behaviors in imperfectly predictable environments. Learning abilities, in other words, are requisite to response invariance, rather than signs of behavioral anarchy.

How many social appraisal mechanisms, dependent on neurophysiologic processes and leading to affective experiences, can be usefully distinguished? Are there, as Watson (1919) argued, only love, hate, and fear in the human affective repertoire? Or are there innumerable affects, distinguishable only by fine nuances? And, however many there are, how may they be classified? The discussion thus far suggests that affectively experienced social appraisal processes may be classified on at least three dimensions. The first of these is the social situation eliciting the affectively experienced state and whether the affect is such as to maintain or interrupt that situation. Affectively experienced appraisals elicited by the same social situation and carrying the same valence are likely to play functionally overlapping roles in maintenance of at least one genetically transmitted response strategy. Insofar as these same appraisals may also be elicited by differing social situations, or carry opposite valences with respect to common ones, then one will also subserve strategies in which the other plays no role. Depression and anger, for example, are both aversive affects elicited by disruption of certain social bonds (Chapter 13), and therefore play similar roles in social strategies calling for the maintenance of those bonds. However, anger also occurs alone in response to certain social situations, and then it contributes to social strategies little dependent on the appraisal experienced as depression.

The second dimension on which social appraisal processes can be classified is the neurophysiologic. Since appraisal processes of this type depend on neurophysiologic processes leading to affectively experienced states, they may be classified according to the biochemistry and physiology known to be associated with them. Not only will differences between appraisal processes emerge in the neurophysiologic dimension, but certain evolutionary and functional relationships between appraisal processes may be indicated by sharing of common physiologic pathways. Classified according to their physiology, for example, depression and euphoria appear as polar opposites. Apparently, the neurophysiologic states subjectively experienced as depression and euphoria rely on opposite changes in common neurochemical mechanisms (Berger and Barchas, 1977). Thus, pharmacologic treatment of depression may cause euphoria, and vice versa. Similar sharing of physiologic pathways may typify other appraisal processes as well. Love and hatred, for example, may turn out to be dependent on common brain mechanisms, as may fear and rage. Depending on their overlap along dimensions other than the neurophysiologic, some affectively different states may even be considered referable to single, but multivalent, appraisal processes rather than to be wholly separate phenomena. This, however, is more a matter of terminology than substance.

The third dimension according to which appraisal processes may be categorized is that of feeling tone, or subjective experience. With regard to affective nuances, though, little agreement can be expected between differing individuals or across differing cultures.

Other bases for categorization of valuative processes include expressive gestures (Tomkins, 1962), autonomic activation patterns, and various experimental paradigms. As for expressive gestures, although evidence points to a finite number of discrete *phylogenetically ritualized* affective signals, a one-to-one relationship between these gestures and underlying appraisal processes cannot be assumed. Those affectively experienced valuations that are profitably communicated may be associated with more than one ritualized gesture, while other valuations may be associated with none. Similarly, autonomic activation may or may not accompany specific valuative judgments or may accompany several at once. Pugh's (1977) suggestion that autonomic measures can reveal components in the human valuative system assumes a simple relationship that may or may not characterize affective experiences. The same considerations apply to experimental paradigms. Although Pugh (1977) suggests that highly refined choice box paradigms might be used to study valuative processes, behavioral experiments are hardly likely to yield data of superior consistency to that coming from other experimental methods. If an experimental, rather than naturalistic, classification of appraisal processes is desired, priority should be given to studies using neurophysiologic, rather than behavioral, dependent variables.

Statistical methods may reduce complex behaviors to their underlying components (Van Hoof, 1973; Dawkins, 1976), but the relation between behavioral components discovered with these methods and single appraisal processes is far from obvious. Therefore, statistical methods alone are unlikely to prove useful in studying underlying valuative dimensions.

Deciding which alternative classification is superior depends on one's purposes. Throughout this study appraisal processes are categorized according to their social elicitors and functional valences. This method of categorization emphasizes the social function of appraisal processes and their role as proximate mechanisms promoting adherence to genetically transmitted social response strategies. A neurophysiologist, who is less interested in psychosocial functioning than in accurate delineations of brain states, might categorize appraisal processes according to their neurophysiologic substrates. Social elicitors might enter the field of neurophysiologic inquiry only as provocative stimuli. Lastly, an artist may be totally disinterested in neurophysiology and interested in social elicitors only as background for the exploration of subjective experience. For him or her, phenomenologic distinctions between finely shaded affects are of paramount importance.

Other theoretical points are also worth mentioning. Since given social configurations may activate several appraisal processes, each of which must be simultaneously optimized, output of appraisal mechanisms must be combined to form a superordinate *utility function.* As described in Chapter 5, utility functions are summary indices used for evaluating various response options. They (algebraically) summarize many variables (in this case, the valuations of specific appraisal mechanisms) that are then expressed along a common numerical dimension. Central decision mechanisms, by acting to maximize (or minimize, depending on the polarity convention) the anticipated superordinate utility function, ensure that behavior pursues maximally adaptive ends. In many situations, tactical subroutines optimizing the superordinate utility function will also optimize each individual appraisal process. In other cases, though, appraisal processes, through their varying contributions to the utility function, may actually compete for behavioral control. But the relative weight given to each appraisal process in the superordinate utility function—the influence that process will have over behavioral decisions—must itself be a product of natural selection. By way of illustration, individuals who failed to heed panic when also angry would no doubt have perished from ancestral human populations. Combination of individual appraisal processes into a superordinate utility function also embodies their hierarchical integration, which was postulated for stopping rules by Dawkins (1976). It also recalls Wilson's (1978a) argument that the mind must be structured as a "republic" of innate schemata competing among themselves for control of behavioral "decision centers." Piaget (1978), too, stressed the importance of "innate combinatorial mechanisms" through which elementary tendencies are combined into purposive wholes.

If individual appraisal processes, each of which promotes adherence to one or several social response strategies, influence behavioral decisions only through their weight in a superordinate utility function, then many tactical subroutines will likely accomplish several different strategic purposes. Behavior, that is, will tend to be overdetermined in relation to its deep strategic structures, a point that was also made, but in rather different terms, by psychoanalysts (Fenichel, 1945). In the following section, tactical subroutines are treated as strategically unidimensional, subserving single strategic purposes at any one time. Yet the actual overdetermination of their selection, and the compromise that selection represents between competing appraisal processes, should not be forgotten. These are fundamental consequences of having at least several social appraisal mechanisms, two or more of which may be simultaneously activated.

Finally, the central role given by the model of Chapter 5 to an appraisal process based utility function is of some historical interest. Essentially, the anticipated rate of positively valued change for this function drives behavior, just as anticipated discharge of libidinal energy was said to drive behavior in the Freudian model. Nor did Freud originate this basic idea. The history of psychologic thought is largely the history of successive "quantity theories," each of which attributed behavioral motivation to the vicissitudes of some inner substance (see Gray, 1978). Hippocrates, for example, thought that both somatic and behavioral disturbances were caused by superabundance of one or another "humor," a theory passed on to future generations through Galen. Hippocratic pathophysiology, in fact, is strongly reminiscent of the psychoanalytic theory of so-called "actual neuroses" (Fenichel, 1945). To release excess "vapors," Paracelsus scarified the toes, fingers, and scalp of manic patients. Willis, after whom the cerebral blood vessels are named, regarded the flow of "animal spirits" from blood to brain as the cause of certain mental disorders. Cullen, who first used the term "neurosis," attributed mental illness to abnormalities in the quantity of cerebrospinal fluid, and Mesmer believed that "animal magnetism," his term for what is now called hypnosis, cured illness by inducing movements of fluids within the body. Like Freud, Janet founded his dynamic psychiatry on the notion of psychic energy, and he coined the term "psychasthenic" to denote those patients in whom it seemed depleted. In an effort to replenish psychasthenic patients, nineteenth century practitioners applied electrical devices to limbs, head, neck, or other bodily parts. Meyer's theory of reaction types also centered on the notion of psychic energy, and he incorporated the root "erg" in the names he gave for mental illnesses. Thus, merergasia, parergasia, thymergasia, anergasia, and oligergasia denoted neurosis, psychosis, affective illness, organic brain syndrome, and mental subnormality, respectively.

In ethology, too, virtually every innate behavior was once thought to require its own "action specific energy" (Lorenz, 1950), an idea now in disrepute (see Hinde, 1960).

Undoubtedly, the various quantity theories cited above are historically interrelated. Furthermore, other scientific developments, such as those in nineteenth century physical science, are responsible for the specific forms in which these theories appear. Yet, the intuitive appeal of quantity theories must be considerable, for quantitative formulations of behavioral vitality actually antedated development of analogous physical concepts (Lifton, 1979). Nor are quantitative formulations restricted to psychologic theorists, who are likely to be more aware of scientific fashion and history. Lay persons, too, explicitly formulate motivation in essentially quantitative terms. Thus, individuals are said to possess or lack "energy," or to become temporarily "exhausted," suggesting they have run out of something. Alternatively, they may be "drained" or even "depleted." "Running on empty," "running on reserves," or even "running out of steam" describe deeply felt analogies between malfunctions of modern machinery and subjective experiences of fatigue. The appeal of quantity theories for both medical and lay psychologists may well be metaphoric, based on familiar needs for food, fluid, and air, but it may also result from the real importance of a utility function in behavioral motivation. That is, individuals may appreciate that their behavior is driven by an internal quantity, albeit a quantity associated with distinctive qualitative features corresponding to each affectively experienced appraisal process. Subjective appreciation of an internal utility function might produce a bias in favor of quantitative motivational models, these being more or less direct representations of the utility function itself. Pugh (1977), for instance, points out that "negative" multicomponent utility functions activate purposive behavior while "positive" ones inhibit it, exactly as reputed for other psychic quantities although with a conventionally inverted polarity.

Identification of utility function and psychic quantity, moreover, reveals the model of Chapter 5 as one of a long line of similar theories, each cast in the form appropriate to its age. Following the discovery of cerebral ventricles, fluid replaced humors, vapors, and animal spirits as quantities responsible for behavior. In the era of thermodynamics, psychic energy replaced fluids. Now, in an age of computers, utility functions might replace psychic energy. Progress, however, occasionally consists in saying the same thing, but with words chosen for their more accurate implications.

Behavioral Subroutines

If behavioral subroutines are activated to optimize an anticipated future utility function, composed in turn from separate social appraisal processes, then the logic that guides this choice is of great psychologic interest. Individual differences in this regard, or in the same individual over time, may account for at least some abnormal behaviors. Implicitly, the predictive optimization of an affective utility function, and consequent selection of tactical subroutines, has been treated as a process akin to that which Galanter and Gerstenhaber (1956) term "imaginal thinking." As defined by these authors, imaginal thinking consists in devising a model of the environment, defining for it certain initial conditions—which from the present viewpoint might include certain response specifications—and running the model forward in faster than real time. If the model accurately represents environmental forces, the environment should behave, given any set of hypothetical conditions or response specifications, approximately as the model has behaved during simulation runs. However, certain aspects of the environmental response to given initial conditions may be more reliably modeled than are other aspects, and knowledge of the predictive reliability of the model in these respects is important for optimizing a utility function. Imagine, for example, that the probability of finding game on any single hunting expedition is only fifty percent. Then modeling of the consequences of a hunting expedition, if it is to be accurate, must produce not one outcome, but at least two outcomes, each with an assigned probability faithfully mirroring the actual probabilities of finding food.

If the data available from environmental modeling, however, is not one outcome but two or more, each with assigned probabilities, then means must exist for choosing among these outcomes what will be considered representative of the behavioral choice being simulated. Consider, for example, a slightly more realistic hunting expedition, on which not only the probability of finding game is less than certain, but on which there is also the possibility of serious injury. Four different outcomes, each with an assigned probability, should result from accurate environmental modeling of this expedition. These are not finding game but escaping injury, not finding game and being injured, finding game and escaping injury, and finding game but being injured. If one of these outcomes had an assigned probability so high as to be nearly certain, then there would be little difficulty in assigning that outcome to the behavioral tactic—"hunting expedition"—from the simulation of which it emerged. If one or more outcomes were equiprobable, however, then which should be taken as representative of hunting expeditions? If the second—coming home empty-handed with an injury—were chosen, then a hunting expedition would be passed over in favor of other behaviors with a more favorable outcome. If the third—finding game without injury—were chosen, then a hunting expedition might very well be mounted.

Given equiprobable predicted outcomes, the choice of which outcome is considered representative of the behavior being simulated may be wholly dependent upon their transient relative utility. Starving individuals, for example, may positively value the possibility of finding game more than they negatively value the possibility of injury. As a result, outcomes featuring successful hunting will loom larger than those featuring injury. In part, however, choices between more or less equiprobable outcomes may reflect enduring personal traits. Some individuals, for example, may habitually attend to positively valued outcomes while ignoring equally possible negatively valued ones. Others may attend to negatively valued outcomes rather than to those that are positively valued. Individuals with the first attentional preference will choose tactical subroutines to maximize gains; individuals with the latter preference will choose subroutines to minimize losses. The former will be recognized as habitual optimists, the latter as habitual pessimists. In between the two extreme patterns—maximum gain and mininum loss—will be mixed attentional preferences that are neither particularly optimistic nor particularly pessimistic. Tendencies toward preferential recall of pleasant or unpleasant events also occur and are probably closely related to optimism and pessimism, respectively (Waldvogel, 1982).

Why some individuals may habitually attend to positively valued and others to negatively valued equiprobable predicted outcomes is an extraordinarily important but little understood psychologic issue. Tiger (1979a) discusses the adaptive function of optimism and concludes that selective attention to positive outcomes may be necessary for the initial activation of otherwise problematic long-term projects. Hunting forays, technical innovations, and agricultural labors are among the profitable long-term projects Tiger has in mind. The sheer unpredictability of human life might prove daunting to individuals who attend equally to positively and negatively valued outcomes. However, even if the normal innate decision bias is optimistic, or maximum gain, under specific conditions more conservative biases should also be adaptive. In particular, if environmental conditions are such that major losses appear probable, then it should never be adaptive to ignore these very negatively valued outcomes. Optimism, or preferential attention to positively valued outcomes, should always yield to pessimism, or preferential attention to negatively valued outcomes, if the perceived probability of major loss is high. Rubenstein (1982) has shown that suboptimal payoffs are likely to be accepted if potential losses are more important than potential gains. Studies in economic anthropology (see Lumsden and Wilson, 1981) support the notion that minimum loss strategies determine group decisions precisely when major losses are thought possible. Clinical evidence suggests that the subjective probability of major loss is high, too, for many habitual pessimists. However, the manner in which such perceptions, which can often be traced to abnormal self-estimations, interact with genetically determined dispositional factors remains unknown. Identical twins with little or no history of contact manifest striking similarities in their tendencies toward optimism or pessimism (Farber, 1981), suggesting significant genetic influence over maximum gain, minimum loss attentional preferences. Learned helplessness, response-contingent reinforcement, resource holding power, and pathologic narcissism are topics closely related to pessimistic, or minimum loss, response selection patterns. Each of these is discussed in Chapters 13 through 15.

Given, however, that social appraisal processes are somehow combined to form a utility function, and that some procedure, however biased, predicts its future value for each tactical alternative, then behavioral control must be passed to the tactical subroutine that gives the best predicted results. The tactical subroutine itself is a behavioral prescription. Encoded in the nervous system, it must be represented in a form capable of being "read out" so as to control motor activity. Subroutines of this sort are essential for performance of motor tasks not anatomically built into bodily form. Logically, they may be categorized according to any number of characteristics, but only two distinctions are likely to prove valuable for psychologic purposes. The first of these is between what may, for purposes of discussion, be called "innate" and "learned" subroutines. Innate subroutines are those manifested by universal and stereotypic behaviors. Like all innate behavioral prescriptions, their development also requires environmental collaboration, usually in the form of experiences that are ubiquitous in the environment of adaptation. Learned subroutines, by contrast, are highly individualized and occur only within certain subtypes of the environment of adaptation. Like all learned behavioral prescriptions, their acquisition depends on innate factors responsible for learning capacities in the first place. Examples of innate and learned subroutines are those that control male sexual movements and the use of firearms, respectively. Pelvic thrusting movements during sexual intercourse are highly stereotypic, occur in response to definable stimuli, and are performed by males raised in anything resembling a normal environment. Use of firearms, by contrast, occurs only in certain subtypes of the developmentally "normal" environment: Those societies with access to guns and without prohibitions on their ownership.

The second distinction of value to psychopathology is between tactical subroutines manifested as diverse behaviors and those manifested specifically as communicative gestures. Both ethologically and psychologically, somewhat different rules may apply to the generation and maintenance of behavioral subroutines in these two categories. Subroutines in the first category, for example, contain inherent cognitive models, and most of them also feature *set goals.* Neither set goals nor inherent cognitive models are salient aspects of behavioral subroutines manifested as communicative acts. These, however, may be formed by *ritualization* processes that are of interest in their own right.

Behavioral subroutines manifested as diverse behaviors may be simple and repetitive, such as that responsible for pelvic thrusting, or highly elaborate and extended over many years. Extremes of this latter type include pursuing educational or career goals, seeking revenge, or building a home. Extremely complex behavioral subroutines are themselves hierarchically arranged groupings of more or less complex subroutines (see Dawkins, 1976) capable of interruption, resumption, and flexible channel sharing of the sort achieved with modern computers. Miller, Galanter, and Pribram (1960) provide the classic introduction to how complex behaviors may be constructed in this fashion, and the growth of computer science has demonstrated its feasibility.

The least complex diverse behavioral subroutines tend to be innate. Their manifestations include the somatic appetitive behaviors that Freud considered the foundations of social life (Chapter 2). In other cases, the only manifestations are motoric preferences. Salk (1973), for example, found that both right- and left-handed mothers carried their newborn infants with the head against their left breast. This motor preference, which exposes the infant to potentially soothing maternal heart sounds, appears to occur cross culturally (Lockhard, et al., 1979) and is represented in works of art from numerous historical periods (Finger, 1975). It can fail to develop if mother and infant are separated during the postpartum period (Trowell, 1982) or if the mother is very anxious (DeChateau, 1983). Evidence also exists for distinct male-female styles in methods of carrying inanimate objects. These styles, moreover, develop before adolescence and therefore cannot be attributed solely to anatomic sex differences (Jenni and Jenni, 1976).

If the least complex diverse behavioral subroutines tend to be innate, the more complex ones tend to be learned. As expected, the latter are also highly dependent upon personal history. "Climbing the corporate ladder," for instance, manifests a complex tactical subroutine into which numerous other subroutines are, of necessity, nested. The decision to seek corporate advancement, and the methods with which it is pursued, are dependent upon idiosyncracies of personal history too complex to describe with any simple formula. These personal factors, of course, interact with cultural factors that make corporate ladders available in the first place. Once a decision is made, the capacity to sustain long-term tactical subroutines may depend upon age-related factors, such as the ability to recall step-wise actions (see Meacham and Leiman, 1982; Kreutzer, et al., 1982), as well upon idiosyncratic factors, such as the strength of anticipated benefits. Also, very strongly activated behavioral subsystems in general may be immune to interference by other behavioral components (Fentress, 1976). The self-sustaining character of strongly activated subroutines could play a role in pathologic monomanias or in the psychology of "workaholics." Typically, monomanias of this sort are associated with reduced behavioral flexibility and with attrition of competing activities.

Innate and learned tactical subroutines manifested as diverse behaviors differ not only in their complexity, but also in that the latter tend to incorporate tools. Contrary to previous anthropologic opinion, tool use characterizes not just homo sapiens, but nonhuman primates as well. In fact, tool use is most likely dependent on elaboration of object-manipulation skills evolutionarily continuous with instrumental programs controlling bodily parts (Reynolds, 1981). These latter programs are shared by all higher animals, but are further developed in humans as the result of improved iconic and spatial capacities, among other cognitive advantages. Thus, incorporation of tools into learned tactical subroutines differs from the tactical use of bodily parts manifested by all organisms only in degree and not necessarily in concept.

Characteristic of all but the simplest diverse behavioral subroutines, whether innate or learned, is dependence on what Bowlby (1969), following the cybernetic custom, refers to as *set goals.* Set goals are definable states, either of the organism, the environment, or the relation between them, that form terminal or homeostatic set points for those subroutines governing behavior. Tactical set goals are analogous to what Pugh (1977) calls *secondary values.* These are surrogates instrumentally related to higher level primary values, or set goals associated with what is here termed strategic functioning. Tactical set goals may be nested, or arranged sequentially or in parallel, depending on the complexity and nature of the specific subroutines in which they function. More complex subroutines undoubtedly require their hierarchical integration (Dawkins, 1976), while sequential and parallel arrangements may suffice for simpler ones. Specific set goals, moreover, may be innate or learned, consistent with the subroutines that they inform. Intromission, for example, is an innate tactical set goal, in the stereotypic sense already described, and serves to initiate male pelvic thrusting. Becoming rich, by contrast, is a learned set goal closely related to corporate ambitions. Tactical set goals may also be more or less conscious. Individuals, that is, may avow or disavow particular set goals, just as they avow or disavow the behaviors leading to them (Schafer, 1978).

Finally, an interesting facet of subroutines manifested as diverse behaviors is their cognitive aspect. That is, since use of any behavioral subroutine to optimize a utility function implies specific expectations, cognitive models are implicit in its employment. In using any tactic, the individual acts as if he or she possessed certain models, regardless of whether discrete intrapsychic representations of those models occur separately from the behavioral prescriptions and set goals comprising the tactic. Every tactical subroutine, in other words, is inherently one or more cognitive models, and every manifested model is a tactical subroutine. Mental processes depicted in Chapter 5 as antecedent and consequent to affectively experienced utility functions—cognitive and tactical processes, respectively—are actually facets of a unitary process both cognitive and motoric. The model of Chapter 5, which features neatly categorized mental processes acting sequentially to produce adherence to social response rules, is merely an heuristic device. It may suffice for psychologic purposes, and for the integration of ultimate and proximate causal viewpoints, but not for others. The indistinctness of what may be called "descriptive" and "prescriptive" mental elements is of a logical kind, moreover, and not based on a particular theory of thought, such as the behaviorist theories that identify thinking with subliminal motor activity (see Wertheimer, 1979).

Behavioral subroutines that are manifested as gestures are usefully distinguished from those manifested as diverse behaviors in several dimensions. The most important of these concerns their symbolic, as opposed to purely instrumental, content. Behavioral subroutines manifested as gestural acts serve to produce symbols, the significance of which may be either phylogenetically or culturally determined. Eibl-Eibesfeldt (1979a) has studied these symbols and their accretion and makes several important points. First, ritualized symbols permit social interactions in situations where signals are essential to prevent disruption. The most significant of these situations are those involving potential hostilities, which can be prevented only by redundant, mutually understood gestures. Some of these, such as smiling, direct eye contact, and head tossing, may be genetically fixed in humans by *phylogenetic ritualization.* Phylogenetic ritualization is a process by which fragments of species-stereotypic behavioral sequences come to represent the whole. Direct eye contact, for example, is part of primate threat displays, so the ability to maintain eye contact in interactions not overtly agonistic has, through phylogenetic ritualization, come to represent power. That genes predispose to production of specific gestures is evidenced by the extraordinary expressive and manneristic similarities of identical twins raised with little or no contact (Farber, 1981). Twins having no exposure to common models may nonetheless share dramatically similar nervous gestures, handshakes, facial expressions, and even postural habits. Other symbolic gestures have their meanings fixed by *cultural ritualization,* a process akin to phylogenetic ritualization, but here fragments of culturally typical behaviors come to represent the whole. To demonstrate peaceful intent, for example, members of various societies shake hands, display arrows, discharge rifles into the ground, or even provide twenty-one gun salutes. All these acts employ references to culturally or historically familiar hostile practices, but in a setting that signifies their renunciation.

The number of phylogenetically or culturally ritualized gestural subroutines is potentially unlimited, and their execution occupies more of daily life than is readily appreciated. Roughly, they may be categorized as either verbal or nonverbal, depending on whether they employ the articulatory apparatus, and the latter may be further subdivided into the purely gestural and the dramatic, depending on the salience of pantomimic components. Ritualized greetings of the sort described by Eibl-Eibesfeldt (1979a), including spear throwing, rifle shooting, and twenty-one gun salutes, belong in the class of nonverbal dramatic gestures, since they enact the larger behaviors the renunciation of which they represent. Culturally ritualized gestures intended to save face following a social faux pas also belong in this category. By way of example, individuals tripping in public predictably glance at the ground, shake their head, look disgusted, and in other ways imitate the behavior of someone suffering an imposed nuisance (Goffmann, 1979). In this way they lead onlookers to assume that their having tripped was both extraordinary and the result of someone else's negligence. Cultures mandate a range of pantomimic gestural routines for individuals faced with a variety of similar exigencies.

Emotional and conversational gestures comprise the category of nonverbal, purely gestural subroutines. Emotional gestures are largely facial, appear early in the neonatal period (Trevarthen, 1979), develop without visual experience (Eibl-Eibesfeldt, 1973), and universally signify particular affective states (Ekman, 1979). Their universal interpretation probably results from phylogenetic ritualization of facial movements. Ekman (1979), for instance, argues that at least some eyebrow gestures may have adaptive value during the emotional states they have come to signify. Smiling may also be derivative from agonistic grimacing (Reynolds, 1981) and may serve to renounce hostile intentions. Conversational gestures, by contrast, are used to indicate emphasis, punctuation, or interrogation, rather than internal states, and are probably of cultural origin (Ekman, 1979). Hand movements, too, play a larger role in conversational than in emotional gestures, further distinguishing the two types of signals.

Finally, verbal gestural subroutines include Goffmann's (1979) "response cries." These are noises ("ahh," "phew," "oops"), imprecations ("hell," "damn"), and phrases ("what on earth?") intended to reveal the mental state of the speaker. Other verbal gestural subroutines are culturally ritualized greetings of the sort described by Eibl-Eibesfeldt (1979a). These include comments on the weather, to which assenting replies are expected ("hot day today"), and queries on well-being ("How do you do?"), among many others. Innocuous remarks on the weather early in the course of renewed interpersonal contact, for example, serve to enact amicable consensus. Although in the form of linguistic acts, these remarks are actually culturally ritualized pantomimes signifying the amicable intentions of individuals meeting each other under somewhat uncertain conditions. In a similar fashion, queries on health and well-being pantomime friendly intentions. To respond to these with detailed self-revelations, in fact, is considered socially inept. Phylogenetically ritualized verbal gestures include crying, laughter, moaning, and other nonlinguistic stereotypic auditory signs. Infantile cries, for example, are stereotypically specific to their inciting cause. They reliably indicate to the caretaker the source of the infant's distress (Wolf, 1973). Laughter is elicited from infants by expectational or perceptual mismatch (Kagan, 1970), a factor also important for adult jokes (Pugh, 1977). Moaning, like the specific cries of infants, serves to indicate somatic distress, illness, or injury.

In general, tactical subroutines manifested as gestural acts are of particular psychologic significance. Both their appropriate execution and interpretation, for example, are flawed in some psychiatric disorders. That execution and interpretation tend to be jointly defective is of some theoretical interest and may suggest that gestural interpretation occurs by a process analogous to the sympathetic motor matching hypothesized by some to account for phonemic decoding. If so, the individual might interpret gestures by reference to the circumstances and intentional states under which he or she would produce the same signals. Failure to gesture appropriately would then result in flawed perception of the circumstances or intentional states causing others to gesture.

Perhaps the least well-characterized disorder related to gestural tactics is shyness. Essentially, the shy person goes through life fearing that his or her gestures—verbal, nonverbal, and dramatic—will give the wrong impression. The shy person has little confidence in his or her ability to manage gestural communications in a way that will produce a favorable impact. This lack of confidence is consciously manifested by a preoccupation with appearances, with real or potential social missteps, and with real or imagined social rejection. The fear of making stupid remarks, which is also frequently expressed by shy persons, is not so much a dread of producing intellectually fatuous statements as of being marked incompetent. Communicative defense of reputation is of considerable significance for pursuit of higher level social strategies (see, in particular, Chapters 7, 8, 10, and 11), so that lack of faith in one's gestural abilities could result in social inhibitions of a diffuse nature. Significantly, persons not ordinarily shy frequently become so when placed in situations where the impression they make is especially critical to strategic goals. Inhibitions concerning public speaking, job interviews, and dating are situation-specific failures of gestural confidence.

Appendix F
A Third Type of Parent-Child Conflict

Two types of parent-child conflict are described in Chapter 6. Trivers (1978), however, described yet a third type, which, like the first two, can also be explicated from an inclusive fitness viewpoint. This last, though it falls outside the purview of infant-caretaker attachment, is outlined here for the sake of completeness. Also, its consideration—together with that of sibling incest (Chapter 9)—illustrates the view of ideology taken in Chapter 3. As described by Trivers, the conflict concerns intersibling altruistic or egocentric acts. The parent—being equally related to all offspring—should desire that they be mutually altruistic whenever the benefits to the recipient exceed the cost to the altruist. Intersibling altruistic acts that meet this criteria are certain to enhance the inclusive fitness of parental genes. Contrariwise, the parent should desire that offspring mutually refrain from egocentric acts whenever the costs to the victim exceed the benefits to the perpetrator. Intersibling egocentric acts that meet this criteria are certain to reduce the inclusive fitness of parental genes.

However, insofar as they maximize the inclusive fitness of their own genes, children will take a rather different view of both intersibling altruism and egocentrism. Because a given child is genetically more perfectly related to himself or herself than to a sibling, he or she will have a higher threshold for intersibling altruism and a lower threshold for intersibling egocentrism than the parent would prefer. While the parent encourages altruistic acts yielding more benefit than cost, a given child should be willingly altruistic only when benefits are greater than twice the cost. This is based on the fact that the altruist has twice as many of his or her own genes as a full-sibling recipient. Altruistic benefits received by half-siblings should be discounted by a further factor of two, so that they must exceed four times the cost before they are willingly conferred. While the parent discourages egocentric acts costing the victim more than they benefit the perpetrator, a given child should willingly refrain from egocentric acts only when costs are more than twice the expected benefits. This also results from discounting full-sibling costs by a factor of two. Egocentric costs incurred by half-siblings should be discounted by a further factor of two, so that they must exceed four times the anticipated benefit before that will be voluntarily surrendered.

In effect, when the benefit-to-cost ratios of intersibling altruistic acts are between one and two, or the benefit-to-cost ratios of intersibling egocentric acts are between one-half and one, then the parent and the decision-making child will prefer different behaviors. These zones of conflict, moreover, are even broader when altruistic or egocentric behaviors will effect half-, rather than full-siblings. Given such a conflict, parents might reward altruistic acts and punish egocentric acts in an effort to change the benefits and costs of these behaviors as they appear to the child. In response, the child might become adept at hiding altruistic failures and disguising egocentrism. Parents, in turn, might become even more alert to dissembled egocentrism or to hidden failures of altruistic purpose.

Eventually, the cycle of punishment, reward, and evasion should be transferred to an ethical arena. Parental injunctions against egocentrism and in favor of sibling altruism should become ideologic. This, of course, has already occurred. In our own culture, the popular story of Cain and Abel enjoins children to become their brother's keeper, while the story of Joseph contrasts unacceptable sibling egocentrism with Joseph's own altruism.

Due to an age-related shift in inclusive fitness interests, ethical ideologies in favor of sibling altruism have more of an appeal to adults than to the children whose behavior they are intended to influence. Among adults, in fact, these ideologies serve purposes far outside the family circle. Thus, the widespread religious notion that individuals stand as siblings before a God who enjoins them from harming each other, and who rewards good deeds, can be understood as an attempt—by hypothesizing a universal parent in relation to which all are siblings—to find in recalled and now fully accepted parental ideologies a metaphoric basis for the amelioration of hostility between unrelated adults. Nor are ethical ideologies likely to be the only adult vestiges of this last type of parent-child conflict. Parent-child conflicts over altruism and egocentrism are potentially important in the etiology of certain psychologic disorders, such as excessive generosity or niggardliness. The dogmatic reduction of mental life to somatic and hostile impulses may have prevented recognition of the psychologic importance of "brotherly love" or, in any event, of its absence.

Appendix G Special Aspects of Human Female Sexuality

Menopause

General features of human female sexual patterns, and their relation to male sexual patterns, are discussed in Chapter 8. Here, attention is drawn to special aspects of human female sexuality, the inclusive fitness effects of which are far less clear. These are well summarized by Symons (1979), to whom the reader is referred for more complete discussions, and include menopause, orgasm, and "anestrous" sexuality. Concerning menopause, the postmenopausal woman is in a selectively unique position: Her inclusive fitness can be promoted only through the enhanced reproductive success of others, because her own reproductive possibilities are now nil. Since postmenopausal females, like everyone else, are expected on theoretical grounds to behave to maximize their inclusive fitness, the changed composition of inclusive fitness after menopause might logically be reflected in behavioral change. Greater altruism, absence of the desire for male affection, or willingness to please males promiscuously are among the potential changes that might result from loss of reproductive potential.

That these behavioral changes largely fail to materialize could signify that menopause itself has not been the object of selective pressures. Instead, it might be a degenerative process experienced by women living longer than expected in the environment of adaptation. Yet, there are those who argue that ancestral human females did reach the age of menopause (Mellen, 1981), and that a postreproductive period in late female life could itself enhance inclusive fitness (Campbell, 1971). In particular, Dawkins (1976a) points out that when the probability that a grandchild will achieve reproductive success becomes more than twice the probability that a late-born child will achieve it, it becomes more profitable for grandparents to invest in grandchildren than in another child. This follows from the genetic-relatedness of parents, children, and grandchildren. The older mother's relative inability to make parental investments, together with her reduced reproductive efficiency, manifested by a higher incidence of birth defects, may sufficiently deteriorate the chances of late-born children so that enforced sterility becomes selectively advantageous. Furthermore, although female behavior shows little evidence of previous adaptation to the postmenopausal state, the same cannot be said of male behavior. Male preferences for younger females do imply that ancestral human females lived sufficiently long lives that the older among them suffered at least some loss of reproductive capacity. Among shorter-lived nonhuman primates males fail to demonstrate such preferences (Simonds, 1974). Given the intensity of male sexual selection, evolved male preferences may provide more sensitive indicators of past selective pressures than postmenopausal female behaviors, which may be difficult to document in any event. Further studies of postmenopausal selective pressures are of great psychologic interest, to help explain both the extraordinary social position of postmenopausal women in many societies (Bart, 1980) and the occurrence of distinctive psychopathologic syndromes in women of advancing age.

Orgasm

Somewhat similar remarks apply to female orgasms. Whether their distinctiveness is absolute or merely quantitative (see Alexander and Noonan, 1979), orgasmic women are sexually different from other mammalian females. Although nonhuman female mammals solicit and initiate copulation, there is little evidence that they experience orgasms. The single exception to this rule is offered by nonhuman female primates living in captivity. Captive primates engage in more varied and frequent sexual activity than their free living counterparts, and at least some captive females of these species will seek prolonged clitoral stimulation leading to apparent orgasm. Even among human females, orgasms are only variably experienced and are generally dependent upon culturally determined sexual practices involving prolonged clitoral stimulation. Aside from the obvious psychologic significance of experiencing or not experiencing orgasms, and from personal or ideological biases about what "kinds" of orgasm are appropriate to what situation, occurrence of female orgasms raises issues relevant to inclusive fitness and, therefore, to genetically transmitted strategic tendencies.

Essentially, five competing models variably describe the interrelationship of female orgasm with inclusive fitness. First, Symons (1979) argues that female orgasms serve no adaptive functions but result instead from the same vestigial bisexuality responsible for development of male nipples. Those women with clitoral-neural mechanisms more homologous to those of the male sexual organ, and who live in cultures providing for prolonged clitoral foreplay, will experience orgasms. Those with neural mechanisms less akin to the masculine, or who live in cultures less amenable to prolonged foreplay, will be anorgasmic. In any event, female orgasm will be without reproductive consequences. While it does seem plausible that structures underlying female orgasms evolved largely because of their essential role in male sexual physiology, to assert that their resultant functional properties have no incremental influence on inclusive fitness is, in fact, the strongest form of evolutionary hypothesis. Since experience of orgasms cannot help but play some proximate role in sexual attitude formation, to assert that it has neither an adaptive nor adverse effect on female reproductive success seems unlikely on the face of it. Symons himself points out another difficulty when he mentions the possible adverse effects of orgasms on female fertility (see also Bernds and Barash, 1979), and he attends, too, to the communicative function of female orgasm, which will be discussed here.

The second and third models of female orgasms are also reviewed by Symons (1979). The first of these treats the female orgasm, which can occur following a very short refractory period, as evidence of an insatiable female sexual drive. This drive, according to proponents of this theory, has been suppressed by postagricultural male-dominated societies. Symons properly points out that this highly polemic model serves more political than scientific purposes. Sexual drives equal in intensity to the male's, much less insatiable, could hardly have served the reproductive interests of ancestral human females, whose inclusive fitness depended less on sexual access than on discriminating allocation of their reproductive capacity. The second of these two models treats the female orgasm as a social reinforcer, which, by motivating the female to engage in sexual intercourse, strengthens the bond with her mate. This model, which is not implausible, might be further strengthened if orgasmic women could be shown to form more durable relationships. Establishing that point is greatly complicated by cultural and other factors affecting sexual life, but should not be impossible.

Finally, there are two "communicative" models of the female orgasm and of its effects on inclusive fitness. These may be of more immediate clinical relevance than the three models discussed so far. The first of these, mentioned by Symons (1979), notes that once a woman experiences orgasm, then the willingness and ability of her male partner to engage in the type of foreplay leading to orgasm becomes a test of his affection and intentions. Those partners unwilling to help her achieve orgasm are likely to be more interested in their own sexual pleasure than in her well-being. Male performance with respect to the possibility of female orgasm therefore becomes a source of useful information to the female in her quest for reliable partners. Orgasmic women, consequently, might be incrementally advantaged with respect to their nonorgasmic counterparts by their ability to make finer discriminations of male sexual intentions. This, of course, is also a potentially testable hypothesis.

The second communicative model, closely related to the first, notes that the behavioral manifestations of female orgasm may signal sexual satisfaction in a form easily understood by male partners. Insofar as they mimic behavioral manifestations of male orgasm, which is associated with a temporary cessation of sexual drive, behavioral manifestations of female orgasm may reassure the male of his mate's sexual satiation and therefore likely fidelity (Alexander and Noonan, 1979). The female able to reassure her mate in this fashion is more likely to avoid both punitive aggression and abandonment (Chapter 8) and may therefore enhance her own inclusive fitness.

Significantly, affective responses to female orgasm do support the two communicative models of its adaptive function. The man on the street, if he may be called to testify, seems to believe that orgasmic women do use sexual climax as a measure of male competence and intentions. The modern male's performance anxiety, in fact, is now widely considered a major cause of psychogenic impotence. On the other hand, that manifested female orgasms raise male paternity confidence making the male more friendly—explains why women frequently mimic orgasms to satisfy male egos. The various signal functions served by female orgasm, in fact, may also explain the extraordinary duration of human sexual intercourse compared to that of nonhuman primates. Sexual intercourse between chimpanzees, for example, typically lasts only a few seconds before being terminated by male ejaculation (Mellen, 1981). Human intercourse of that duration may result from premature ejaculation, but would leave the female anorgasmic, would be considered a poor reflection on the male, whose pride and jealousy would be simultaneously aroused, and in some societies would be counted a sufficient cause for female infidelity.

Anestrous Sexuality

Like those of menopause and orgasm, the behavioral and inclusive fitness implications of "anestrous" female sexuality are also largely unclear. Females of nonhuman mammalian species, including primates, experience "estrual" periods coincident with ovulation. Only during estrual periods are they either sexually attractive to members of the opposite sex or receptive to their overtures. Human females, by contrast, remain continuously attractive to males of the species, and there is no definite evidence that receptivity and sexual interest vary in a cyclical fashion. Spuhler (1979) argues that continual female receptivity evolved in homo sapiens as an incidental effect of hormonal changes requisite to endurance running, the capacity for which sets humans apart from all other mammals. Symons (1979), however, treats anestrous sexuality as an evolved involuntary behavior and cites two hypotheses of how it might enhance inclusive fitness. First, citing evidence that cooperatively hunting nonhuman primate males share meat selectively with sexually attractive estrous females, Symons conjectures that continuously "feigning" fertility may allow the human female to obtain more resources from males of the species. If only to be certain of paternity (Chapter 8), indeterminate periods of female fertility force human males to be continually attentive to their mates. Second, Symons speculates that anestrous sexuality might give the female advantages in male-dominated societies, if only by preventing their sexually jealous mates from sequestering them during fertile periods. Both of these theories, therefore, consider scenarios in which loss of clearly identifiable fertile periods enhances female power with respect to males.

The only time at which the premenopausal human female is demonstrably less fertile—and therefore, perhaps, in a more disadvantaged position—is during the menstrual period. However, whether infertility per se has anything to do with menses-related psychopathology (Ivey and Bardwick, 1968; Rosenthal, et al., 1972; Halbreich, et al., 1983) is entirely problematic. Most of these syndromes may best be explicated in proximate causal, and most probably hormonal, terms. As for related issues, inclusive fitness explanations are also lacking for the apparent menstrual synchronization of young women living in close proximity (McClintock, 1971) and for the common male fear of menstruating women. The latter is frequently encountered in unconscious material from male psychotherapy patients and is also manifested in cultural dictates of primitive peoples (see Lifton, 1979), but the present conceptual framework seems unable to shed light on it.

Appendix H
Inclusive Fitness Aspects of Infanticide

Although both male and female sexual choices are largely predictable from the competitive exigencies determining inclusive fitness for each sex (Chapter 8), they occasionally culminate in what seems at first an astonishing act. After making sexual choices, delineating their relationship with a marriage ceremony, and remaining more or less faithful, according to the dictates of their society, parents occasionally murder the very children they were supposedly seeking! Infanticide, moreover, is neither culturally nor temporally restricted but has been periodically practiced in numerous human societies (Chagnon, et al., 1979), even during times of plenty. Although murdered infants are frequently deformed, so that further parental investments would yield few benefits, in other instances their murder seems to violate reproductive logic entirely. That these latter victims are usually female is of great theoretical importance. For example, because female reproductive potential is the limiting factor in human population growth, various theorists have explained preferential female infanticide as a primitive means of population control. Divale and Harris (1976), to take one extreme, speculate that warfare regulates population growth by providing the ideologic rationale for female infanticide, thus serving important ecologic functions.

A more plausible line of inquiry into preferential female infanticide comes from a proposal by Trivers and Willard (1973). These authors noted that whenever the reproductive success of either sex is in any way predictable, parental inclusive fitness interests would be served by varying the sex ratio of their offspring accordingly (see Clutton-Brock and Albon, 1982). Although Trivers and Willard considered only physiologic means of varying sex ratios, Alexander (1974) extended their line of reasoning to include culturally sanctioned infanticide. According to Alexander, culturally successful males—insofar as their own reproductive success could be passed on to their sons—should be particularly prone toward female infanticide. Since the reproductive success of daughters is always limited by physiologic factors, these high-ranking males should be loathe to invest resources in them that might be reserved for sons with unlimited reproductive potential. Similar tendencies might be manifested by female mates of high-ranking males, but their enthusiasm for female infanticide would be tempered by the enormous parental investments they have already made by the time sex is determined. Chagnon and co-workers (1979) have demonstrated that the predicted relationship between preferential female infanticide and paternal social rank fails to materialize in so-called egalitarian societies. However, in such societies adult success depends more on personal characteristics than social status at birth, so that reproductive success is less than perfectly predictable. In stratified societies, by contrast, the reproductive success of sons of high-ranking males is highly predictable, and preferential female infanticide tends to be characteristic of the highest social classes (Dickemann, 1979).

Appendix I Kinship Systems and Genetic Relatedness

As noted in Chapter 9, culturally determined kinship and genetically measured relationship are only imperfectly correlated. Patrilineal kinship systems, for instance, forbid marriage between genetic relatives on the paternal side, while permitting equally inbred matings with maternal relatives. Matrilineal systems do the reverse. In many societies, cross-cousins are considered marriageable, whereas equally related parallel-cousins are not. From an inclusive fitness point of view, either the disadvantages of any given inbred mating are sufficiently small that individuals should be treated as unrelated, or they are sufficiently large that individuals should be treated as kin. Discrepancies of this sort therefore raise questions about the real functions of kinship and exogamy rules. Now, contrary claims exist as to the extent of genetic misclassifications resulting from kinship systems as they actually operate (see, for example, Sahlins, 1976; Chagnon and Bugos, 1979; Alexander, 1979), but that kinship and exogamy rules may serve functions additional to that of genetic incest avoidance is not at all implausible.

First, insofar as males in any given culture exert sexual control over female first degree relatives, matrilineal and patrilineal classification systems embody different solutions to the conflict between fathers and sons. Patrilineal kinship systems generally confer control over female offspring on the father, who, subject only to cultural and economic restraints, may dispose of their reproductive potential to maximize his own inclusive fitness. Matrilineal systems, by contrast, confer control over female offspring on the mother's brother, who may also channel "parental" investments toward his uterine kin. In some matrilineal societies, control over the mother's sexuality also rests in the hands of her brother. Therefore, matrilineal and patrilineal kinship classifications embody symbolic victories of son and father, respectively, in their competition for control over daughters.

Second, kinship systems direct the flow of altruistic acts toward those who, in a particular society, are most assuredly genetic kin. Kurland (1979) has shown that when paternity confidence falls below 26.8 percent, the *paternity threshold,* the offspring of a man's uterine sister are more related to him on the average than those of his own wife. As described in Chapter 8, paternity confidence is the man's certainty that his mate's offspring are also his own. Therefore, when paternity confidence is below 26.8 percent, kinship systems should feature avuncular, rather than paternal, investments, and possibly control as well. When paternity confidence is low, regardless of whether it is actually below the paternity threshold, matrilateral kin classification would in general assure that altruistic acts by both sexes are directed toward those more closely related. Only in societies with very high paternity confidence might equivalent patrilineal and matrilineal relatives be given equal value for altruistic purposes. Factors affecting paternity confidence in a given society include economic, political, and cultural exigencies. Societies in which some or all males are frequently absent for trading, hunting, fishing, or military expeditions, for example, would tend to have lower paternity confidence than those in which males are largely at home. Culturally sanctioned sexual promiscuity also reduces paternity confidence, while severe strictures against adultery may increase it. Avuncular investment itself, insofar as it diminishes male interest in policing female fidelity, may further reduce paternity confidence in the societies in which it occurs (see Barkow, 1980).

Finally, kinship classification systems serve military, economic, and political functions of sufficient importance to survival that they may well overshadow inclusive fitness disadvantages accruing from genetically inaccurate classifications. Kinships are such major social units in most primitive societies that any given individual would do better belonging to even a genetically incorrect kinship group than to none at all. These functions, moreover, affect the forms taken by kinship systems, since some are more easily accomplished in league with one set of relatives than with another. Chagnon (1979), for instance, points out that due to greater male reproductive potential, kinship groups composed of reproductively successful males will outreproduce groups composed of reproductively successful females. Therefore, successful patrilineal kinship groups will have more individuals at their disposal for economic, political, and military purposes than successful matrilineal groups. The apparent replacement of matrilineal by patrilineal kinship systems in evolving primitive societies may result from the competitive advantages offered to successful patrilines by their greater human resources. Bilateral kinship systems may promote the unity of very large groups. When kin are counted bilaterally, no two persons other than siblings have the same kinship group. Fragmentation of society into groups of related individuals is therefore minimal (Alexander, 1979).

Numerous local factors also affect the inclusive fitness consequences of various departures from genetically accurate kin classifications. Readers interested in ethnographic examples illustrating the operation of these factors are referred to Chagnon and Irons (1979).

In light of the numerous universal and local functions served by kinship classification systems, it is clear why exogamy rules, while functioning to prevent inbred matings, may nonetheless not be genetically accurate. Kinship functions other than genetic incest avoidance force compromises in the structure of kinship systems, which, although genetically inaccurate, nonetheless best serve the inclusive fitness interests of those with powers of selective retention (Chapter 3; also Chagnon, 1982). Even so, kinship classifications do largely coincide with genetic relatedness, and exogamy rules therefore signify a widespread preference for using reproductive potential of opposite sex relatives for other than inbred matings (Chapter 9). This is particularly evident, too, for first degree relatives, with whom inbred matings would have the gravest consequences. Both matrilineal and patrilineal kinship systems, for instance, count brother and sister in the same kinship group and differ only in their classifications of second degree or more distant relatives.

Bibliography

Abrams, R., and Taylor, M.A. 1976. Catatonia: A prospective clinical study. *Archives of General Psychiatry* 33:579.

Adam, K.S. 1982. Loss, suicide, and attachment. In *The place of attachment in human behavior.* C.M. Parkes, and J. Stevenson-Hinde, editors. New York: Basic Books.

Adler, G. 1979. The myth of the alliance with borderline patients. *American Journal of Psychiatry* 136:642.

Adorno, T.W.; Frenkel-Brunswik, E.; Levinson, D.J., et al. 1950. *The authoritarian personality.* New York: Harper and Brother.

Ainsworth, M.D.S. 1982. Attachment: Retrospect and prospect. In *The place of attachment in human behavior.* C.M. Parkes, and J. Stevenson-Hinde, editors. New York: Basic Books.

Akhtar, S., and Byrne, J.P. 1983. The concept of splitting and its clinical relevance. *American Journal of Psychiatry* 140:1013.

Akiskal, H.S.; Hirschfeld, R.M.A.; and Yerevanian, B.I. 1983. The relationship of personality to affective disorders. *Archives of General Psychiatry* 40:801.

Alexander, F., and French, T. 1946. *Psychoanalytic theory: Principles and applications.* New York: Ronald Press.

Alexander, R.D. 1974. The evolution of social behavior. *Annual Review of Ecology and Systematics* 5:325.

Alexander, R.D. 1975. The search for a general theory of behavior. *Behavioral Science* 10:77.

Alexander, R.D. 1979. *Darwinism and human affairs.* Seattle: Univ. of Washington Press.

Alexander, R.D., and Borgia, G. 1978. Group selection, altruism, and the levels of organization of life. *Annual Review of Ecological Systems* 9:449

Alexander, R.D.; Hoogland, J.L.; Howard, R.D., et al. 1979. Sexual dimorphisms and breeding systems in pinnipeds, ungulates, primates, and humans. In *Evolutionary biology and human social behavior: An anthropological perspective.* N.A. Chagnon, and W. Irons, editors. North Scituate, Mass.: Duxbury.

Alexander, R.D., and Noonan, K.M. 1979. Concealment of ovulation, parental care, and human social evolution. In *Evolutionary biology and human social behavior: An anthropological perspective.* N.A. Chagnon, and W. Irons, editors. p. 436. North Scituate, Mass.: Duxbury.

Allen, M.G. 1976. Twin studies of affective illness. *Archives of General Psychiatry* 33:1476.

Allodi, F. 1982. Acute paranoid reaction (Boufee Delirante) in Canada. *Canadian Journal of Psychiatry* 27:366.

American Psychiatric Association, 1980. *Diagnostic and statistical manual of mental disorders.* 3rd ed.

Anderson, J.R., and Bower, G.H. 1973. *Human associative memory.* Washington, D.C.: Winston and Sons.

Andrew, R.J. 1976. Attentional processes and animal behaviour. In *Growing points in ethology.* P.P.G. Bateson, and R.A. Hinde, editors. New York: Cambridge Univ. Press.

Andreasen, N.C. 1979. Thought, language, and communication disorders: I. Clinical assessment, definition of terms, and evaluation of their reliability. *Archives of General Psychiatry* 36:1315.

Andreasen, N.C. 1979a. Thought, language, and communication disorders: II. Diagnostic significance. *Archives of General Psychiatry* 36:1325.

Andreasen, N.C., and Olsen, S. 1982. Negative vs. positive schizophrenia: Definition and validation. *Archives of General Psychiatry* 39:789.

Ansbacher, H.L., and Ansbacher, R.R. 1956. *The individual psychology of Alfred Adler: A systematic presentation in selections from his writings.* New York: Basic Books.

Antelman, S.M., and Caggiula, A.R. 1977. Norepinephrine-dopamine interactions and behavior. *Science* 195:646.

Anthony, E.J. 1968. The developmental precursors of adult schizophrenia. *Journal of Psychiatric Research* 6:293.

Arieti, S., and Bemporad, J. 1978. *Severe and mild depression: The psychotherapeutic approach.* New York: Basic Books.

Asch, S. 1956. Studies of independence and conformity: A minority of one against a unanimous majority. *Psychological Monographs* 70(9).

Astrup, C.; Fossum, A.; and Holmboe, R. 1962. *Prognosis in functional psychoses.* Springfield, Mo.: Charles C. Thomas.

Audy, J.R. 1980. Man the lonely animal: Biological roots of loneliness. In *The anatomy of loneliness.* J. Hartog; J.R. Audy; and Y.A. Cohen, editors. New York: International Universities Press.

Bacon, M.; Child, I.; and Barry, H. 1963. A cross-cultural study of the correlates of crime. *Journal of Abnormal and Social Psychology* 66:291.

Bandura, A. 1973. *Aggression: A social learning analysis.* Englewood Cliffs, N.J.: Prentice-Hall.

Bandura, A. 1979. Psychological mechanisms of aggression. In *Human ethology: Claims and limits of a new discipline.* M. von Cranach; K. Foppa; W. Lepenies, et al., editors. p. 316. New York: Cambridge Univ. Press.

Barash, D.P. 1977. Sociobiology and behavior. New York: Elsevier.

Barkow, J.H. 1980. Sociobiology: Is this the new theory of human nature. In *Sociobiology examined.* A. Montagu, editor. Oxford: Oxford Univ. Press.

Barnett, S.A. 1980. Biological determinism and the Tasmanian native hen. In *Sociobiology examined.* A. Montagu, editor. Oxford: Oxford Univ. Press.

Baron, M.; Gruen, R.; Asnis, L., et al. 1983. Familial relatedness of schizophrenia and schizotypal traits. *American Journal of Psychiatry* 140:1437.

Baron, M.; Klotz, J.; Mendlewicz, J., et al. 1981. Multiple-threshold transmission of affective disorders. *Archives of General Psychiatry* 38:79.

Bart, P. 1980. Loneliness of the long-distance mother. In *The anatomy of loneliness.* J. Hartog; J.R. Audy; and Y.A. Cohen, editors. New York: International Universities Press.

Bateson, P.P.G. 1976. Rules and reciprocity in behavioural development. In *Growing points in ethology.* P.P.G. Bateson, and R.A. Hinde, editors. New York: Cambridge Univ. Press.

Bateson, P.P.G. 1982. Behavioural development and evolutionary processes. In *Current problems in sociobiology.* King's College Sociobiology Group, editors. Cambridge: Cambridge Univ. Press.

Beardslee, W.R.; Bemporad, J.; Keller, M.B., et al. 1983. Children of parents with major affective disorder: A review. *American Journal of Psychiatry* 140:825.

Beck, A.T. 1976. Cognitive therapy and the emotional disorders. New York: International Universities Press.

Bell, A.P.; Weinberg, M.S.; and Hammersmith, S.K. 1981. *Sexual preference: Its development in men and women.* Bloomington: Indiana Univ. Press.

Berger, P.A., and Barchas, J.D. 1977. Biochemical hypotheses of affective disorders. In *Psychopharmacology: From theory to practice.* J.D. Barchas; P.A. Berger; R.D. Ciaranello, et al., editors. New York: Oxford Univ. Press.

Berger, P.L., and Luckmann, T. 1966. *The social construction of reality: A treatise in the sociology of knowledge.* Garden City, N.J.: Doubleday.

Bernds, W.P., and Barash, D.P. 1979. Early termination of parental investment in mammals, including humans. In *Evolutionary biology and human social behavior: An anthropological perspective.* N.A. Chagnon, and W. Irons, p. 487. North Scituate, Mass.: Duxbury.

Bertelsen, A.; Harvald, B.; and Hauge, M. 1977. A Danish twin study of manic-depressive disorders. *British Journal of Psychiatry* 130:330.

Bertram, B.C.R. 1976. Kin selection in lions and in evolution. In *Growing points in ethology.* P.P.G. Bateson, and R.A. Hinde, editors. New York: Cambridge Univ. Press.

Bertram, B.C.R. 1982. Problems with altruism. In *Current problems in sociobiology.* King's College Sociobiology Group, editors. Cambridge: Cambridge Univ. Press.

Bettelheim, B. 1966. *The empty fortress.* New York: Macmillan.

Bettelheim, B. 1969. *The children of the dream.* New York: MacMillan.

Binswanger, L. 1958. The case of Ellen West: An anthropological-clinical study. In *Existence.* R. May; E. Angel; and H.F. Ellenberger, editors. New York: Simon and Schuster.

Bischof, N. 1978. On the phylogeny of human morality. In *Morality as a biological phenomenon.* G.S. Stent, editor. Berlin: Dahlem Konferenzen.

Blanck, G., and Blanck, R. 1974. *Ego Psychology: Theory and Practice.* New York: Columbia Univ. Press.

Blinder, B.J.; Freeman, D.M.A.; and Stunkard, A.J. 1970. Behavior therapy of anorexia nervosa: Effectiveness of activity as a reinforcer of weight gain. *American Journal of Psychiatry* 126:77.

Blumer, D., and Benson, D.F. 1975. Personality changes with frontal and temporal lobe lesions. In *Psychiatric aspects of neurologic disease.* New York: Grune and Stratton.

Bock, K. 1980. *Human nature and history: A response to sociobiology.* New York: Columbia Univ. Press.

Bowden, D.M., and McKinney, W.T. 1972. Behavioral effects of peer separation, isolation, and reunion on adolescent male rhesus monkeys. *Developmental Psychobiology* 5:353.

Bower, T.G.R. 1974. *Development in infancy.* San Francisco: W.H. Freeman.

Bowlby, J. 1969. *Attachment and loss: Volume I, Attachment.* New York: Basic Books.

Bowlby, J. 1973. *Attachment and loss: Volume II, Separation.* New York: Basic Books.

Bowlby, J. 1980. *Attachment and loss: Volume III, Loss.* New York: Basic Books.

Bradley, S.J. 1979. The relationship of early maternal separation to borderline personality in children and adolescents: A pilot study. *American Journal of Psychiatry* 136:424.

Brandt, E.M.; Stevens, C.W.; and Mitchell, G. 1971. Visual and social communication in adult isolate-reared monkeys. *Primates* 12:105.

Brazelton, T.; Tronick, E.; Adamson, L., et al. 1975. Early mother-infant reciprocity. *Ciba Foundation Symposium* 33:137.

Brenner, C. 1973. *An elementary textbook of psychoanalysis.* rev. ed. Garden City, N.J.: Anchor Books.

Breuer, G. 1982. *Sociobiology and the human dimension.* Cambridge: Cambridge Univ. Press.

Brown, G.W. 1982. Early loss and depression. In *The place of attachment in human behavior.* C.M. Parkes, and J. Stevenson-Hinde, editors. New York: Basic Books.

Brown, G.W., and Harris, T. 1978. *The social origins of depression: A study of psychiatric disorder in women.* London: Tavistock.

Bruch, H. 1973. *Eating disorders: Obesity, anorexia nervosa, and the person within.* New York: Basic Books.

Buchsbaum, M.S. 1979. Neurophysiological aspects of the schizophrenic syndrome. In *Disorders of the schizophrenic syndrome.* L. Bellak, editor. New York: Basic Books.

Bursten, B. 1982. Narcissistic personalities in DSM III. *Comprehensive Psychiatry* 23:409.

Byrne, D. 1969. Attitudes and attraction. In *Advances in experimental social psychology.* L. Berkowitz, editor. New York: Academic Press.

Calhoun, J.B. 1980. Seven steps from loneliness. In *The anatomy of loneliness.* J. Hartog; J.R. Audy; and Y.A. Cohen, editors. New York: International Universities Press.

Campbell, B. 1971. *Human evolution: An introduction to man's adaptations.* Chicago: Aldine.

Campbell, D.T. 1978. Social morality norms as evidence of conflict between biological human nature and social system requirements. In *Morality as a biological phenomenon.* G.S. Stent, editor. Berlin: Dahlem Konferenzen.

Cannon, W.B. 1942. Voodoo death. *American Anthropologist* 44:169.

Caplan, A.L. 1978. Introduction. In *The sociobiology debate.* A.L. Caplan, editor. New York: Harper and Row.

Caplan, N. 1970. The new ghetto man: A review of recent empirical studies. *Journal of Social Issues* 23:59.

Carpenter, W.T., and Strauss, J.S. 1979. Diagnostic issues in schizophrenia. In *Disorders of the schizophrenic syndrome.* L. Bellak, editor. New York: Basic Books.

Chagnon, N.A. 1979. Is reproductive success equal in egalitarian societies? In *Evolutionary biology and human social behavior: An anthropological perspective.* N.A. Chagnon, and W. Irons, editors. p. 374. North Scituate, Mass.: Duxbury.

Chagnon, N.A. 1979a. Mate competition, favoring close kin, and village fissioning among the Yanomamo indians. In *Evolutionary biology and human social behavior: An anthropological perspective.* N.A. Chagnon, and W. Irons, editors. p. 86. North Scituate, Mass.: Duxbury.

Chagnon, N.A. 1982. Nepotism in tribal populations. In *Current problems in sociobiology.* King's College Sociobiology Group, editors. Cambridge: Cambridge Univ. Press.

Chagnon, N.A., and Bugos, P.E. 1979. Kin selection and conflict: An analysis of a Yanomamo ax fight. In *Evolutionary biology and human social behavior: An anthropological perspective.* N.A. Chagnon, and W. Irons, editors. p. 213. North Scituate, Mass.: Duxbury.

Chagnon, N.A.; Flinn, M.V.; and Melancon, T.F. 1979. Sex-ratio variation among the Yanomamo indians. In *Evolutionary biology and human social behavior: An anthropological perspective.* N.A. Chagnon, and W. Irons, editors. p. 290. North Scituate, Mass.: Duxbury.

Chagnon, N.A., and Irons, W., editors. 1979. *Evolutionary biology and human social behavior: An anthropological perspective.* North Scituate, Mass.: Duxbury.

Chance, M.R.A. 1962. Social behaviour and primate evolution. In *Culture and the evolution of man.* A. Montagu, editor. New York: Oxford Univ. Press.

Charlesworth, W.R. 1979. Ethology: Understanding the other half of intelligence. In *Human ethology: Claims and limits of a new discipline.* M. von Cranach; K. Foppa; W. Lepenies, et al., editors. Cambridge: Cambridge Univ. Press.

Chepko-Sade, B.D. 1979. Monkey group splits up. *New Scientist* 82:348.

Chomsky, N. 1957. *Syntactic structures.* The Hague: Mouton.

Chomsky, N. 1975. *Reflections on language.* New York: Random House.

Christian, J.J. 1964. Actions of ACTH in intact and corticoid-maintained adrenalectomized female mice with emphasis on the reproductive tract. *Endocrinology* 75:653.

Clark, H.H., and Clark, E.V. 1977. *Psychology and language: An introduction to psycholinguistics.* New York: Harcourt Brace Jovanovich.

Clutton-Brock, T.H., and Albon, S.D. 1982. Parental investment in male and female offspring in animals. In *Current problems in sociobiology.*

King's College Sociobiology Group, editors. Cambridge: Cambridge Univ. Press.

Clutton-Brock, T.H., and Harvey, P.H. 1976. Evolutionary rules and primate societies. In *Growing points in ethology.* P.P.G. Bateson, and R.A. Hinde, editors. New York: Cambridge Univ. Press.

Clutton-Brock, T.H., and Harvey, P.H. 1978. Primate ecology and social organization. In *Readings in sociobiology.* T.H. Clutton-Brock, and P.H. Harvey, editors. San Francisco: W.H. Freeman.

Cohen, L.J. 1974. The operational definition of human attachment. *Psychological Bulletin* 81:207.

Cohen, Y.A. 1980. You're OK, how am I?: Loneliness and its institutional frames. In *The anatomy of loneliness.* J. Hartog; J.R. Audy; and Y.A. Cohen, editors. New York: International Universities Press.

Cohen, B.P., and Camhi, J. 1967. Schizophrenic performance in a word communication task. *Journal of Abnormal Psychology* 72:240.

Cole, M.; Hood, L.; and McDermott, R. 1982. Ecological niche picking. In *Memory observed: Remembering in natural contexts.* U. Neisser, editor. San Francisco: W.H. Freeman.

Coryell, W., and Norten, S.G. 1981. Briquet's syndrome (Somatization disorder) and primary depression: Comparison of background and outcome. *Comprehensive Psychiatry* 22:249.

Cottle, T.J.; Edwards, C.N.; and Pleck, J.H. 1970. The relationship of sex identity and social and political attitudes. *Journal of Personality* 38:435.

Crook, J.H. 1980. Social change in Indian Tibet. *Social Science Information* 19:139.

Crook, T., and Eliot, J. 1980. Parental death during childhood and adult depression: A critical review of the literature. *Psychological Bulletin* 87:252.

Crowe, R.R.; Pauls, D.L.; Venkatesh, A., et al. 1979. Exercise and anxiety neurosis. *Archives of General Psychiatry* 36:652.

Daly, M., and Wilson, M. 1979. Sex and strategy. *New Scientist* 81:15.

Darwin, C. 1859. *The origin of species by means of natural selection.*

Darwin, C. 1872. *The expression of the emotions in man and animals.*

Darwin, C. 1874. *The descent of man and selection in relation to sex.* 2d ed.

Davies, N.B. 1982. Behaviour and competition for scarce resources. In *Current problems in sociobiology.* King's College Sociobiology Group, editors. Cambridge: Cambridge Univ. Press.

Dawkins, R. 1976. Hierarchical organizations: A candidate principle for ethology. In *Growing points in ethology.* P.P.G. Bateson, and R.A. Hinde, editors. New York, Cambridge Univ. Press.

Dawkins, R. 1976a. *The selfish gene.* Oxford: Oxford Univ. Press.

Dawson, D.F.L.; Bartolucci, G.; and Blum, H.M. 1980. Language and schizophrenia: Towards a synthesis. *Comprehensive Psychiatry* 21:81.

D'Azevedo, W.L. 1982. Tribal history in Liberia. In *Memory observed: Remembering in natural contexts.* U. Neisser, editor. San Francisco: W.H. Freeman.

Dealy, R.S.; Ishiki, D.M.; Avery, D.H., et al. 1981. Secondary depression in anxiety disorders. *Comprehensive Psychiatry* 22:612.

DeCasper, A.J., and Fifer, W.P. 1980. Of human bonding: Newborns prefer their mothers' voices. *Science* 208:1174.

DeChateau, P. 1983. Left-side preferences for holding and carrying newborn infants: Parental holding and carrying during the first week of life. *Journal of Nervous and Mental Disease* 171:241.

DeLozier, P.P. 1982. Attachment theory and child abuse. In *The place of attachment in human behavior.* C.M. Parkes, and J. Stevenson-Hinde, editors. New York: Basic Books.

Dickemann, M. 1979. Female infanticide, reproductive strategies, and social stratification: A preliminary model. In *Evolutionary biology and human social behavior: An anthropological perspective.* N.A. Chagnon, and W. Irons, editors. p. 321. North Scituate, Mass.: Duxbury.

Divale, W.T., and Harris, M. 1976. Population, warfare, and the male supremacist complex. *American Anthropologist* 78:521.

Dohrenwend, B.P., and Dohrenwend, B.S. 1974. Psychiatric disorders in urban settings. In *American handbook of psychiatry.* 2d ed, vol. II. S. Arieti, editor. New York: Basic Books.

Donovan, W.L.; Leavitt, L.A.; and Balling, J.D. 1978. Maternal physiological responses to infant signals. *Psychophysiology* 15:68.

Dunham, H.W. 1976. Society, culture, and mental disorder. *Archives of General Psychiatry* 33:147.

Dunn, J. 1979. Understanding human development: Limitations and possibilities in an ethological approach. In *Human ethology: Claims and limits of a new discipline.* M. Von Cranach; K. Foppa; W. Lepenies, et al., editors. Cambridge: Cambridge Univ. Press.

Durham, W.H. 1979. Toward a coevolutionary theory of human biology and culture. In *Evolutionary biology and human social behavior: An anthropological perspective.* N.A. Chagnon, and W. Irons, editors. p. 39. North Scituate, Mass.: Duxbury.

Durkheim, E. 1950. *The rules of sociological method.* Glencoe: Free Press.

Eibl-Eibesfeldt, I. 1973. The expressive behaviour of the deaf-and-blind born. In *Social communication and movement.* M. von Cranach, and I. Vine, editors. New York, Academic Press.

Eibl-Eibesfeldt, I. 1975. *Ethology: The biology of behavior.* 2d ed. New York: Holt, Rinehart and Winston.

Eibl-Eibesfeldt, I. 1979. Reply to Harre's comments. In *Human ethology: Claims and limits of a new discipline.* M. von Cranach; K. Foppa; W. Lepenies, et al., editors. p. 81. New York: Cambridge Univ. Press.

Eibl-Eibesfeldt, I. 1979a. Ritual and ritualization from a biological perspective. In *Human Ethology: Claims and limits of a new discipline.* M. von Cranach; K. Foppa; W. Lepenies, et al., editors. p. 3. New York: Cambridge Univ. Press.

Eimas, P.D.; Siqueland, E.R.; Jusczyk, P., et al. 1971. Speech perception in infants. *Science* 171:303.

Eisenberg, L. 1972. The 'human' nature of human nature. *Science* 176:123.

Eitinger, L. 1960. The symptomatology of mental disease among refugees in Norway. *Journal Mental Science* 106:947.

Ekman, P. 1979. About brows: Emotional and conversational signals. In *Human ethology: Claims and limits of a new discipline.* M. von Cranach; K. Foppa; W. Lepenies, et al., editors. p. 169. New York: Cambridge Univ. Press.

Elias, M. 1981. Serum cortisol, testosterone, and testosterone-binding globulin responses to competitive fighting in human males. *Aggressive Behavior* 7:215.

Epstein, A.W. 1980. Familial imperative ideas and actions: How encoded? *Biological Psychiatry* 15:489.

Epstein, A.W., and Collie, W.R. 1976. Is there a genetic factor in certain dream types? *Biological Psychiatry* 11:359.

Ewing, A.W. 1963. Attempts to select for spontaneous activity in Drosophila Melanogaster. *Animal Behavior* 2:369.

Fabre-Nys, C.; Meller, R.E.; and Keverne, E.B. 1982. Opiate antagonists stimulate affiliative behaviour in monkeys. *Pharmacology, Biochemistry, and Behavior* 16:653.

Farber, S.L. 1981. *Identical twins reared apart: A reanalysis:* New York: Basic Books.

Farborow, N.L., and Shneidman, E.S. 1959. Suicide and death. In *The meaning of death.* H. Feifel, editor. New York: McGraw-Hill.

Farris, R.E.L., and Dunham, H.W. 1939. *Mental disorders in urban areas: An ecological study of schizophrenia and other psychoses.* Chicago: Univ. of Chicago Press.

Fenichel, O. 1945. *The psychoanalytic theory of neurosis.* New York: W.W. Norton.

Fentress, J.C. 1976. Dynamic boundaries of patterned behaviour: Interaction and self-organization. In *Growing points in ethology.* P.P.G. Bateson, and R.A. Hinde, editors. New York: Cambridge Univ. Press.

Festinger, L. 1957. *A theory of cognitive dissonance.* Palo Alto, Calif.: Stanford Univ. Press.

Finger, S. 1975. Child-holding patterns in western art. *Child Development* 46:267.

Finkelstein, P.; Wenegrat, B.; and Yalom, I. 1982. Large group awareness training. *Annual Review of Psychology* 33:515.

Fisher, R.A. 1930. *The genetical theory of natural selection.* 2d ed. New York: Dover.

Flaherty, J.A.; Gaviria, F.M.; Black, E.M., et al. 1983. The role of social support in the functioning of patients with unipolar depression. *American Journal of Psychiatry* 140:473.

Fox, R. 1979. Kinship categories as natural categories. In *Evolutionary biology and human social behavior: An anthropological perspective.* N.A. Chagnon, and W. Irons, editors. p. 132. North Scituate, Mass.: Duxbury.

Fox, R. 1980. *The red lamp of incest.* New York: E.P. Dutton.

Frances, A.; Brown, R.P.; Kocsis, J.H., et al. 1981. Psychotic depression: A separate entity? *American Journal of Psychiatry* 138:831.

Freeman, D. 1980. Sociobiology: The 'antidiscipline' of anthropology. In *Sociobiology examined.* A. Montagu, editor. Oxford: Oxford Univ. Press.

Freud, S. 1911. Psychoanalytic notes upon an autobiographical account of a case of paranoia. standard ed., vol. 12. London: Hogarth Press.

Freud, S. 1912. Contributions to the psychology of love: The most prevalent form of degration in erotic life. standard ed., vol. 11. London: Hogarth Press.

Freud, S. 1913. *Totem and taboo.* standard ed., vol. 13. London: Hogarth Press.

Freud, S. 1915. Thoughts for the times on war and death. standard ed., vol. 14. London: Hogarth Press.

Freud, S. 1916. Mourning and melancholia. standard ed., vol. 14. London: Hogarth Press.

Freud, S. 1917. *Introductory lectures on psychoanalysis.* standard ed., vol. 15 & 16. London: Hogarth Press.

Freud, S. 1920. Beyond the pleasure principle. standard ed., vol. 18. London: Hogarth Press.

Freud, S. 1923. *The ego and the id.* standard ed., vol. 19. London: Hogarth Press.

Freud, S. 1924. The loss of reality in neurosis and psychosis. standard ed., vol. 19. London: Hogarth Press.

Freud, S. 1927. *The future of an illusion.* standard ed., vol. 21. London: Hogarth Press.

Freud, S. 1933. *New introductory lectures on psychoanalysis.* standard ed., vol. 23. London: Hogarth Press.

Freud, S. 1939. *Moses and monotheism.* standard ed., vol. 23. London: Hogarth Press.

Freud, S. 1940. *An outline of psychoanalysis.* standard ed., vol. 23. London: Hogarth Press.

Fried, C. 1978. biology and ethics: Normative implications. In *Morality as a biological phenomenon.* G.S. Stent, editor. Berlin: Dahlem Konferenzen.

Galanter, E., and Gerstenhaber, M. 1956. On thought: The extrinsic theory. *Psychological Review* 63:218.

Galanter, M. 1978. The "Relief Effect": A sociobiological model for neurotic distress and large-group therapy. *American Journal of Psychiatry* 135:588.

Galanter, M. 1983. Unification church ("Moonie") dropouts: Psychological readjustment after leaving a charismatic religious group. *American Journal of Psychiatry* 140:984.

Galanter, M. 1983a. Engaged members of the Unification Church: Impact of a charismatic large group on adaptation and behavior. *American Journal of Psychiatry* 140:1197.

Galanter, M., and Buckley, P. 1978. Evangelical religion and meditation: Psychotherapeutic effects. *Journal of Nervous and Mental Disease* 166:685.

Galanter, M.; Rabkin, R.; Rabkin, J., et al. 1979. The "Moonies": A psychological study of conversion and membership in a contemporary religious sect. *American Journal of Psychiatry* 136:165.

Gallup, G.G. 1970. Chimpanzees: Self-recognition. *Science* 167:86.

Gallup, G.G. 1977. Self-recognition in primates. A comparative approach to the bidirectional properties of consciousness. *American Psychologist* 32:329.

Gardner, B.T., and Wallach, L. 1965. Shapes of figures identified as a baby's head. *Perceptual and Motor Skills* 20:135.

Gershon, E.S.; Baron, M.; and Leckman, F. 1975. Genetic models of the transmission of affective disorders. *Journal of Psychiatric Research* 12:301.

Geshwind, N. 1979. Specializations of the human brain. *Scientific American* 241:180.

Godelier, M. 1979. Territory and property in primitive society. In *Human ethology: Claims and limits of a new discipline.* M. von Cranach; K. Foppa; W. Lepenies, et al., editors. p. 133. New York: Cambridge Univ. Press.

Goffman, E. 1979. Response cries. In *Human ethology: Claims and limits of a new discipline.* M. von Cranach; K. Foppa; W. Lepenies, et al., editors. p. 203. New York: Cambridge Univ. Press.

Gold, M.S., and Bowers, M.B. 1978. Neurobiological vulnerability to low-dose amphetamine psychosis. *American Journal of Psychiatry* 135:1546.

Goldberg, A., editor. 1978. *The psychology of the self: A casebook.* New York: International Universities Press.

Goodall, J. 1971. *In the shadow of man.* London: Collins.

Goodall, J. 1979. Life and death at Gombe. *National Geographic Magazine* 155:591.

Goodman, A.B.; Siegel, C.; Craig, T.J., et al., 1983. The relationship between socioeconomic class and prevalence of schizophrenia, alcoholism, and affective disorders treated by inpatient care in a suburban area. *American Journal of Psychiatry* 140:166.

Goody, J. 1978. Literacy and moral rationality. In *Morality as a biological phenomenon.* G.S. Stent, editor. Berlin: Dahlem Konferenzen.

Gottesman, I.I., and Shields, J. 1982. *Schizophrenia: The epigenetic puzzle.* Cambridge: Cambridge Univ. Press.

Gottlieb, G. 1976. Early development of species-specific auditory perception in birds. In *Neural and behavioral specificity. Studies on the development of behavior and the nervous system.* vol. 3. G. Gottlieb, editor. New York: Academic Press.

Gould, S.J. 1980. Sociobiology and human nature: A postpanglossian vision. In *Sociobiology examined.* A. Montagu, editor. Oxford: Oxford Univ. Press.

Gouldner, A. 1960. The norm of reciprocity: A preliminary statement. *American Sociological Review* 47:73.

Gray, M. 1978. *Neuroses: A comprehensive and critical view.* New York: Van Nostrand Reinhold.

Green, D.M., and Swets, J.A. 1966. *Signal detection theory and psychophysics.* New York: Wiley.

Greenberg, J.R., and Mitchell, S.A. 1983. *Object relations in psychanalytic theory.* Cambridge: Harvard Univ. Press.

Griffin, D.R. 1981. *The question of animal awareness: Evolutionary continuity of mental experience.* rev. ed. Los Altos, Calif.: Kaufmann.

Grinker, R.R.; Werble, B.; and Drye, R.C. 1968. *The borderline syndrome.* New York: Basic Books.

Grosz, H.J., and Farmer, B.B. 1972. Pitts and McClure's lactate-anxiety study revisited. *British Journal of Psychiatry* 120:415.

Grumet, G.W. 1983. Eye contact: The core of interpersonal relatedness. *Psychiatry* 46:172.

Grunhaus, L.; Gloger, S.; and Weisstub, E. 1981. Panic attacks: A review of treatments and pathogenesis. *Journal of Nervous and Mental Disease* 169:608.

Gunderson, J.G. 1979. Individual psychotherapy. In *Disorders of the schizophrenic syndrome.* L. Bellak, editor. New York: Basic Books.

Gunderson, J.G.; Kerr, J.; and Englund, D.W. 1980. The families of borderlines. *Archives of General Psychiatry* 37:27.

Gunderson, J.G., and Kolb, J.E. 1978. Discriminating features of borderline patients. *American Journal of Psychiatry* 135:792.

Gunderson, J.G.; Siever, L.J.; and Spaulding, E. 1983. The search for a schizotype: Crossing the border again. *Archives of General Psychiatry* 40:15.

Guze, S.B.; Woodruff, R.A., and Clayton, P.J. 1975. The significance of psychotic affective disorders. *Archives of General Psychiatry* 32:1147.

Halbreich, U.; Endicott, J.; and Nee, J. 1983. Premenstrual depressive changes. *Archives of General Psychiatry* 40:535.

Haldane, J.B.S. 1932. *The Causes of evolution.* London: Longmans, Green.

Hamilton, W.D. 1964. The genetical evolution of social behavior. *The Journal of Theoretical Biology* 7:1.

Hamilton, W.D. 1978. Geometry for the selfish herd. In *Readings in sociobiology.* T.H. Clutton-Brock, and P.H. Harvey, editors. San Francisco: W.H. Freeman.

Harlow, H.F., and Zimmerman, R.R. 1959. Affectional responses in the infant monkey. *Science* 130:421.

Harre, R. 1979. Comments on papers by Eibl-Eibesfeldt and Luckman. In *Human ethology: Claims and limits of a new discipline.* M von Cranach; K. Foppa; W. Lepenies, et al., editors. p. 75. New York: Cambridge Univ. Press.

Harris, M. 1979. *Cultural materialism: The struggle for a science of culture.* New York: Random House.

Hartmann, H. 1952. The mutual influences in the development of ego and id. *Psychoanalytic Study of the Child* 7:9.

Hartmann, H. 1953. Contribution to the metapsychology of schizophrenia. *Psychoanalytic Study of the Child* 8:177.

Hartog, J. 1980. The anlage and ontogeny of loneliness. In *The anatomy of loneliness.* J. Hartog; J.R. Audy; and Y.A. Cohen, editors. New York: International Universities Press.

Haviland, S.E., and Clark, H.H. 1974. What's new? Acquiring new information as a process in comprehension. *Journal of Verbal Learning and Verbal Behavior* 13:512.

Heider, F. 1958. *The psychology of interpersonal relations.* New York: Wiley.

Henderson, N.D. 1982. Human behavior genetics. *Annual Review of Psychology* 33:403.

Henderson, S. 1982a. The significance of social relationships in the etiology of neurosis. In *The place of attachment in human behavior.* C.M. Parkes, and J. Stevenson-Hinde, editors. New York: Basic Books.

Heston, L.L. 1966. Psychiatric disorders in foster home reared children of schizphrenic mothers. *British Journal of Psychiatry* 112:819.

Heston, L., and Denny, D 1969. Interactions between early life experiences and biological features in schizophrenia. In *Transmissions of schizophrenia.* D. Rosenthal, and S.S. Kety, editors. Oxford: Pergamon Press.

Heston, L., and Shields, J. 1968. Homosexuality in twins. *Archives of General Psychiatry* 18:149.

Hill, J.L. 1974. Peromyscus: Effect of early pairing on reproduction. *Science* 186:1042.

Hinde, R.A. 1960. Energy models of motivation. *Symposia of the Society for Experimental Biology* 14:199.

Hinde, R.A. 1982. Attachment: Some conceptual and biological issues. In *The place of attachment in human behavior.* C.M. Parkes, and J. Stevenson-Hinde, editors. New York: Basic Books.

Hinde, R.A., and Spencer-Booth, Y. 1971. Effects of brief separation from mother on rhesus monkeys. *Science* 173:111.

Hinde, R.A., and Stevenson-Hinde, J. 1976. Towards understanding relationships: Dynamic stability. In *Growing points in ethology.* P.P.G. Bateson, and R.A. Hinde, editors. New York: Cambridge Univ. Press.

Hirschfeld, R.M.A.; Klerman, G.L.; Clayton, P.J., et al. 1983. Personality and depression. *Archives of General Psychiatry* 40:993.

Horney, K. 1950. *Neurosis and human growth.* New York: W.W. Norton.

Humphrey, N.K. 1976. The social function of intellect. In *Growing points in ethology.* P.P.G. Bateson, and R.A. Hinde, editors. New York: Cambridge Univ. Press.

Huxley, T.H. 1894. *Evolution and ethics.* New York: Appleton and Co.

Iacono, W.G.; Tuason, V.B.; and Johnson, R.A. 1981. Dissociation of smooth-pursuit and saccadic eye tracking in remitted schizophrenics. *Archives of General Psychiatry* 38:991.

Imperato-McGinley, J.; Peterson, R.E.; Gautier, T., et al. 1979. Androgens and the evolution of male-gender identity among male pseudohermaphrodites with 5-alpha-reductase deficiency. *New England Journal of Medicine* 300:1233.

Inouye, E. 1963. Similarity and dissimilarity of schizophrenia in twins. In *Proceedings of the third world congress of psychiatry.* Montreal: Univ. of Toronto Press.

Irons, W. 1979. Natural selection, adaptation, and human social behavior. In *Evolutionary biology and human social behavior: An anthropological perspective.* N.A. Chagnon, and W. Irons, editors. p. 4. North Scituate, Mass: Duxbury.

Irons, W. 1979a. Cultural and biological success. In *Evolutionary biology and human social behavior: An anthropological perspective.* N.A. Chagnon, and W. Irons, editors. p. 257. North Scituate, Mass: Duxbury.

Irons, W. 1979b. Investment and primary social dyads. In *Evolutionary biology and human social behavior: An anthropological perspective.* N.A. Chagnon, and W. Irons, editors. p. 181. North Scituate, Mass: Duxbury.

Irons, W. 1979c. Kinship. In *Evolutionary biology and human social behavior: An anthropological perspective.* N.A. Chagnon, and W. Irons, editors. p. 79. North Scituate, Mass: Duxbury.

Itani, J., and Nishimura, A. 1973. The study of infrahuman culture in Japan: A review. In *Precultural primate behavior.* E.W. Menzel, editor. Basel, Switzerland: Karger.

Ivey, M., and Bardwick, J. 1968. Patterns of affective fluctuation in the menstrual cycle. *Psychosomatic Medicine* 30:336.

Jaspers, K. 1963. *General psychopathology.* Chicago: Univ. of Chicago Press.

Jaynes, J. 1977. *The origin of consciousness in the breakdown of the bicameral mind.* Boston: Houghton Mifflin.

Jenner, F.A. 1978. Psychiatry, biology and morals. In *Morality as a biological phenomenon.* G.S. Stent, editor. Berlin: Dahlem Konferenzen.

Jenni, D.A., and Jenni, M.A. 1976. Carrying behavior in humans: Analysis of sex differences. *Science* 194:859.

Johansen, K.H. 1983. Transitional experience of a borderline patient. *Journal of Nervous and Mental Disease* 171:126.

Johnson, C., and Berndt, D.J. 1983. Preliminary investigation of bulimia and life adjustment. *American Journal of Psychiatry* 140:774.

Jung, C.G. 1953. *Two essays on analytical psychology.* Princeton: Princeton Univ. Press.

Kagan, J. 1970. Attention and psychological change in the young child. *Science* 170:826.

Kahn, M.W. 1951. The effect of severe defeat at various age levels on the aggressive behavior of mice. *Journal of Genetic Psychology* 79:117.

Kallman, F.J. 1954. Genetic principles in manic-depressive psychosis. In *Depression.* P.H. Hock, and J. Zubin, editors. New York: Grune and Stratton.

Kanner, L. 1943. Autistic disturbances of affective contact. *Nervous Child* 2:217.

Karl, F.R. 1979. *Joseph Conrad: The three lives.* New York: Farrar, Straus and Giroux.

Karlsson, J. 1966. *The biological basis for schizophrenia.* Springfield: Charles C. Thomas.

Kauffman, C.; Grunebaum, H.; Cohler, B., et al. 1979. Superkids: Competent children of psychotic mothers. *American Journal of Psychiatry* 136:1398.

Kaufman, I.C., and Rosenblum, L.A. 1967. Depression in infant monkeys separated from their mothers. *Science* 155:1030.

Keane, T.M., and Fairbank, J.A. 1983. Survey analysis of combat-related stress disorders in Viet Nam veterans. *American Journal of Psychiatry* 140:348.

Kelley, H.H., and Michela, J.L. 1980. Attribution theory and research. *Annual Review of Psychology* 31:457.

Kendler, K.S. 1980. The nosologic validity of paranoia (simple delusional disorder). *Archives of General Psychiatry* 37:699.

Kernberg, O.F. 1967. Borderline personality organization. *Journal of the American Psychoanalytic Association* 15:641.

Kernberg, P.F. 1979. Childhood schizophrenia and autism: A selective review. In *Disorders of the schizophrenic syndrome.* L. Bellak, editor. New York: Basic Books.

Kety, S.S. 1983. Mental illness in the biological and adoptive relatives of schizophrenic adoptees: Findings relevant to genetic and environmental factors in etiology. *American Journal of Psychiatry* 140:720.

King, J.C. 1980. The genetics of sociobiology. In *Sociobiology examined.* A. Montagu, editor. Oxford: Oxford Univ. Press.

Kintsch, W. 1972. Notes on the structure of semantic memory. In *Organization of memory.* E. Tulving, and W. Donaldson, editors. New York: Academic Press.

Klaus, M.H.; Jerauld, R.; Kreger, N.C., et al. 1972. Maternal attachment: Importance of the first post-partum days. *New England Journal of Medicine* 286:460.

Klein, D.F. 1967. Importance of psychiatric diagnosis in prediction of clinical drug effects. *Archives of General Psychiatry* 16:118.

Klein, D.F. 1975. Psychopharmacology and the borderline patient. In *Borderline states in psychiatry.* J.E. Mack, editor. New York: Grune and Stratton.

Klein, D.F. 1980. Anxiety reconceptualized: Early experience with imipramine and anxiety. *Comprehensive Psychiatry* 21:411.

Klein, M. 1948. On the theory of anxiety and guilt. In *Envy and gratitude and other works* (1975). New York: Dell.

Knoedel, J. 1977. Breast-feeding and population growth. *Science* 198:1111.

Knowlton, N. 1982. Parental care and sex role reversal. In *Current problems in sociobiology.* King's College Sociobiology Group, editors. Cambridge: Cambridge Univ. Press.

Kohut, H. 1971. The analysis of the self. New York: International Universities Press.

Kohut, H. 1977. The restoration of the self. New York: International Universities Press.

Kolodny, R.C.; Masters, W.H.; Hendryx, J., et al. 1971. Plasma testosterone and semen analysis in male homosexuals. *New England Journal of Medicine* 285:1170.

Konner, M. 1982. *The tangled wing: Biological constraints on the human spirit.* New York: Harper and Row.

Kosslyn, S.M. 1975. Information representation in visual images. *Cognitive Psychology* 7:341.

Kramlinger, K.G.; Swanson, D.W.; and Maruta, T. 1983. Are patients with chronic pain depressed? *American Journal of Psychiatry* 140:747.

Kreutzer, M.A.; Leonard, C.; and Flavell, J.H. 1982. Prospective remembering in children. In *Memory observed: Remembering in natural contexts.* U. Neisser, editor. San Francisco: W.H. Freeman.

Kruuk, H. 1964. Predators and anti-predator behaviour in the black-headed gull. *Behaviour Supplement* 11:1.

Kuhn, R. 1958. The attempted murder of a prostitute. In *Existence.* R. May; E. Angel, and H.F. Ellenberger, editors. New York: Simon and Schuster.

Kummer, H. 1968. *Social organization of hamadryas baboons: A field study.* Chicago: Univ. of Chicago Press.

Kummer, H. 1978. Analogs of morality among nonhuman primates. In *Morality as a biological phenomenon.* G.S. Stent, editor. Berlin: Dahlem Konferenzen.

Kummer, H. 1979. Reply to von Cranach's comments. In *Human Ethology: Claims and limits of a new discipline.* M. von Cranach; K. Foppa; W. Lepenies, et al., editors. p. 428. New York: Cambridge Univ. Press.

Kummer, H. 1979a. On the value of social relationships to nonhuman primates: A heuristic scheme. In *Human ethology: Claims and limits of a new discipline.* M. von Cranach; K. Foppa; W. Lepenies, et al., editors. p. 381. New York: Cambridge Univ. Press.

Kunz, P.R., Brinkerhoff, M.B.; and Hundley, V. 1973. Relationship of income and childlessness. *Social Biology* 20:139.

Kurland, J.A. 1979. Paternity, mother's brother, and human sociality. In *Evolutionary biology and human social behavior: An anthropological perspective.* N.A. Chagnon, and W. Irons, editors. p. 145. North Scituate, Mass: Duxbury.

Latane, B., and Darley, J. 1968. Group inhibition of bystander intervention in emergencies. *Journal of Personality and Social Psychology* 10:215.

Leak, G.K., and Christopher, S.B. 1982. Freudian psychoanalysis and sociobiology: A synthesis. *American Psychologist* 37:313.

LeBoeuf, B.J. 1974. Male-male competition and reproductive success in elephant seals. *American Zoology* 14:163.

Leckman, J.F.; Merikangas, K.R.; Pauls, D.L., et al. 1983. Anxiety disorders and depression: Contradictions between family study data and DSM-III conventions. *American Journal of Psychiatry* 140:880.

Levi-Strauss, C. 1969. *Elementary structures of kinship*. Boston: Beacon Press.

Lewis, A.J. 1934. Melancholia. *Journal of Mental Science* 80:277.

Lewis, M., and Goldberg, S. 1969. Perceptual-cognitive development in infancy: A generalized expectancy model as a function of mother-infant interaction. *Merrill-Palmer Quarterly* 15:81.

Leyhausen, P. 1973. On the function of the relative hierarchy of moods (as exemplified by the phylogenetic and ontogenetic development of prey-catching in carnivores). In *Motivation of human and animal behavior: An ethological view.* K. Lorenz, and P. Leyhausen, editors. New York: Van Nostrand Rheingold.

Liberman, A.M. 1979. An ethological approach to language through the study of speech perception. In *Human ethology: Claims and limits of a new discipline*. M. von Cranach; K. Foppa; W. Lepenies, et al., editors. p. 682. New York: Cambridge Univ. Press.

Lifton, R.J. 1979. *The broken connection: On death and the continuity of life*. New York: Simon and Schuster.

Lindelius, R., and Kay, D.W.R. 1973. Some changes in the pattern of mortality in schizophrenia in Sweden. *Acta Psychiatrica Scandinavica* 49:315.

Lindemann, E. 1944. The symptomatology and management of acute grief. *American Journal of Psychiatry* 101:141.

Lindemann, E. 1960. Psychosocial factors as stress agents. In *Stress and psychiatric disorder.* J.M. Tanner, editor. Oxford: Blackwell.

Lipowski, Z.J. 1975. Organic brain syndromes: Overview and classification. In *Psychiatric aspects of neurological disease*. D.F. Benson, and D. Blumer, editors. New York: Grune and Stratton.

Lipton, M.A., and Burnett, G.B. 1979. Pharmacological treatment of schizophrenia. In *Disorders of the schizophrenic syndrome.* L. Bellak, editor. New York: Basic Books.

Lockhard, J.; Daley, P.C.; and Gunderson, V.M. 1979. Maternal and paternal differences in infant carrying: U.S. and African data. *American Naturalist* 113:235.

Lomnicki, A. 1982. Individual heterogeneity and population regulation. In *Current problems in sociobiology.* King's College Sociobiology Group, editors. Cambridge: Cambridge Univ. Press.

Loranger, A.W.; Oldham, J.M.; and Tulis, E.H. 1982. Familial transmission of DSM-III borderline personality disorder. *Archives of General Psychiatry* 39:795.

Lorenz, K. 1950. The comparative method in studying innate behaviour patterns. *Symposia of the Society for Experimental Biology* 4:221.

Lorenz, K. 1957. The nature of instinct. In *Instinct: The development of a modern concept.* C.H. Schiller, editor. London: Methuen.

Lorenz, K. 1960. *On Aggression.* New York: Harcourt, Brace and World.

Loy, J. 1970. Behavioral responses of free-ranging rhesus monkeys to food shortage. *American Journal of Physical Anthropology* 33:263.

Lubin, A.J. 1980. Loneliness, creativity, and Vincent Van Gogh. In *The anatomy of loneliness.* J. Hartog; J.R. Audy; and Y.A. Cohen, editors. New York: International Universities Press.

Luckman, T. 1979. Personal identity as an evolutionary and historical problem. In *Human ethology: Claims and limits of a new discipline.* M. von Cranach; K. Foppa; W. Lepenies, et al., editors. p. 56. New York: Cambridge Univ. Press.

Lumsden, C.J., and Wilson, E.O. 1981. *Genes, mind, and culture: The coevolutionary process.* Cambridge: Harvard Univ. Press.

Lumsden, C.J., and Wilson, E.O. 1983. *Promethean fire: Reflections on the origin of the mind.* Cambridge: Harvard Univ. Press.

Luria, A.R. 1981. *Language and cognition.* New York: Wiley.

Maccoby, E.E., and Jacklin, C.N. 1974. *The psychology of sex differences.* Palo Alto, Calif.: Stanford Univ. Press.

Mahler, M.S. 1971. A study of the separation-individuation process and its possible application to borderline phenomena in the psychoanalytic situation. *Psychoanalytic Study of the Child* 26:403.

Mahler, M.S., and Furer, M. 1972. Child psychosis: A theoretical statement and its implications. *Journal of Autism and Childhood Schizophrenia* 2:213.

Mahler, M.S.; Pine, F.; and Bergman, A. 1975. *The psychological birth of the human infant.* New York: Basic Books.

Main, M., and Weston, D.R. 1982. Avoidance of the attachment figure in infancy: Descriptions and interpretations. In *The place of attachment in human behavior.* C.M. Parkes, and J. Stevenson-Hinde, editors. New York: Basic Books.

Malinowski, B. 1927. *Sex and repression in savage society.* Cleveland: Meridian.

Margolese, M.S., and Janiger, O. 1973. Androsterone/etiocholanone ratios in male homosexuals. *British Medical Journal* 3:207.

Mark, V.H., and Ervin F.R. 1970. *Violence and the brain.* New York: Harper and Row.

Markl, H.S.; Butenandt, E.; Campbell, D.T., et al. 1978. Evolution of morals? Morals of evolution?: Group report. In *Morality as a biological phenomenon.* G.S. Stent, editor. Berlin: Dahlem Konferenzen.

Marler, P. 1979. Development of auditory perception in relation to vocal behavior. In *Human ethology: Claims and limits of a new discipline.* M. von Cranach; K. Foppa; W. Lepenies, et al., editors. p. 663. New York: Cambridge Univ. Press.

Marmor, J. 1954. Orality in the hysterical personality. *Journal of the American Psychoanalytic Association* 1:656.

Mason, W.A. 1979. Maternal attributes and primate cognitive development. In *Human ethology: Claims and limits of a new discipline.* M. von Cranach; K. Foppa; W. Lepenies, et al., editors. p. 437. New York: Cambridge Univ. Press.

Mason, W.A.; Davenport, R.K.; and Menzel, E.W. 1968. Early experience and the social development of rhesus monkeys and chimpanzees. In *Early experience and behavior.* G. Newton, and S. Levine, editors. Springfield, Mo.: Charles C. Thomas.

Mason, W.A., and Green, P.C. 1962. The effects of social restriction on the behavior of rhesus monkeys: IV. responses to a novel environment and to an alien species. *Journal of Comparative and Physiological Psychology* 55:363.

Mason, W.A., and Kenney, M.D. 1974. Redirection of filial attachments in rhesus monkeys: Dogs as mother surrogates. *Science* 183:1209.

Mathews, A.M.; Gelder, M.G.; and Johnston, D.W. 1981. *Agoraphobia: Nature and treatment.* New York: Guilford Press.

Matussek, P., and Feil, W.B. 1983. Personality attributes of depressive patients. *Archives of General Psychiatry* 40:783.

May, R. 1958. Contributions of existential psychotherapy. In *Existence.* R. May; E. Angel, and H.F. Ellenberger, editors. New York: Simon and Schuster.

Maynard Smith, J. 1978. Parental investment: A prospective analysis. In *Readings in sociobiology.* T.H. Clutton-Brock, and P.H. Harvey, editors. San Francisco: W.H. Freeman.

Maynard Smith, J. 1978a. Evolution and the theory of games. In *Readings in sociobiology.* T.H. Clutton-Brock, and P.H. Harvey, editors. San Francisco: W.H. Freeman.

Maynard Smith, J. 1978b. The concepts of sociobiology. In *Morality as a biological phenomenon.* G.S. Stent, editor. Berlin: Dahlem Konferenzen.

Maynard Smith, J. 1982. *Evolution and the theory of games.* Cambridge: Cambridge Univ. Press.

Maynard Smith, J. 1982a. The evolution of social behaviour—a classification of models. In *Current problems in sociobiology.* King's College Sociobiology Group, editors. Cambridge: Cambridge Univ. Press.

Mayr, E. 1976. *Evolution and the diversity of life: Selected essays.* Cambridge: Belknap Press.

McClintock, M. 1971. Menstrual synchrony and suppression. *Nature* 229:229.

McGuire, M.T., and Essock-Vitale, S.M. 1981. Psychiatric disorders in the context of evolutionary biology: A functional classification of behavior. *Journal of Nervous and Mental Disease* 169:672.

McGuire, M.T.; Essock-Vitale, S.M.; and Polsky, R.H. 1981. Psychiatric disorders in the context of evolutionary biology: An ethological model of behavioral changes associated with psychiatric disorders. *Journal of Nervous and Mental Disease* 169:687.

McKinney, W.T., and Moran, E.C. 1981. Animal models of schizophrenia. *American Journal of Psychiatry* 138:478.

Meacham, J.A., and Leiman, B. 1982. Remembering to perform future actions. In *Memory observed: Remembering in natural contexts.* U. Neisser, editor. San Francisco: W.H. Freeman.

Medawar, P.B. 1976. Does ethology throw any light of human behaviour? In *Growing points in ethology.* P.P.G. Bateson, and R.A. Hinde, editors. New York: Cambridge Univ. Press.

Mellen, S.L.W. 1981. *The evolution of love.* San Francisco: W.H. Freeman.

Meltzer, H.Y. 1979. Biochemical studies in schizophrenia. In *Disorders of the schizophrenic syndrome.* L. Bellak, editor. New York: Basic Books.

Menzel, E.W. 1973. Chimpanzee spatial memory organization. *Science* 182:943.

Menzel, E.W. 1975. Natural language of young chimpanzees. *New Scientist* 65:127.

Midgley, M. 1980. Gene-juggling. In *Sociobiology examined.* A. Montagu, editor. Oxford: Oxford Univ. Press.

Milgram, S. 1963. Behavioral study of obedience. *Journal of Abnormal and Social Psychology* 67:371.

Miller, A. 1981. *The drama of the gifted child: How narcissistic parents form and deform the emotional lives of their talented children.* New York: Basic Books.

Miller, G; Galanter, I.; and Pribram, K. 1960. *Plans and the structure of behavior.* New York: Holt, Rhinehart and Winston.

Miller, R.E. 1971. Experimental studies of communication in the monkey. *Primate Behaviour* 2:139.

Minkowski, E. 1958. Findings in a case of schizophrenic depression. In *Existence.* R. May; E. Angel; and H.F. Ellenberger, editors. New York: Simon and Schuster.

Montagu, A. 1966. *On being human.* 2d ed. New York: Hawthorn Books.

Montagu, A. 1980. Introduction. In *Sociobiology examined.* A. Montagu, editor. Oxford: Oxford Univ. Press.

Morsbach, G., and Bunting, C. 1979. Maternal recognition of their neonates' cries. *Developmental Medicine and Child Neurology* 21:178.

Mosher, L.R., and Gunderson, J.G. 1979. Group, family, milieu, and community support systems treatment for schizophrenia. In *Disorders of the schizophrenic syndrome.* L. Bellak, editor. New York: Basic Books.

Murdock, G.P. 1949. *Social structure.* New York: Macmillan.

Murray, L.G., and Blackburn, I.M. 1974. Personality differences in patients with depressive illness and anxiety neurosis. *Acta Psychiatrica Scandinavica* 50:189.

Myers, M.F. 1982. Homosexuality, sexual dysfunction, and incest in male identical twins. *Canadian Journal of Psychiatry* 27:144.

Nagel, T. 1978. Ethics as an autonomous theoretical subject. In *Morality as a biological phenomenon.* G.S. Stent, editor. Berlin: Dahlem Konferenzen.

Neisser, U. 1982. Preface. In *Memory observed: Remembering in natural contexts.* U. Neisser, editor. San Francisco: W.H. Freeman.

Newman, H.H.; Freeman, F.N.; and Holzinger, K.J. 1937. *Twins: A study of heredity and environment.* Chicago: Univ. of Chicago Press.

Nickerson, R.S., and Adams, M.J. 1982. Long-term memory for a common object. In *Memory observed: Remembering in natural contexts.* U. Niesser, editor. San Francisco: W.H. Freeman.

Norman, D.A. 1976. *Memory and attention: Introduction to human information processing.* 2ed. New York: Wiley.

O'Connor, S.M.; Vietze, P.M.; Hopkins, J.B., et al. 1977. Post-partum extended maternal-infant contact: Subsequent mothering and child health. *Pediatric Research* 11:380.

Ornitz, E.M. 1971. Disorders of perception common to early infantile autism and schizophrenia. In *The schizophrenic syndrome annual review.* R. Cantro, editor. New York: Brunner/Mazel.

Ostrov, E., and Offer, D. 1980. Loneliness and the adolescent. In *The anatomy of loneliness.* J. Hartog; J.R. Audy; and Y.A. Cohen, editors. New York: International Universities Press.

Packer, C. 1978. Reciprocal alturism in olive baboons. In *Readings in sociobiology.* T.H. Clutton-Brock, and P.H. Harvey, editors. San Francisco: W.H. Freeman.

Paivio, A. 1971. *Imagery and verbal processes.* New York: Holt, Rinehart and Winston.

Panksepp, J.; Herman, B.; Conner, R., et al. 1978. The biology of social attachments: Opiates alleviate separation distress. *Biological Psychiatry* 13:607.

Papousek, H., and Papousek, M. 1979. Early ontogeny of human social interaction: Its biological roots and social dimensions. In *Human ethology: Claims and limits of a new discipline.* M. von Cranach; K. Foppa; W. Lepenies, et al., editors. New York: Cambridge Univ. Press.

Park, R.E. 1928. Human migration and the marginal man. *American Journal of Sociology* 33:881.

Parker, G. 1983. Parental 'affectionless control' as an antecedent to adult depression. *Archives of General Psychiatry* 40:956.

Parker, G.A. 1978. Assessment strategy and the evolution of fighting behaviour. In *Readings in sociobiology.* T.H. Clutton-Brock, and P.H. Harvey, editors. San Francisco: W.H. Freeman.

Parker, G.A. 1982. Phenotype-limited evolutionarily stable strategies. In *Current problems in sociobiology*. King's College Sociobiology Group, editors. Cambridge: Cambridge Univ. Press.

Parkes, C.M. 1970. The first year of bereavement. *Psychiatry* 33:444.

Parkes, C.M., and Weiss, R.S. 1983. *Recovery from bereavement.* New York: Basic Books.

Parkinson, T. 1980. Loneliness of the poet. In *The anatomy of loneliness.* J. Hartog; J.R. Audy; and Y.A. Cohen, editors. New York: International Universities Press.

Pastore, N. 1949. *The nature-nurture controversy.* New York: King's Crown Press.

Patterson, G.R.; Littman, R.A.; and Bricker, W. 1967. Assertive behavior in children: A step toward a theory of aggression. *Monographs of the Society for Research in Child Development* 32(5), serial no. 113.

Pfohl, B.; Stangl, DD.; and Tsuang, M.T. 1983. The association between early parental loss and diagnosis in the Iowa 500. *Archives of General Psychiatry* 40:965.

Phillips, J.L. 1975. *The origin of intellect: Piaget's Theory* 2ed. San Francisco: W.H. Freeman.

Piaget, J. 1954. *The construction of reality in the child.* New York: Basic Books.

Piaget, J. 1955. *The language and thought of the child.* Cleveland: World Publishing.

Piaget, J. 1978. *Behavior and evolution.* New York: Pantheon.

Pilowsky, I., and Bassett, D. 1980. Schizophrenia and the response to facial emotions. *Comprehensive Psychiatry* 21:236.

Pilowsky, I., and Spence, N.D. 1975. Hostility and depressive illness. *Archives of General Psychiatry* 32:1154.

Pitts, F.N., and McClure, J.N. 1967. Lactate metabolism in anxiety neurosis. *New England Journal of Medicine* 227:1329.

Pleck, J.H. 1981. *The myth of masculinity.* Cambridge: MIT Press.

Ploog, D. 1979. Comments on papers by Marler and Liberman. In *Human ethology: Claims and limits of a new discipline.* M. von Cranach; K. Foppa; W. Lepenies, et al., editors. New York: Cambridge Univ. Press.

Pope, H.G.; Jonas, J.M.; Hudson, J.I., et al. 1983. The validity of DSM-III borderline personaltiy disorder: A phenomenologic, family history, treatment response, and long-term follow-up study. *Archives of General Psychiatry* 40:23.

Pope, H.G., and Lipinski, J.F. 1978. Diagnosis in schizophrenia and manic-depressive illness. *Archives of General Psychiatry* 35:811.

Pound, A. 1982. Attachment and maternal depression. In *The place of attachment in human behavior.* C.M. Parkes, and J. Stevenson-Hinde, editors. New York: Basic Books.

Prosen, M.; Clark, D.C.; Harrow, M., et al. 1983. Guilt and conscience in major depressive disorders. *American Journal of Psychiatry* 140:839.

Pugh, G.E. 1977. *The biological origin of human values.* New York: Basic Books.

Rabin, A.I.; Doneson, S.L.; and Jentons, R.L. 1979. Studies of psychological functions in schizophrenia. In *Disorders of the schizophrenic syndrome.* L. Bellak, editor. New York: Basic Books.

Rapaport, D.; Gill, M.M.; and Schafer, R. 1968. *Diagnostic psychological testing.* rev. ed. New York: International Universities Press.

Raphael, B. 1983. *The anatomy of bereavement.* New York: Basic Books.

Reich, W. 1949. *Character analysis.* New York: Farrar, Straus and Giroux.

Reynolds, P.C. 1981. *On the evolution of human behavior.* Berkeley: Univ. of California Press.

Rheingold, H.L., and Hay, D.F. 1978. Prosocial behavior of the very young. In *Morality as a biological phenomenon.* G.S. Stent, editor. Berlin: Dahlem Konferenzen.

Rieff, P. 1968. *The triumph of the therapeutic: Uses of faith after Freud.* New York: Harper and Row.

Rizzuto, A. 1979. *The birth of the living god: A psychoanalytic study.* Chicago: Univ. of Chicago Press.

Robinson, D.N. 1979. *Systems of modern psychology: A critical sketch.* New York: Columbia Univ. Press.

Rogers, C.M. 1973. Implications of a primate early rearing experiment for the concept of culture. In *Precultural primate behavior.* E.W. Menzel, editor. New York: Karger.

Rose, R.M.; Gordon, T.P.; and Bernstein, I.S. 1971. Plasma testosterone levels in the male rhesus: Influences of sexual and social stimuli. *Science* 178:643.

Rose, R.M.; Holaday, J.W.; and Bernstein, I.S. 1971. Plasma testosterone, dominance rank, and aggressive behavior in rhesus monkeys. *Nature* 231:366.

Rose, S. 1980. It's only human nature: The sociobiologist's fairyland. In *Sociobiology examined.* A. Montagu, editor. Oxford: Oxford Univ. Press.

Rosenblatt, J.S. 1976. Stages in the early behavioural development of altricial young of selected species of non-primate mammals. In *Growing points in ethology.* P.P.G. Bateson, and R.A. Hinde, editors. New York: Cambridge Univ. Press.

Rosenthal, R.J.; Rinzler, C.; Wallsh, R., et al. 1972. Wrist-cutting syndrome: The meaning of a gesture. *American Journal of Psychiatry* 128:1363.

Roth, L.H. 1971. Territoriality and homosexuality in a male prison population. *American Journal of Orthopsychiatry* 41:510.

Rothenberg, A. 1983. Psychopathology and creative cognition. *Archives of General Psychiatry* 40:937.

Rubenstein, C.M., and Shaver, P. 1980. Loneliness in two northeastern cities. In *The anatomy of loneliness.* J. Hartog; J.R. Audy; and Y.A. Cohen, editors. New York: International Universities Press.

Rubenstein, D.I. 1982. Risk, uncertainty and evolutionary strategies. In *Current problems in sociobiology.* King's College Sociobiology Group, editors. Cambridge: Cambridge Univ. Press.

Rumelhart, D.E.; Lindsay, P.H.; and Norman, D.A. 1972. A process model for long-term memory. In *Organization of memory.* E. Tulving, and W. Donaldson, editors. New York: Academic Press.

Rutter, M., and Bartak, L. 1971. Causes of infantile autism: Some considerations from recent research. *Journal of Autism and Childhood Schizophrenia* 1:20.

Saghir, M.T., and Robins, E. 1973. *Male and female homosexuality: A comprehensive investigation.* Baltimore: Williams and Wilkins.

Sahlins, M.D. 1976. *The use and abuse of biology: An anthropological critique of sociobiology.* Ann Arbor: Univ. of Michigan Press.

Salk, L. 1973. The role of the heartbeat in the relations between mother and infant. *Scientific American* 228:24.

Salzen, E.A. 1979. Social attachment and a sense of security. In *Human ethology: Claims and limits of a new discipline.* M. von Cranach; K. Foppa; W. Lepenies, et al., editors. New York: Cambridge Univ. Press.

Sameroff, A.J.; Seifer, R.; and Zax, M. 1982. Early development of children at risk of emotional disorder. *Monographs of the Society for Research in Child Development* 47(7).

Sartorius, N.; Jablensky, A.; and Shapiro, R. 1978. Cross-cultural differences in the short-term prognosis of schizophrenic psychoses. *Schizophrenia Bulletin* 4:102.

Schachtel, E.G. 1947. On memory and childhood aphasia. *Psychiatry* 10:1.

Schafer, R. 1976. *A new language for psychoanalysis.* New Haven: Yale Univ. Press.

Schafer, R. 1978. *Language and insight.* New Haven: Yale Univ. Press.

Schneider, K. 1959. *Clinical psychopathology.* New York: Grune and Stratton.

Schneirla, T.C. 1966. Behavioral development and comparative psychology. *Quarterly Review of Biology* 41:283.

Schwartz, S. 1982. Is there a schizophrenic language? *Behavioral and Brain Sciences* 5:579.

Searle, J.R. 1969. *Speech acts.* New York: Cambridge Univ. Press.

Seligman, M.E. 1975. *Helplessness: On depression, development, and death.*

San Francisco: W.H. Freeman.

Sennett, R. 1981. *Authority.* New York: Random House.

Sermat, V. 1980. Some situational and personality correlates of loneliness. In *The anatomy of loneliness.* J. Hartog; J.R. Audy; and Y.A. Cohen, editors. New York: International Universities Press.

Shapiro, T. 1979. *Clinical psycholinguistics.* New York: Plenum Press.

Shepard, R.N.; Kilpatric, D.W.; and Cunningham, J.P. 1975. The internal representation of numbers. *Cognitive Psychology* 1:1.

Shepher, J. 1983. *Incest: A biosocial view.* New York: Academic Press.

Sherif, M. 1966. *Group conflict and cooperation: Their social psychology.* London: Routledge and Kegan Paul.

Shields, J. 1962. *Monozygotic twins brought up apart and brought up together.* London: Oxford Univ. Press.

Silverstone, J.T., and Russell, G.F.M. 1967. Gastric "hunger" contractions in anorexia nervosa. *British Journal of Psychiatry* 113:257.

Simon, M.A. 1980. Biology, sociobiology, and the understanding of human social behavior. In *Sociobiology examined.* A Montagu, editor. Oxford: Oxford Univ. Press.

Simonds, P.E. 1974. *The social primates.* New York: Harper and Row.

Simpson, M.J.A. 1976. The study of animal play. In *Growing points in ethology.* P.P.G. Bateson, and R.A. Hinde, editors. New York: Cambridge Univ. Press.

Skinner, B.F. 1948. *Walden II.* New York: Macmillan.

Slater, E., and Roth, M. 1969. *Clinical psychiatry.* London: Bailliere, Tindall and Cassell.

Sloane, R.B.; Staples, F.R.; Cristol, A.H., et al. 1975. *Psychotherapy versus behavior therapy.* Cambridge: Harvard Univ. Press.

Sloman, L. 1983. Inclusive fitness, altruism, and family adaptation. *Canadian Journal of Psychiatry* 28:18.

Sloman, L.; Konstantareas, M.; Dunham, D.W. 1979. The adaptive role of maladaptive neurosis. *Biological Psychiatry* 14:961.

Soloff, P.H., and Millward, J.W. 1983. Psychiatric disorders in the families of borderline patients. *Archives of General Psychiatry* 40:37.

Spencer-Booth, Y., and Hinde, R.A. 1971. Effects of brief separations from mothers during infancy on behaviour of rhesus monkeys 6-24 months later. *Journal of Child Psychology and Psychiatry* 12:157.

Sperber, M.A., and Jarvik, L.F. 1976. *Psychiatry and genetics.* New York: Basic Books.

Spiegel, H., and Spiegel, D. 1978. *Trance and treatment: Clinical uses of hypnosis.* New York: Basic Books.

Spitz, R.A. 1965. *The first year of life.* New York: International Universities Press.

Spitzer, R.L.; Endicott, J.; and Gibbon, M. 1979. Crossing the border into borderline personality and borderline schizophrenia. *Archives of General Psychiatry* 36:17.

Spotnitz, H. 1976. *Psychotherapy of preoedipal conditions.* New York: Jason Aronson.

Spuhler, J.N. 1979. Continuities and discontinuities in anthropoid-hominid behavioral evolution: Bipedal locomotion and sexual receptivity. In *Evolutionary biology and human social behavior: An anthropological perspective.* N.A. Chagnon, and W. Irons, editors. p. 454. North Scituate, Mass.: Duxbury.

Stekel, W. 1930. *Sexual aberrations: The phenomena of fetishism in relation to sex.* vol. I. New York: Liveright.

Stent, G.S. 1978. Introduction: The limits of the naturalistic approach to morality. In *Morality as a biological phenomenon.* G.S. Stent, editor. Berlin: Dahlem Konferenzen.

Stephens, J.H.; Shaffer, J.W.; and Carpenter, W.T. 1982. Reactive psychoses. *Journal of Nervous and Mental Disease* 170:657.

Stoller, R.J. 1976. Sexual excitement. *Archives of General Psychiatry* 33:899.

Stoller, R.J. 1979. Centerfold: An essay on excitement. *Archives of General Psychiatry* 36:1019.

Stone, M.H. 1980. *The borderline syndromes: Constitution, personality, and adaptation.* New York: McGraw-Hill.

Strauss, J.S., and Carpenter, W.T. 1979. The prognosis of schizophrenia. In *Disorders of the schizophrenic syndrome.* L. Bellak, editor. New York: Basic Books.

Stunkard, A. 1959. Obesity and the denial of hunger. *Psychosomatic Medicine* 21:281.

Sulloway, F.J. 1979. *Freud, biologist of the mind: Beyond the psychoanalytic legend.* New York: Basic Books.

Suomi, S., and Harlow, H.F. 1972. Social rehabilitation of isolate-reared monkeys. *Developmental Psychology* 6:487.

Surman, O.S.; Sheehan, D.V.; Fuller, T.C., et al. 1983. Panic disorder in genotypic HLA identical sibling pairs. *American Journal of Psychiatry* 140:237.

Symons, D. 1979. *The evolution of human sexuality.* New York: Oxford Univ. Press.

Szasz, T. 1961. *The myth of mental illness: Foundations of a theory of personal conduct.* New York: Hoeber-Harper.

Tajfel, H. 1979. Human intergroup conflict: Useful and less useful forms of analysis. In *Human ethology: Claims and limits of a new discipline.* M. von Cranach; K. Foppa; W. Lepenies, et al., editors. New York: Cambridge Univ. Press.

Tennant, C.; Bebbington, P.; and Hurry, J. 1980. Parental death in childhood and risk of adult depressive disorders: A review. *Psychological Medicine* 10:289.

Tennant, C.; Smith, A; Bebbington, P., et al. 1981. Parental loss in childhood. *Archives of General Psychiatry* 38:309.

Thompson, E.A. 1982. Gene competition without selection. In *Current problems in sociobiology.* King's College Sociobiology Group, editors. Cambridge: Cambridge Univ. Press.

Tiger, L. 1979. Biology, psychology, and incorrect assumptions of cultural relativism. In *Evolutionary biology and human social behaviour: An anthropological perspective.* N.A. Chagnon, and W. Irons, editors. North Scituate, Mass.: Duxbury.

Tiger, L. 1979a. *Optimism: The biology of hope.* New York: Simon and Schuster.

Tinbergen, N. 1968. On war and peace in animals and men. *Science* 160:1411.

Tinbergen, N. 1976. Ethology in a changing world. In *Growing points in ethology,* P.P.G. Bateson, and R.A. Hinde, editors. New York: Cambridge Univ. Press.

Tinbergen, W.A., and Tinbergen, N. 1972. Early childhood autism: An ethological approach. *Zeitschrift Fur Tierpsychologie* (suppl.) 10:1.

Tolman, E.C. 1932. *Purposive behavior in animals and men.* New York: Appleton-Century-Crofts.

Tomkins, S.S. 1962. *Affect, imagery, consciousness.* New York: Springer.

Torrey, E.F. 1979. Epidemiology. In *Disorders of the schizophrenic syndrome.* L. Bellak, editor. New York: Basic Books.

Trevarthen, C. 1974. Conversations with a 2 month old. *New Scientist* 62:230.

Trevarthen, C. 1979. Instincts for human understanding and cultural cooperation: Their development in infancy. In *Human ethology: Claims and limits of a new discipline.* M. von Cranach; K. Foppa; W. Lepenies, et al., editors. New York: Cambridge Univ. Press.

Trimmer, E. 1978. *Basic sexual medicine: A textbook of sexual medicine and an introduction to sex counselling techniques.* London: William Heinemann.

Trivers, R.L. 1971. The evolution of reciprocal altruism. *Quarterly Review of Biology* 46:35.

Trivers, R.L. 1978. Parent-offspring conflict. In *Readings in sociobiology.* T.H. Clutton-Brock, and P.H. Harvey, editors. San Francisco: W.H. Freeman.

Trivers, R.L. 1978a. Parental investment and sexual selection. In *Readings in sociobiology.* T.H. Clutton-Brock, and P.H. Harvey, editors. San Francisco: W.H. Freeman.

Trivers, R.L., and Willard, D.E. 1973. Natural selection of parental ability to vary the sex ratio of offspring. *Science* 179:90.

Trowell, J. 1982. Effects of obstetric management on the mother-child relationship. In *The place of attachment in human behavior.* C.M. Parkes, and J. Stevenson-Hinde, editors. New York: Basic Books.

Tulving, E. 1972. Episodic and semantic memory. In *Organization of memory.* E. Tulving, and W. Donaldson, editors. New York: Academic Press.

Turiel, E. 1978. The development of moral concepts. In *Morality as a biological phenomenon.* G.S. Stent, editor. Berlin: Dahlem Konferenzen.

Turnbull, C.M. 1973. The mountain people. London: Cape.

Van Hoof, J.A.R.A.M. 1973. A structural analysis of the social behaviour of a semi-captive group of chimpanzees. In *Social communication and movement.* M. von Cranach, and I. Vine, editors. New York: Academic Press.

Volkan, V. 1970. Typical findings in pathological grief. *Psychiatric Quarterly* 44:231.

Vygotsky, L.S. 1962. *Thought and language.* Cambridge: M.I.T. Press.

Waddington, C.H. 1956. Principles of embryology. London: Allen and Unwin.

Waldvogel, S. 1982. Childhood memories. In *Memory observed: Remembering in natural contexts.* U. Neisser, editor. San Francisco: W.H. Freeman.

Wallach, M.A., and Wallach, L. 1983. *Psychology's sanction for selfishness: The error of egotism in theory and therapy.* San Francisco: W.H. Freeman.

Waller, J.V.; Kaufman, R.M.; and Deutsch, F. 1940. Anorexia nervosa: A psychosomatic entity. *Psychosomatic Medicine* 2:3.

Warner, R. 1983. Recovery from schizophrenia in the third world. *Psychiatry* 46:197.

Washburn, S.L. 1980. Human behavior and the behavior of other animals. In *Sociobiology examined.* A. Montagu, editor. Oxford: Oxford Univ. Press.

Watson, J. 1919. *Psychology from the standpoint of a behaviorist.* Philadelphia: Lippincott.

Watson, J.S. 1971. Cognitive-perceptual development in infancy: Setting for the seventies. *Merrill-Palmer Quarterly* 17:139.

Waxler, N.E. 1979. Is outcome for schizophrenia better in nonindustrialized societies?: The case of Sri Lanka. *Journal of Nervous and Mental Disease* 167:144.

Weiss, R.S. 1982. Attachment in adult life. In *The place of attachment in human behavior.* C.M. Parkes, and J. Stevenson-Hinde, editors. New York: Basic Books.

Weitkamp, L.R.; Stancer, H.C.; Persad, E., et al. 1981. Depressive disorders and HLA: A gene on chromosome 6 that can affect behavior. *New England Journal of Medicine* 305:1301.

Wender, P.H.; Rosenthal, D.; and Kety, S.S. 1968. A psychiatric assessment of the adoptive parents of schizophrenics. In *The transmission of schizophrenia*. D. Rosenthal, and S.S. Kety, editors. Oxford: Pergamon Press.

Wender, P.H.; Rosenthal, D.; Kety, S.S., et al. 1974. Cross-fostering: A research strategy for clarifying the role of genetic and experiential factors in the etiology of schizophrenia. *Archives of General Psychiatry* 30:121.

Wertheimer, M. 1979. *A brief history of psychology.* rev. ed. New York: Holt, Rinehart and Winston.

Wetzel, R.D.; Cloninger, C.R.; Hong, B., et al. 1980. Personality as a subclinical expression of the affective disorders. *Comprehensive Psychiatry* 21:197.

Whiting, J.W.M.; Kluckhohn, R.; and Anthony, A.S. 1958. The function of male initiation ceremonies at puberty. In *Readings in social psychology.* E.E. Maccoby, editor. New York: Henry Holt.

Wiley, R.H. 1973. Territoriality and non-random mating in sage grouse. *Animal Behaviour Monographs* 6:85.

Wilson, D.S. 1980. *The natural selection of populations and communities.* Menlo Park, Calif.: Benjamin/Cummings.

Wilson, E.O. 1971. *The insect societies.* Cambridge: Harvard Univ. Press.

Wilson, E.O. 1975. *Sociobiology: The new synthesis.* Cambridge: Belknap Press.

Wilson, E.O. 1978. Academic vigilantism and the political significance of sociobiology. In *The sociobiology debate.* A.L. Caplan, editor. New York: Harper and Row.

Wilson, E.O. 1978a. *On human nature.* Cambridge: Harvard Univ. Press.

Winokur, G. 1980. Is there a common genetic factor in bipolar and unipolar affective disorder? *Comprehensive Psychiatry* 21:460.

Wise, L.A., and Zimmerman, R.R. 1973. The effect of protein deprivation on dominance measured by shock and avoidance competition and food competition. *Behavioural Biology* 9:317.

Wolf, A.P. 1966. Childhood association, sexual attraction, and the incest taboo: A Chinese case. *American Anthropology* 68:883.

Wolf, A.P. 1968. Adopt a daughter-in-law, marry a sister; A Chinese solution to the problem of the incest taboo. *American Anthropology* 70:864.

Wolf, P.H. 1973. The natural history of crying and other vocalizations in early infancy. In *The social infant.* L.J. Stone; H.T. Smith, and L.B. Murphy, editors. New York: Basic Books.

Wolff, P.H. 1978. The biology of morals from a psychological perspective. In *Morality as a biological phenomenon.* G.S. Stent, editor. Berlin: Dahlem Konferenzen.

Wolman, B.B. 1979. Dreams and Schizophrenia. In *Handbook of dreams: Research, theories and applications.* B.B. Wolman, editor. New York: Van Nostrand Rheinhold.

Woodruff, R.A.; Goodwin, D.W.; and Guze, S.B. 1974. *Psychiatric diagnosis.* New York: Oxford Univ. Press.

Wrangham, R.W. 1982. Mutualism, kinship and social evolution. In *Current problems in sociobiology.* King's College Sociobiology Group, editors. Cambridge: Cambridge Univ. Press.

Wynne, L.C.; Toohey, M.L.; and Doane, J. 1979. Family studies. In *Disorders of the schizophrenic syndrome.* L. Bellak, editor. New York: Basic Books.

Wynne-Edwards, V.C. 1980. Ecology and the evolution of social ethics. In *The sociobiology debate.* A.L. Caplan, editor. New York: Harper and Row.

Yalman, N. 1971. *Under the bo tree: Studies in caste, kinship and marriage in the interior of Ceylon.* Berkeley: Univ. Of California Press.

Yalom, I.D. 1980. *Existential Psychotherapy.* New York: Basic Books.

Young, F. 1962. The function of male initiation ceremonies: A cross-cultural test of an alternative hypothesis. *American Journal of Sociology* 67:379.

Young, L.D.; Suomi, S.S.; Harlow, H.F., et al. 1973. Early stress and later response to separation in rhesus monkeys. *American Journal of Psychiatry* 130:400.

Zwerling, I. 1979. Community psychiatric treatment. In *Disorders of the schizophrenic syndrome.* L. Bellak, editor. New York: Basic Books.

Index